"Shinn and Khadduri's new book is a thorough yet concise examination of what we know about the nature and causes of homelessness, and the crucial lessons learned. This critically important work provides a roadmap to restoring basic housing and income security as viable policy options, in the face of our daunting inequality divide that otherwise threatens millions with destitution and homelessness."

Dennis Culhane, *Dana and Andrew Stone Professor of Social Policy,*
University of Pennsylvania

"Marybeth Shinn and Jill Khadduri have combined their significant expertise to create an essential guide about the history of modern homelessness and to offer a clear path forward to end this American tragedy. Their policy recommendations on ending homelessness are culled from the best about what we know works."

Barbara Poppe, *Executive Director US Interagency Council on Homeless,*
2009–2014

"The authors of this book have a deep knowledge of its subject, and anyone with a serious interest in ending homelessness would benefit from reading it. The book describes a wide range of approaches that have been used to alleviate homelessness and provides a thoughtful assessment of the evidence on their effectiveness."

Edgar O. Olsen, *Professor of Economics & Public Policy,*
University of Virginia

"The book provides an excellent overview of the causes of homelessness and a hard-headed assessment of the efficacy of different policies to address it. The authors offer a clear and balanced summary of research evidence and suggest both incremental reforms to existing programs as well as major, but still politically plausible, expansions. Readers will walk away with a much richer understanding of homelessness along with some hope that with the right set of policies, government can reduce it."

Ingrid Gould Ellen, *Paulette Goddard Professor of Urban Policy and*
Planning, Wagner School, New York University

As California grapples with the growing humanitarian crisis of homelessness, Shinn and Khadduri's book is eagerly anticipated by researchers and policy makers alike. Even in its draft stages, this highly credible and rigorously researched book has informed local strategies to prevent homelessness.

Janey Rountree, *Executive Director of the California Policy Lab*

D0139685

In the Midst of Plenty

Contemporary Social Issues

Contemporary Social Issues, a book series authored by leading experts in the field, focuses on psychological inquiry and research relevant to social issues facing individuals, groups, communities, and society at large. Each volume is written for scholars, students, practitioners, and policy-makers.

Series Editor: Brian D. Christens

In the Midst of Plenty

Homelessness and What to Do About It

Marybeth Shinn
Jill Khadduri

WILEY Blackwell

This edition first published 2020
© 2020 Marybeth Shinn and Jill Khadduri

Registered Offices
John Wiley & Sons, Inc., 111 River Street, Hoboken, NJ 07030, USA
John Wiley & Sons Ltd, The Atrium, Southern Gate, Chichester, West Sussex, PO19 8SQ, UK

Editorial Office
111 River Street, Hoboken, NJ 07030, USA

For details of our global editorial offices, customer services, and more information about Wiley products visit us at www.wiley.com.

Wiley also publishes its books in a variety of electronic formats and by print-on-demand. Some content that appears in standard print versions of this book may not be available in other formats.

Library of Congress Cataloging-in-Publication Data

Names: Shinn, Marybeth, editor. | Khadduri, Jill,- editor.
Title: In the midst of plenty : homelessness and what to do about it /
    edited by Marybeth Shinn, Jill Khadduri.
Description: Hoboken, NJ : Wiley-Blackwell, [2020] | Series: Contemporary
    social issues | Includes bibliographical references and index.
Identifiers: LCCN 2019053468 (print) | LCCN 2019053469 (ebook) | ISBN
    9781405181259 (hardback) | ISBN 9781405181242 (paperback) | ISBN
    9781119104766 (adobe pdf) | ISBN 9781119104759 (epub)
Subjects: LCSH: Homelessness–United States. | Homeless persons–United
    States.
Classification: LCC HV4505 .I52 2020 (print) | LCC HV4505 (ebook) | DDC
    362.5/920973–dc23
LC record available at https://lccn.loc.gov/2019053468
LC ebook record available at https://lccn.loc.gov/2019053469

Cover Design: Wiley
Cover Image: © Alessandro Conti/Getty Images

Set in 10/12pt Galliard by SPi Global, Pondicherry, India

10   9   8   7   6   5   4   3   2   1

For Dave and Tom, with thanks for their love and support, and many dinners cooked along the way.

Contents

Foreword

Though many dispute it, we have not always had widespread homelessness in the United States. I know this because my first job out of graduate school was working for a policy advocacy organization (National Association of Neighborhoods) in Washington, DC whose major concern was residential displacement. At the time, in the 1970s, cities were just exiting a period of intense urban change characterized by slum removal, highway construction, and urban renewal. Many affordable urban housing units had been lost. And our organization felt that more losses were to come. Single Room Occupancy (SRO) hotels that could be paid for by the day, or week, or month were vanishing. Multifamily rental housing (and other than in New York City almost all multifamily housing was rental) was disappearing—converted to ownership in the condominium boom of the 1970s. Cities were sitting on properties acquired through tax foreclosure, and with no resources to repair them they were being lost to the affordable market. In short, federal policies and social movements were resulting in a declining supply of affordable housing, and we feared that the result would be homelessness among very poor people. At the time, this position was viewed as alarmist in the extreme. There was no way, we were told by a prominent liberal senator, that the American people would tolerate widespread homelessness. It simply could not happen.

If only he had been correct. When we started, if someone poor and down on their luck needed a place to live, one could probably be found that same day. If a day laborer spent his earnings at the bar instead of on the nightly rent for an SRO room, he might sleep on the street—for a night or two. But being homeless for weeks or months on end was nearly unheard of.

All of this changed relatively quickly. Affordable housing continued to be lost, and starting in the early 1980s, the relatively robust federal subsidies to replace it were slashed. What had been a national surplus of affordable housing relative to the number of poor households that needed it had turned into a growing national gap. Around 1982, people started sleeping on the steam grates of Washington, DC and the cities across the nation, and homelessness emerged as a national problem.

Over the years since then, the nation has dug itself into a deeper hole on housing, seen homelessness grow and take hold, and moved from short-term responses like "a hot and a cot" to more effective and sophisticated ones like permanent supportive housing. It has seen the number of people who are homeless recede—but not go away. Homelessness has settled in, and to many it now seems inevitable and unsolvable.

But my experience leads me to believe that it is neither inevitable nor unsolvable in a nation with the resources and capacity of ours. And the knowledgeable and thoughtful authors of this book—two brilliant women who know as much as anyone in the country about the nature of homelessness and its solutions—have done a great service by taking us on a journey through the history of homelessness, how our responses have changed, and how we can end it.

Chapter 1 describes the problem of homelessness in terms of the number, characteristics and trajectories of people who experience it. It describes how people use the various programs that constitute the emerging homelessness system, and looks at how this system has changed over time. It also reflects on the very important fact that homelessness is an experience that a wide variety of mostly poor people face: not a characteristic that defines a person.

In Chapter 2 the authors explore whether homelessness is the result of personal characteristics or outside factors—or an interaction of the two. Here they make the case that housing affordability (a combination of the cost of housing and people's incomes), while not accounting for everything, is the primary driver of homelessness to which personal characteristics or experiences (mental illness, gender identity, criminal records, etc.) contribute. They examine how the U.S. experience of homelessness compares to that of other countries, and why.

Chapter 3 looks at what it takes to end homelessness for people who experience it. If homelessness is defined by not having a home, then acquiring a home must be its solution. The authors describe two approaches to providing that home: long-term housing subsidies for families and individuals whose problem is largely affordability; and permanent supportive housing (also referred to as Housing First and Pathways to Housing) which provides a long-term housing subsidy plus services to people with chronic health disorders. They also look at what services people may need to maintain their housing. Chapter 4 explores how the various homelessness interventions are being brought together into homelessness systems, with the goal of coordinating resources to reduce and end homelessness. The authors point out the strong and weak elements of these systems and the challenges not only of delivering quality assistance, but delivering it to scale.

Getting people who have become homeless back into housing is one way to solve the problem. Another is to prevent them from becoming homeless in the first place. Chapter 5 explores this option, pointing out that prevention must first figure out who is going to become homeless and then intervene in a way that stops them from having that experience (the first being harder to achieve than the second). Housing-focused prevention is examined, as is preventing homelessness for people exiting public systems such as foster care and criminal justice, and geographic targeting.

Finally, in Chapter 6 the authors present a more wide-ranging vision of a social contract that would ensure all the people of our nation could afford decent housing. They propose various ways to accomplish this from both the housing and the income side. They also point out that making sure people have resources to support a decent standard of living would help to mitigate other problems such as racial discrimination. And they recognize that ensuring everyone has decent affordable housing will require significant political will: will that has not been present over the past 30 years of widespread national homelessness.

Marybeth Shinn and Jill Khadduri have provided us with a full-fledged history of homelessness and what has been done about it—successfully and otherwise. They make a strong case that ensuring the most vulnerable people have safe, decent and affordable housing would probably cost less and certainly yield far more than allowing tens of thousands of people to become homeless every year. Their wise and educated voices provide a rational vision of how homelessness can be ended. It is to be hoped that this vision will be widely adopted.

Nan Roman
President and CEO of the National Alliance to End Homelessness

Acknowledgments

Many people helped improve the quality of this book—its accuracy, its clarity, the force of its presentation.

Four people were kind enough to read the entire manuscript, and they made helpful comments and corrections throughout: Paul Dornan, formerly responsible for research on homelessness at the U.S. Department of Housing and Urban Development (HUD); Lucie Khadduri, who lives in Olympia WA, a city with a recent upsurge in homelessness; Daniel Perlman, Series Editor for the Society for the Psychological Study of Social Issues, who provided encouragement throughout the book's long gestation period; and Nan Roman, President and CEO of the National Alliance to End Homelessness. Zach Glendening, Molly Richard, and Jason Rodriguez at Vanderbilt University read portions of the manuscript and provided comments that improved clarity and pointed to additional sources of information.

Meghan Henry, project director for the Annual Homeless Assessment Reports at Abt Associates, commented extensively on Chapter 1 and confirmed numbers. John Miller, an experienced journalist, also read Chapter 1 and, along with Meghan, helped us make the chapter more readable. Jill's Abt colleagues Anna Jefferson and Hannah Thomas helped identify and expand the vignettes about people experiencing homelessness that begin Chapter 1. Sally B. Lott described her work as a housing navigator in Chapter 5. Kathryn P. Nelson, who designed HUD's ongoing reports on "worst case" housing problems and needs for assistance, read Chapter 2 and suggested additions and corrections. Barbara Sard of the Center on Budget and Policy Priorities read Chapter 6 and provided comments on the housing side of the social safety net. She also enlisted her colleagues at the Center to review portions of Chapter 6 on the income side of the safety net: Ed Bolen, Brendan Duke, Chye-Ching Huang, LaDonna Pavetti, Kathleen Ronig, and Chad Stone. We thank them for their comments and for their identification of literature that we had missed.

Janine Christiano, Gavin Crowell-Williamson, Kayle DeCant, and Rebecca Huppi provided help with references, and David Krantz drew several of the figures.

Many thanks to them all. As always, all errors belong to us.

Beth was hosted in turn by the Urban Institute and the Rockefeller Foundation Bellagio Center and wrote portions of the book during those visits and during a sabbatical from Vanderbilt.

Jill would like to thank her employer, Abt Associates, for the many research projects on homelessness in which she has participated and for access to wonderful colleagues. Beth had the privilege of working with Jill and Abt colleagues on a couple of these.

In the Midst of Plenty

Introduction

And homeless near a thousand homes I stood,
And near a thousand tables pined and wanted food.
William Wordsworth, 1842
(Guilt and Sorrow Verse XLI)

In the late 1980s, *The New York Times* ran a series of editorials dubbed "New Calcutta," lamenting the rise of homelessness on New York City streets and urging the City to action (e.g. "New Calcutta," 1988). The editorial writers may have chosen their foil poorly—wags complained with some justice that the *Times* was unfair to Calcutta (Gordon, 1989; Roeper, 1989). But the point of the metaphor was clear. How, the *Times* asked, could such abject poverty be permitted in a wealthy land?

An entire generation has grown up since homelessness spilled out of skid rows and into the nation's consciousness. Young people have no memories of the days when they did not have to pick their way around their fellow citizens dwelling in the streets, and older adults can scarcely recapture their shocked disbelief that homelessness should arise here, in the United States.

This book argues that the United States and other wealthy, industrialized countries have the resources to end homelessness, if we make the policy choices to do so. Further, there is a good deal of evidence about what works—and what does not work—to prevent and end homelessness for different groups of people. The recent halving of homelessness among veterans (Henry et al., 2018) shows what can be done with will and resources. But to end homelessness it is important to understand more about it and where it comes from.

The book is organized around four questions: Who becomes homeless? Why do people become homeless? How do we end homelessness? How do we prevent it?

In the Midst of Plenty: Homelessness and What to Do About It, First Edition.
Marybeth Shinn and Jill Khadduri.
© 2020 Marybeth Shinn and Jill Khadduri. Published 2020 by John Wiley & Sons Ltd.

Chapter 1 asks who becomes homeless in the United States, focusing on people living in homeless shelters, on the streets, and in other places not intended to be lived in, and on particular groups such as single adults, families, youth on their own, veterans, and people with chronic patterns of homelessness. The chapter also provides estimates of the number of people who experience homelessness each year and shows that, because homelessness is a transient experience, the number is much larger over a longer period of time such as five years or a lifetime.

Chapter 2 asks why people become homeless. Some writers have assumed that the characteristics of homeless people are in themselves a sufficient explanation. This chapter challenges this assumption and examines causes in social policies and sociocultural attitudes, including patterns of social exclusion, as well as individual characteristics. International comparisons help us understand why rates of homelessness are higher in the United States than in most of Western Europe. The chapter argues that homelessness is essentially a housing problem, marshaling evidence on how the current crisis of homelessness came to be.

Chapter 3 asks how to end homelessness for particular groups of people who experience it, focusing on programs with strong evidence of effectiveness for resolving homelessness and improving the lives of families with children and of individuals who have challenges such as severe and persistent mental illness. Chapter 4 expands on this question, by examining comprehensive efforts to end homelessness. It introduces and assesses the components of the homeless services "system" that has grown up to address the problem and describes efforts to act strategically and with sufficient resources.

The final two chapters ask how to prevent homelessness. Chapter 5 considers targeted prevention efforts directed at groups that are at special risk, and Chapter 6 proposes broader policy changes to end the structural conditions that give rise to homelessness.

Some of the findings in each chapter may be surprising. For example, Chapter 1 shows that the age at which people are at highest risk of entering a homeless shelter in the United States is infancy and that half of adults who experience sheltered homelessness over the course of a year do not suffer from severe mental illness or have any other type of disability.

Chapter 2 suggests that the structural factors (e.g. income inequality, housing costs) that cause high rates of homelessness are rather different from the individual vulnerabilities (e.g. having a young child, mental illness) that affect which particular individual or family will succumb. Chapter 4 notes that even service providers with long experience working with homeless people sometimes design ineffective policies and programs. And Chapter 5 shows that prevention programs with more failures may also have more impact (because programs that rarely fail are offering services to people unlikely to become homeless to begin with).

Some may find the title of this book odd—many Americans do not feel that they are living "in the midst of plenty" and so have little to spare for those with even less. Or they may not feel that those with less are deserving of their aid.

As we endeavor to show in Chapters 2 and 6, the fact that too many Americans are struggling to get by is also a result of social choices such as recent changes in the tax code that provided most of the benefits to the wealthy.

Throughout this book, our basic theme is that homelessness stems from failures of social policy, in particular policies that fail to provide affordable housing for the many people for whom other social policies fail to provide adequate income either from jobs or (when they are unable to work) from income supports.

Does the United States have the resources to prevent homelessness? We think the answer is yes. To take just one example, America pays far more to subsidize housing for the wealthy than for the poor. Housing subsidies for rich people are written into the tax code, primarily in the form of the income tax deduction for mortgage interest. A series of proposals made over several decades would have capped those subsidies and distributed the savings to moderate income homeowners and renters (in the form of a tax credit rather than a deduction); they would also have been used to provide housing subsidies for people whose poverty-level incomes mean that they cannot afford basic shelter and are at risk of falling into homelessness.

The final chapter of this book, Chapter 6, describes a number of policy options that would allow the United States to end homelessness. The United Nations included a right to housing in the Universal Declaration of Human rights 70 years ago (United Nations, 1948). Not all countries are wealthy enough to make that right a reality. In the United States, it is within our power to realize that right today.

1

Who Becomes Homeless?

Victor, a mason in his 50s, had run a family business repairing swimming pools and owned a large house and a car. After a heart attack and triple bypass surgery, he was prescribed the opioid oxycodone to manage the pain. He became addicted, then switched to heroin when the cost of oxycodone became $30 per pill. Estranged from his family as a result of his addiction, and having spent all his savings, Victor lost his home and his rights to visit his daughter as well. After a summer living in woods and parks, he found help at a homeless shelter and has been working on moving past his addiction and rebuilding his life.

Jasmine and her partner moved to North Carolina with their children. She got a job transfer with the same retailer she had been working for full-time in New Jersey, but only a part-time position was available. They lived with her partner's grandmother for some months, but then the grandmother had a stroke and had to move in with her daughter, who could not also house Jasmine's family. Jasmine and the children went to a hotel, which initially let her pay what she could. Then an emergency grant through her employer kicked in some rent. She took a second job at a fast food restaurant, at times leaving the children alone in the hotel. By chance, in the checkout line of the retail store where she works, she met the director of a program that helps homeless people move into rental housing.

William is a 57-year-old veteran with a non-combat-related disability, a back problem that occurred after he had left the service, and was working in the food industry. Without a job for 8 years, Social Security Disability payments were his only source of income, and he understood that they would no longer be available if he tried to work full-time. William had lived in his own apartment for 5 or 6 years, but after drawing down his savings, he could no longer pay the rent. His aunt offered to help out but only if he found something less expensive. William didn't want to leave his home but eventually moved out and became homeless,

In the Midst of Plenty: Homelessness and What to Do About It, First Edition.
Marybeth Shinn and Jill Khadduri.

sometimes staying in a family member's attic. His sister suggested that, because he was a veteran, he might try the Veterans Administration (VA) for help. He did that and started to receive medical care through the VA and also short-term rental assistance.

Bunny, a feisty woman who walks with a cane, struggles with mental health issues related to childhood trauma. Anxiety, depression, and some level of cognitive impairment make it difficult for her to express her needs. At 52, and with a grown son and daughter, she has moved many times, been evicted repeatedly, and had several episodes of homelessness. She is estranged from her son, and her mental health challenges would appear to make it difficult for her to live with her daughter or anyone else. Her daughter does show up from time to time with food and cleaning supplies.

Anthea, a 22-year-old mother to a 3-year-old and a 1-year-old, had never been able to afford a place of her own. She moved out of her mother's home into her partner's mother's double-wide in a small town. The couple intended to buy the trailer, but Anthea's partner became abusive. She left him one Wednesday night and showed up at the door of a shelter with her children. She couldn't get into that shelter, so she and the children prepared to bed down on the street. A passer-by called the police who showed up and helped them get into a different shelter.

Ricardo, a soft-spoken man with glasses perched on top of his head, came to a city in the Northeast from Puerto Rico at age 50, hoping to find work and bring his wife and young son to join him. Finding he could not afford the rent in this very expensive city, he stayed in a shelter for homeless people for a year, working a job during most of the time, and then got into a program that provides help with the rent. His wife and son have managed to get to the same city but are living in a different apartment, having figured out assistance in another way.

Michelle first became homeless as a new mother at 22. She was working two jobs and lost one of them. "My daughter was in daycare. I couldn't get affordable daycare for her. It was like I was stuck and I couldn't afford the rent anymore. I had to move out. Came home to stay with family members, mom, whoever I could at the time." She was evicted from her apartment, the first she'd had in her name. Over the next 8 years, she experienced similar cycles of unstable employment, childcare challenges, births of additional children, and homelessness. Before entering a program that helps homeless people obtain affordable housing, she and her children had spent a year and a half moving between different hotels or shelters when their money ran out. She was paying about $400 a week for hotel stays but could not save enough money for up-front move-in costs (first and last months' rent and security deposit) and had an eviction on her record.

Jermaine left home for the last time at age 15. "I remember my dad used to put me out at the age of like 15. I live with myself and been on my own since I was like 13, in a certain sense. I used to run away. Me and my sisters used to jump out of a window and run away. We used to sleep in abandoned cars. I've been a survivor though." He floated from friend's house to friend's house and between a city in North Carolina and Kansas City, where he had extended family. He became involved with selling drugs at 21 and when he got into trouble in one city, he would move to the other, bouncing back and forth for years and living with family members, friends, on the street, or in his truck. He was staying in his truck at the time a friend of his told him about the rapid re-housing program he entered. Based on that friend's knowledge of the process, he "sucked up my pride" and entered a shelter for the first time, at age 35 so he could put in his application.

These examples may or may not jibe with common views of who becomes homeless in the United States in the twenty-first century, but all the stories in this book are about real people (we have changed their names).[1] In addition to showing the variety of pathways into homelessness, they exemplify categories of people that have been developed to help governments and social service systems respond to homelessness: adults homeless on their own, families homeless together with their children, veterans who become homeless after serving their country, young people who fall into homelessness after leaving their parents, and people whose patterns of homelessness are sustained or "chronic."

Efforts to classify people who become homeless go back half a millennium. In 1528, Martin Luther took a turn. His "Book of Vagabonds and Beggars" cataloged 28 varieties, ranging from "Bregers, or beggars who simply ask an alms for God's or the Holy Virgin's sake" to "Schleppers, or false begging priests" to "Süntregers, or pretended murderers, who say they have taken a man's life in self-defense, and unless they bring money at the right time they will have their heads cut off" (Ribton-Turner, 1887).

Early twentieth-century researchers had the same taxonomic impulse. For example, Solenberger (1911) profiled 1,000 homeless men who sought help from the city of Chicago from 1900 to 1903 in a book with chapters on "homeless old men," "chronic beggars," "confirmed wanderers or 'tramps'," and "homeless, vagrant and runaway boys." She also described their disabilities or deficits, with chapters on "the crippled and maimed," and "the insane, feeble-minded, and epileptic."

The twin foci on classification and deficits remain dominant tropes today, although we prefer "challenges" as a less pejorative term than "deficits" for describing mental illness and other issues that some people who experience homelessness struggle with. For both scholars and citizens who try to make sense of the growth of homelessness in our streets, it is perhaps natural to ask what is wrong with the people we encounter there. The rest of this book suggests that if the goal is to understand the causes of homelessness and come up with solutions, there are more important questions to ask.

---

[1] These examples are from a study of people who entered programs for homeless people called rapid re-housing. Sponsored by the U.S. Department of Housing and Urban Development, the study interviewed people at length in late 2018 and early 2019 (Jefferson, Thomas, Khadduri, & Mahathey, 2019). Authors Anna Jefferson and Hannah Thomas helped us add to the information that appears in that report, based on the transcriptions of the interviews.

One reason is that first impressions are often misleading. For example, contrary to both Luther and Solenberger, most people experiencing homelessness today do not panhandle, and many who panhandle are not homeless (Dordick, O'Flaherty, Brounstein, Sinha, & Yoo, 2018; Lee & Farrell, 2003).

Another reason is that people encountered in the middle of a homeless episode are arguably at the worst point in their lives. Many of the people we introduced at the beginning of the chapter had jobs and social connections before (and sometimes during) the time they were homeless. And as some of their stories show—and others would if we followed them long enough—most people emerge from episodes of homelessness and return to housing. People's characteristics change, along with their housing status.

Because most episodes of homelessness are fairly brief, far more people have encountered homelessness during their lives than are homeless on any given night. Indeed, as we will show later in this chapter, one of every 14 adult Americans living in normal housing told an interviewer in 1990 that there was a time in their lives when they had been homeless and slept in a shelter, abandoned building, or public place (Link et al., 1994). That's so many people that you must know at least one of them.

Before we get to the causes of homelessness in Chapter 2, and the solutions in Chapters 3–6, we need to take the measure of the problem. The remainder of this chapter defines homelessness based on where people sleep and describes groups of people such as families with children, adults, veterans, and how long they remain homeless. We describe characteristics such as age, race, and gender, and show how groups and characteristics have changed over time. We estimate how many people are homeless over a day, a year, or a lifetime, and finally consider the challenges many of them face. Along the way, we explain how we know what we know, and some limitations on our knowledge.

Where People Sleep: Definitions of Homelessness

By the late twentieth century, homelessness looked very different from how it appeared to Martin Luther in the sixteenth century or to researchers active between 1900 and 1980. In 1989, sociologist Peter Rossi described "modern" homelessness to distinguish it from earlier phenomena such as transient workers in the Great Depression and skid rows of family-less working men that were still common as of the 1970s. Rossi distinguished between literal homelessness and precarious housing. Literal homelessness—living on the streets, in a car, in a bus or train station, an encampment of tents or cardboard shacks, or an abandoned building – corresponds to most people's intuitive definitions of homelessness. Europeans call this "living rough." Rossi added those who sleep in shelters intended for homeless people. People who have access to a conventional home but may not be able to continue to stay there are precariously housed but are not literally homeless.[2] The U.S. Department of Housing and Urban Development (HUD) uses essentially Rossi's definition of literal homelessness, both to determine eligibility for programs that it funds to address homelessness and to estimate how many people are homeless.[3]

To limit disruptions in learning that result from precarious housing situations, the U.S. Department of Education takes a more expansive view of what constitutes homelessness to determine eligibility for programs The education definition includes children and youth in families that share housing with other people because of economic hardship (often called doubling up) or who pay to live in hotels or motels because of a lack of alternative accommodations (National Center for Homeless Education, 2017). The more expansive education estimates are reported by school authorities based on answers to questions on a form submitted by parents. In this and other sources of information in the United States, it is difficult to distinguish doubled up situations that are precarious from those that are not.

Europeans have resolved the definitional complexity with a typology that enables the media, policymakers, service providers, and researchers to specify just whom they are talking about, across national borders. The European Typology on Homelessness and Housing Exclusion, with 13 categories and 24 subcategories (European Federation of National Associations Working with the Homeless AISBL, 2017), derives from a conceptual framework that considers a physical domain of housing security (having exclusive possession of an adequate space), a social domain (being able to maintain privacy), and a legal domain (having legal title to occupation). These domains permit consideration of a variety of dimensions of housing insecurity that go beyond literal homelessness, providing that the data exist to support measuring them.

In the U.S., a consensus emerged in the late 1980s that it was useful to know how many people experienced literal homelessness and who they were, in order to design policies to stem the growth of literal homelessness and ultimately end it (Khadduri, 2015). In this book, we follow that consensus, and, when we refer to homelessness, we usually mean literal homelessness in the Rossi and HUD sense. Most research on homelessness refers to some part of this group, typically those who use shelters and other homeless assistance programs, because it is relatively easy to find people in these programs, although there is some information on people who sleep rough—or, in the terminology used in the United States, are "unsheltered."

---

[2] When the telephone survey in 1990 (Link et al., 1994) included people who said they slept in a friend's or relative's home because they were homeless, the number rose to 1 in 7 adult Americans. Although respondents labeled themselves as homeless, Rossi and HUD would classify them as precariously housed.

[3] HUD makes some exceptions for "imminent" homelessness in determining eligibility for its homeless assistance programs, but does not include imminently homeless people in its tallies of those experiencing homelessness, Examples are people fleeing domestic violence with neither a place to go nor resources to find one and people with chronic disabilities who have moved twice or more in the past two months (U.S. Department of Housing and Urban Development, 2018a).

Data Sources

Before describing more about the characteristics of people experiencing homelessness, we review the data that inform our descriptions. These data are extensive but not infallible, especially when considered for a particular city.

The Department of HUD mandates communities and organizations that accept HUD funds to keep records in a Homelessness Management Information System (HMIS) and report both numbers and characteristics of people who used homeless shelters and other assistance programs to the federal government. Communities report numbers in categories, not individual records of people or households, for HUD's national accounting. When the data system was first created, there were major concerns about the privacy and safety of vulnerable households, and the decision was made not to create a single, national data system but instead to have communities report aggregate data to HUD and to share data with each other if they wanted to do that.

The best national data come from these local systems, aggregated into the Annual Homeless Assessment Reports to Congress (Henry, Bishop, de Sousa, Shivji, & Watt, 2018; Henry, Mahathey, et al., 2018). An advantage of a community-wide system is that it allows calculation of the number of people who use some sort of facility over the course of a year and avoids double-counting of people who use more than one program during that time. Even if all homeless-serving organizations in a community cooperate in a single system, someone who moves from a shelter in one town to a shelter in another town could be double-counted. Thirteen states[4] have state-wide homeless management information systems, either because they are small states with only one planning organization for homelessness or because they have succeeded in merging local systems into a statewide system. People who move across state lines are still missed, as are people who move across communities in many of the larger states.

Entities that do not receive federal funds do not have to report data to the HMIS on people who use their facility, leading to estimates in some communities that are based on weighting up the data that is reported based on the number of beds in these other facilities. In Nashville TN, where Beth lives, only 3% of the beds in emergency shelters were included in 2016, because the Rescue Mission and another large faith-based provider did not participate. More recently, both providers agreed to cooperate, but because of incompatibility of computer systems, a city staffer had to reenter their data for 2017 by hand.

Gradually, around the country, systems are improving, as communities overcome the technical difficulties implementing information systems and as additional programs without federal funding agree to submit data to local systems.

---

[4] Alaska, Connecticut, Iowa, Maine, Michigan, Minnesota, Nebraska, New Jersey, Washington, West Virginia, Wisconsin, Wyoming, and Vermont.

An important reason for the improvement is that many communities use the data for local planning and performance measurement and not just responding to a federal requirement. As of 2017, an estimated 70% of people who used emergency shelters and transitional housing programs[5] were included in HMIS reporting (Henry, Bishop, et al., 2018).

In addition to the required reporting about people who use homeless assistance programs, HUD requires communities to do a point-in-time (PIT) count of all people experiencing homelessness, both sheltered and unsheltered, at least every other year, and many communities do one annually. The count happens on a specific night at the end of January, because in cold weather people experiencing homelessness are more likely to sleep indoors, where they are easier to count. But how to count people who are not sleeping in a shelter on that night but instead on the "street?" In most communities, teams of outreach workers and volunteers go to known locations, and ride around in cars in the middle of the night to try to spot and sometimes interview people who are out of doors. However, people experiencing homelessness often have good reasons to remain hidden, and counters are told not to put themselves at risk by searching for them, so such counts are inevitably incomplete.

Together with colleagues, Beth tried to judge just how incomplete the street count was in New York City in 2005 (Hopper, Shinn, Laska, Meisner, & Wanderling, 2008). The City has one of the most sophisticated counts in the country. It divides the entire city into small packets of a few blocks, a transportation hub, or a subway station. It uses the best information available – from police, outreach workers, and previous counts—to estimate whether a homeless person will be found there. It then sends teams of volunteers on foot to all the packets where it expects to find people, and a random sample of the others, in the middle of the night with instructions to interview everyone found there and ascertain whether they are homeless. (People who are sleeping are counted without waking them.) The street count is then the actual number counted in places where people were expected plus a statistical extrapolation from places where they were not.

We did two things to estimate the undercount. First, we planted people masquerading as homeless in locations where we knew counters were assigned to see whether they were counted. (If so the plant gave a sticker to the counting team for its tally sheet, to be sure that the plants were not confused with people actually experiencing homelessness.) By all accounts, the counters accepted finding the plants as a challenge that motivated them to be more thorough. Beth was one such plant: I shivered in a torn coat on the lower level of the Union Square subway station near New York University where I taught at the time, hoping that none of my students would come by, but also hoping the counters would find me so I could go somewhere warmer before my tour of duty ended at 4 a.m.

---

[5] Both of these offer temporary shelter and typically some supportive services.

The counters nabbed me and, overall, 71% of the plants. In most cases that were missed, the counters never showed up. Occasionally there was confusion over boundaries (did the counters' park zone include the bench between the park wall and the street?). Additionally, counters gave more or less plausible reasons (an apparent tryst or undercover stakeout) why they assumed someone was not homeless and did not ask.

Second, we visited soup kitchens, mobile food programs, drop-in centers and the like over the next 2 days, and asked people where they had been on the night of the count. If they were homeless and not in shelter, we asked follow-up questions to ascertain whether they could have been counted, if counters sent to their location had done exactly what they were instructed to do. For example, if people said they were on the subway, we asked whether they went to the end of the line, where counters moved onto cars to interview people who did not get off. Only 70% of people were in places where they could plausibly have been counted. Others—on a rooftop, in an abandoned building or a stairwell of an occupied one, in a parking structure, or on a porch behind shrubbery were not visible to teams walking the streets.

To be included in the street count, a person had both to be in a visible place (as all the plants were) and to be counted. Thus the proportions from the two stages of our study multiply—suggesting that about half of the people who were sleeping rough that night were missed, although that estimate is not precise. Further, people were more likely to be found if they were in Manhattan, where most buildings are flush with sidewalks and most alleys are walled off, than in outer boroughs, where the varied streetscapes provide more hidden places. The rest of the country looks more like the outer boroughs than like Manhattan, suggesting that street counts elsewhere probably miss more. For example, in the huge geography that constitutes the Los Angeles metropolitan area, many people who sleep under freeways and in other dispersed locations probably are missed.

Unsheltered people who are found during the PIT count are added to the numbers in shelters and transitional housing programs that night. New York's overall PIT count is also better than those of many other cities, because people have a legal right to shelter. So a much larger proportion of homeless people in New York stay in facilities where the count is essentially perfect. However, people who are not found, or who are unsheltered on a different night would not be included in the PIT count, although they may appear in annual numbers if they also use shelter during the course of the year.

Despite their shortcomings, the most detailed national information on the characteristics of people who experience literal homelessness come from these two sources—the administrative data in Homeless Management Information Systems and the one-night, PIT counts. The latter are less detailed, because it is hard to ask people a lot of questions about themselves when counting them in unsheltered locations in the middle of the night. What do these data sources tell us?

Groups of People Who Experience Literal Homelessness

The starting point for classifying people who experience homelessness is to distinguish adults and children who experience homelessness together ("families") from people who experience homelessness without an accompanying child ("individuals"). This distinction is made by the U.S. Department of HUD in its annual reports to Congress, by the U.S. Interagency Council on Homelessness in federal strategic plans to end homelessness, and by community-level planners who are responsible for allocating federal and local resources to address homelessness. The distinction between families and individuals is based loosely on the research literature that began to describe modern homelessness in the late 1980s, as well as the arrangements localities made for shelters, especially in the eastern part of the U.S. It has proved useful for policy and practice. Other groupings (veterans, youth, and people with chronic patterns of homelessness) overlap with both families and individuals.

Families with Children

Nationally, on any given night, close to half (46%) of all people experiencing homelessness in shelters are members of families staying in shelters together (Henry, Mahathey, et al., 2018). In contrast, only a third (34%) of people in shelters at some time over the course of a year are in families (Henry, Bishop, et al., 2018; Henry, Mahathey, et al., 2018). Because families stay in shelters for longer periods of time than individuals, they are more likely to be found in shelters on any particular night. Expanding the definition of homelessness beyond literal homelessness—for example, using the Department of Education's definition that includes doubling up—could make the proportion of people with insecure housing that are in families with children rather than individuals even higher. But there is no count of people without children who meet the Department of Education definition, so we really don't know.[6]

More than 290,000 children under the age of 18 used shelters with their families at some time during the most recent year for which we have data (Henry, Bishop, et al., 2018, p. 3.9). Few children show up in the unsheltered counts (only available for a single night), as adults rarely take a child with them to an unsheltered location (Henry, Mahathey, et al., 2018, pp. 1–3 and exhibit 4.1). However, homelessness affects many more families with minor children than the data on people using shelters or found on the streets imply. Many people in shelters for single adults are in fact parents of minor children from whom they have been separated, and the same may be true of people experiencing unsheltered

---

[6] The Department of Education reports that 1,300,957 students aged 3 through grade 12 who were enrolled in public school or preschool programs met its larger definition of homelessness in the 2015–2016 school year; that estimate excludes children too young to enroll in school, as well as adults without children (Henry, Bishop, et al., 2018).

homelessness. In one large national study of people experiencing homelessness conducted in 1996, 47% of the people surveyed reported that they had minor children, but only 15% had a child with them during the episode of homelessness. One third of mothers were separated from all of their minor children (Burt et al., 1999).

In the more recent Family Options Study, a large experiment that enrolled 2,282 families with children 15 or under from 57 homeless shelters in 12 sites,[7] all families had a child with them, but 24% also had a minor child living elsewhere. The vast majority of these separations were informal; less than 1% of respondents reported that a child was in foster care. Over a quarter of families (27%) were headed by a couple, with both partners together in the shelter, but another 10% had a spouse or partner somewhere else (Gubits et al., 2015; Walton, Dunton, & Groves, 2017).

The separation of families is the first example of several we will cite about how demographic and other characteristics of people who are observed during an episode of homelessness may reflect the experience of homelessness and the programs communities use to address it. In in-depth interviews with a subsample of 80 families in the Family Options Study, some parents reported separating from some children to spare them from shelter conditions (often after they had entered shelter together) although they most often described economic hardship as the reason for the separation, like this mother interviewed in Alameda County, California:

> At the time I was pregnant, and we were living in motels. I found myself getting broke. We were eating fast foods. I got paid from my job and I called their dad, and I said, "[Ex-Partner], I love my boys, I know you love them too, but I need help right now." We met and he took the boys... I didn't have a refrigerator or nothing like that, so I don't want my boys to—it was beginning to be too much.[8]

Data for the entire sample show that only about a fifth of separations from children occurred around the time of a shelter entry; most separations happened well before (sometimes during episodes of precarious housing that would be counted as homeless under the broader Department of Education definition), and additional separations happened afterward (Walton et al., 2017). Mothers described separations from current partners or spouses, in contrast, as related to shelter rules that excluded men or couples that were not legally wed. Rules led to other family separations as well. Shelters were sometimes unable to accommodate all minor children, especially older boys (2 families in the group of 80 with

---

[7] Participating sites were: Alameda County, CA; Atlanta, GA; Baltimore, MD;, Boston, MA; Bridgeport, New Haven, Norwalk, Stamford and Fairfield County, CT; Denver, CA; Honolulu, HI; Kansas City, MO; Louisville, KY; Minneapolis, MN; Phoenix, AZ; and Salt Lake City, UT.

[8] Quotations in this section are from the Family Options Study and were previously published in (Shinn, Gibbons-Benton, & Brown, 2015).

in-depth interviews), a 20-year old child who moved back in with his family later, or a three-generational family where the mother and grandmother each took one child so that both adults would be eligible for a family shelter. Altogether, shelters failed to accommodate 12 of the 80 families in their entirety (Shinn et al., 2015). Mothers felt these separations acutely:

> [T]hen I had to move all the stuff out, and there wasn't no help at the time, because it was just a shelter for women and children. He wasn't with me at the time. He was staying with his mom trying to situate stuff, so it was like—if he was here, it would be so much easier, but they didn't allow that.

Shelter policies and programs also shape patterns of homelessness for people who go to shelters. A study of family shelter users in New York City, Philadelphia, Columbus OH, and the State of Massachusetts found that the majority of people had just one fairly short stay, but "fairly short" ranged from episodes of 30 days in Columbus to 131 days in New York. About a fifth have long episodes, ranging from 144 days in Columbus to 467 days in New York. A small group (2–8%) had multiple brief episodes—these families were also more likely to use psychiatric and substance abuse service systems (Culhane, Metraux, Park, Schretzman, & Valente, 2007). Average stays three times as long in New York as in Columbus are unlikely to result from different characteristics of families in the two cities. In the Massachusetts sample, no one had more than two episodes, and no one with a long stay had more than one in the 2-year observation period, because families usually are not permitted to return to Massachusetts shelters within a year of leaving them (Bourquin, 2015). Even relatively sophisticated researchers sometimes confuse patterns engendered by policies with characteristics of people.[9]

Adults on Their Own

Nationally, almost two-thirds (65%) of people who use shelters at some time over the course of a year are individuals—that is, adults without children with them. Similarly, 67% of people homeless on a particular night are individuals, but this includes unsheltered people, 90% of whom are not part of a family with children. Only 54% of those using shelters on a particular night are individuals (Henry, Bishop, et al., 2018; Henry, Mahathey, et al., 2018).

Most of those considered individuals are by themselves—less than 3% of those who use shelters do so together with another adult. Again, this is partly, although certainly not entirely, a consequence of shelter policies. We have already noted that men may be excluded from family shelters, and there are relatively few locales where childless

---

[9] Social psychologists find that people generally attribute too much of human behavior to the characteristics and personality of people who act in some way and too little to the situations that people find themselves in. This mental mistake is so ubiquitous that psychologists call it "the fundamental attribution error."

couples or childless families with other configurations can be accommodated together. In Nashville's 2019 PIT count, for example, over 30% of the 236 unsheltered people interviewed reported that they were homeless with someone else on the night of the count—half with a spouse or partner and the remainder with other relatives, including adult children, and friends (Bernard, 2019). The ability to live with a loved one, or even a beloved pet, is a reason some people stay on the streets.

The national data show that individuals use shelters for only short periods of time, a median of 22 nights over the most recent 1-year period (Henry, Bishop, et al., 2018). Often, those 22 nights are not continuous but instead are interspersed with periods when the individual is housed (perhaps precariously) or is sleeping rough. Most individuals who use shelters do so only once, and relatively briefly, with brevity often depending on the shelter policies of the jurisdiction where they experience homelessness.

By analyzing shelter records, Culhane and colleagues showed that four-fifths of individual adults who entered shelters in Philadelphia and New York City stayed briefly (an average of 20 days in Philadelphia and 57 in New York), and most did not return during the 2- or 3-year follow-up period. The authors dubbed this pattern transitional. The rest were almost evenly divided among people who shuttled in and out of short stays in shelter and a second group with fewer, but longer, episodes. By self-report and administrative records, the latter two groups had more medical and behavioral health problems (Kuhn & Culhane, 1998).[10] This study was groundbreaking in its demonstration that so many individuals experience homelessness in single, brief episodes. Homelessness is not a permanent trait, but a temporary state that most people pass through before returning to housing (Shinn, 1997).

People with Chronic Patterns of Homelessness

The transitory nature of shelter use for many people and the extensive use of the shelter system by individuals who stay for long consecutive periods or come back often gave rise to the concept of "chronic" homelessness. HUD defines chronicity not only by the length of literal homelessness but also by the presence of a disability, on the grounds that people who meet both criteria will need housing with ongoing supports. To meet the definition, an individual must have been homeless for at least a year, either continuously or over at least four episodes in the past 3 years,[11] and also have a diagnosable substance use disorder, serious mental illness, developmental disability, posttraumatic stress disorder, cognitive impairment resulting from a brain injury, or chronic physical illness or disability (U.S. Department of Housing and Urban Development, 2015a).

---

[10] This is in contrast with the parallel study of families, where long stayers were not more troubled than those who used the shelter system briefly.

[11] The definition was revised in 2015 to reflect total time homeless rather than including people with brief episodes that did not total a year.

About a quarter (24%) of all individuals experiencing homelessness on a particular night in 2018 had chronic patterns, and almost two-thirds of them (65%) were staying in unsheltered locations (Henry, Mahathey, et al., 2018). Many fewer families with children have chronic patterns of homelessness. Communities recently began to report that number, and only 5% of people in families would meet the HUD definition of chronic homelessness (Henry, Mahathey, et al., 2018, p. 3.3).

The definition of chronic homelessness focuses on people who are literally homeless –who make extensive use of the shelter system or often sleep in unsheltered locations, or both. For this group, the periods of time not literally homeless may still be remarkably unstable. As Shlay and Rossi (1992) put it, "the line between being homeless and being domiciled is a fuzzy boundary, often and easily crossed." For example, more than half of a small sample of individuals with serious mental illnesses who entered a shelter in Westchester County had spent most of the past 5 years riding an institutional circuit of shelters, jails, detox facilities, psychiatric hospitals, rehabilitation facilities and the street, punctuated by stays in their own place or living doubled up with other households (Hopper, Jost, Hay, Welber, & Haugland, 1997).

Youth

The federal government's 2010 strategic plan to end homelessness (U.S. Interagency Council on Homelessness, 2010) established separate goals for youth, and HUD began to track additional categories: unaccompanied children under the age of 18, youth aged 18–25 not accompanied by parents or their own children (also included in the counts of individuals); and parenting youth under 25 who have children with them but are not accompanied by anyone over 25 (also included in the counts of families if the parent is at least 18). The 2018 national point-in-time counts found around 36,000 unaccompanied children and youth and 8,700 parenting youth. Parenting youth are almost all 18–25 rather than younger than 18, and they make up about 15% of all family households (Henry, Mahathey, et al., 2018).[12]

Among the unaccompanied young people (sheltered and unsheltered), only 11% were children under the age of 18 (4,000 compared to 107,000 children experiencing homelessness in the company of adults (Henry, Mahathey, et al., 2018, pp. 1–3). Overwhelmingly, minor children who experience the literal homelessness reported by HUD do so as part of families.

However, researchers who focus on adolescent homelessness describe the way in which unaccompanied youth experience homelessness as different in kind from that of older adults or of children who are part of families. Instead of sleeping outdoors or going to shelters, young people who have run away or been thrown

---

[12] The most recent Interagency Council Plan continues to set populations-specific goals for youth (U.S. Interagency Council on Homelessness, 2018b).

out by their families often "couch surf" with friends or are in makeshift and, all too often unsafe or exploitative arrangements (Family and Youth Services Bureau, n.d.; Morton, Dworsky, & Samuels, 2017).

Programs that are funded by the U.S. Department of Health and Human Services to serve homeless youth use a definition of homelessness that is broader than the eligibility criteria for HUD programs. The Runaway and Homeless Youth Act (RHYA) counts as homeless anyone up to age 21 "for whom it is not possible to live in a safe environment with a relative and who have no other safe alternative living situation" (U.S. Department of Health and Human Services, 2016a). Claims that adolescence is the age at highest risk of homelessness usually count young people, including young adults, who meet one of these expanded definitions and also count young parents in families. Some of these young parents were formerly unaccompanied youth who became pregnant or bore children while homeless (Toro, Dworsky, & Fowler, 2007) whereas others became home-less only after becoming pregnant or having a child.

HUD's estimates of numbers of youth experiencing unaccompanied home-lessness are almost certainly undercounts, both because youth may use programs other than the shelters included in the administrative data reported by communi-ties and because unsheltered youth may be even more likely than adults to avoid being found by street counts. HUD's estimates also do not include couch-surfing or staying in exploitative situations—for example, as a victim of trafficking (Family and Youth Services Bureau, n.d.). In the Voices of Youth Count, a nationally representative sample of households, 12.5% of households with an 18–25-year-old member reported that at least one such member had experienced homeless-ness (self-defined) or couch surfing without stable housing in the past 12 months. Follow-up interviews with a small sample of individual youth themselves yielded a rate (including couch surfing) of 9.7% (Morton et al., 2017).

The Voices of Youth Count national survey also found that 4.3% of house-holds with children 13–17 had a child who had run away, left home because of being asked to leave, couch surfed, or been homeless, although it is not clear that all these children were homeless on their own (Morton et al., 2017). The reasons that children leave home, including family conflict over sexual orienta-tion, step-parent relationships, and children's behavior (Toro, Dworsky, et al., 2007), are largely different than the reasons that adults become homeless, and the solutions are also quite different. What it takes to resolve homelessness for 13-year-olds who have run away or been forced to leave home are quite differ-ent from what from what it takes for 18-year-olds who are capable of living on their own and holding a lease. In subsequent chapters, we do not consider causes of homelessness or solutions for minor children who become homeless on their own. Young adults ("youth") 18 and over are included—but typically not broken out—in many of the studies we cite later. Some studies concern special populations of young adults, such as youth aging out of the foster care system. As of this writing, evidence on the effectiveness of special programs for young adults is scarce.

Veterans

In the wake of the U.S. military involvement in Iraq and Afghanistan, federal policymakers became concerned that traumatic combat experience elevates the risk of homelessness, and in 2009 HUD began tracking the numbers of veterans among people experiencing homelessness and describing their characteristics. Similar to all veterans, about 90% are men (Henry, Bishop, et al., 2018). They are more likely to be African American or Hispanic and much less likely to be over 62 years of age than all U.S. veterans, a population that as of the early twenty-first century still reflects the era when U.S. military forces were much larger and relied on the draft rather than on self-selection of volunteers.

So far, those in age groups most likely to have served in Iraq or Afghanistan have only slightly higher rates of homelessness, while those with the highest rates are in middle or late middle age. For example, in 2017, 42% of veterans experiencing homelessness were 51–61 years old, compared with only 18% of all U.S. veterans (Henry, Bishop, et al., 2018). Veterans almost always (98%) experience homelessness on their own (Henry, Bishop, et al., 2018). They may have been married or had a partner, but the partner is no longer with them.

Age, Race, and Gender

When asked to imagine a homeless person, most people think of an ill-kempt middle-aged man. It is true that there are more adults than children who are homeless, but the age at which a person in the United States is most likely to spend a night in shelter is infancy. Figure 1.1 shows the percentage of people of different ages who experience sheltered homelessness, calculated by dividing the number of people HUD reports as experiencing sheltered homelessness over the course of the year by the numbers in the same age groups in the total U.S. population.

As the figure shows, infants under the age of one are at higher risk of homelessness than any other age group. Risk remains high during the preschool years and then drops when children enter school and childcare costs go down. Risk continues to fall in adolescence and rises again in early adulthood (the period through age 24 that is included in youth homelessness) and especially the late 20s, when some young people are the parents of those young children. Risk remains nearly as high in middle adulthood and then falls off sharply among older adults. One's picture of a "typical homeless person" may need to be broadened.

Among adults (including youth over 18), more men than women experience homelessness over the course of a year, 62% vs. 38% (Henry, Mahathey, et al., 2018). The numbers are still more uneven among those who do not have children with them, 71% men vs. 29% women among those using a shelter at some time during a year. Even in families, over a fifth (22%) of adults are men, and data from the Family Options experiment suggest this number would be still higher—perhaps 27%—if family shelters did not exclude them.

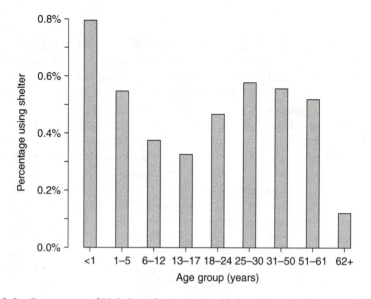

Figure 1.1 Percentage of U.S. Population Using Shelter Over the Course of a Year (2016–2017) by Age Group. Numbers of people experiencing homelessness from Supporting Resources for the 2017 Annual Homeless Assessment Report to Congress Part 2 (Henry, Bishop, et al., 2018). Numbers of people in the U.S. population for 2017 from annual estimates of the resident population by single year of age and sex for the United States, States, and Puerto Rico Commonwealth: April 1, 2010 to July 1, 2017 (U.S. Census Bureau, 2018).

HUD does not include people, overwhelmingly women, who use domestic violence shelters, in these estimates, but the number of beds in domestic violence shelters is not large, so this does not account for the difference (Henry, Bishop, et al., 2018). Women, especially women with children, may be more able than men to persuade kin or non-kin to take them in to doubled-up households,[13] and they have access to some additional safety-net resources. Unaccompanied young people (children and youth under the age of 25) are somewhat more likely to be male, especially if they are on the street, but unaccompanied youth include more women and girls when compared with all adults who are homeless on their own (Henry, Mahathey, et al., 2018; Toro, Dworsky, et al., 2007).

African Americans and Native Americans are especially likely to become homeless (Burt et al., 1999; Hopper & Milburn, 1996). African Americans are particularly heavily represented among families who use shelters, with 52% of that population identifying as black or African American in 2017. By comparison, the African American share of the family population with incomes below the federal poverty

---

[13] Maycock and Bretherton (2016) and the chapter by Pleace (2016) in particular describe the ways that women's homelessness in Europe is often hidden.

level was 23% in the same year. Both shares have dropped somewhat in recent years (Henry, Bishop, et al., 2018).

Homelessness is largely an urban phenomenon. People who experience homelessness over the course of a year are more likely to be in principal cities[14] (72.5%) than either the entire U.S. population (32.5%) or people living in poverty (39.6%), although the number in suburban and rural locations has increased from 23.1 to 27.5% since 2007 (Henry, Bishop, et al., 2018). Here again, homeless services may shape or distort our understanding of people who experience homelessness. Most services are located in cities, so people who become homeless in nearby areas without shelters may migrate there. A study that used HMIS data to look at migration patterns in two states where that was possible, Iowa and Michigan, documented some migration from suburban areas into cities, based on the zip code of the last permanent address before the person entered a shelter. The study found essentially no migration out of rural areas (Leopold, Culhane, & Khadduri, 2017).

Youth who become homeless may or may not differ from the general population in their locale with respect to race or ethnicity (Toro, Dworsky, et al., 2007), but they are disproportionately sexual minorities. Estimates of the proportion of lesbian, gay, bisexual, and transgender (LGBT) youth range from 6 to 40% (Durso & Gates, 2012; Toro, Dworsky, et al., 2007). The 40% estimate comes from a national survey of 354 organizations serving homeless youth (primarily 18 and older) that made special efforts to include agencies serving LGBT youth (Durso & Gates, 2012); the midpoint of earlier estimates is closer to 20% (Toro, Dworsky, et al., 2007). The recent Voices of Youth Count Survey conducted in 2016 and 2017 found no significant difference between urban and rural areas in the prevalence of homelessness for young adults 18–25 (Morton et al., 2018), but that survey also was relatively small and included couch surfing as well as literal homelessness.

Changes Over Time

The patterns seen today by age, gender, race, and family status are a relatively recent phenomenon. After the "Hoovervilles" of the Great Depression (shanty towns of people without jobs) and up until the early 1970s, most people who experienced homelessness were older white men who no longer were able to do the physically demanding work of their younger years, currently had no job or intermittent, poorly paid jobs, and often had disabilities (Bogue, 1963). These men rarely slept on the street, although they were certainly "inadequately housed" in single-room occupancy hotels (with no kitchen and a bathroom down the hall), mission dormitories, or flophouses. Many of the latter were divided into windowless five by seven-foot cubicles with partitions that did not extend to the

---

[14] A U.S. Census Bureau classification.

ceiling or floor. The wire mesh that filled the gap, allowing for minimal privacy and security, gave rise to the moniker "cage hotels" (Rossi, 1989, p. 30). Before public drunkenness was decriminalized, some slept in police stations and jails. Researchers focused more on the men's lack of social ties than on their housing circumstances (Bahr, 1973; Grigsby, Baumann, Gregorich, & Roberts-Gray, 1990). Although several studies estimated that only about a quarter of men were alcoholics, researchers emphasized this problem, for example, entitling a book about New York's skid row *Old Men Drunk and Sober* (Bahr & Caplow, 1973). Many observers thought that the problem of homelessness would disappear as this older generation of men came to the end of their lives (Bogue, 1963).

But homelessness did not die off. It changed. By the late 1970s, "the new homeless," younger men, often African American, along with some women and even families, began to emerge (New York City Commission on the Homeless, 1992). Further, the shrinkage of skid rows associated with urban renewal made the residual "old" homelessness more visible. The decriminalization of vagrancy and public drunkenness meant that people who might once have sobered up in jail were now on the streets (Shlay & Rossi, 1992). Efforts to count and categorize people experiencing homelessness led to wildly differing estimates of the composition and characteristics of people experiencing homelessness during the 1980s. Nevertheless, across 60 studies conducted from 1981 to 1988, 26% of people identified as homeless were women, over 40% were black, and the median age was 37 (Shlay & Rossi, 1992), a far cry from the older white men of the 1960s.

The age distribution of homelessness has continued to change, quite separately for single men and for parents in families. Men born in the latter half of the baby boom, from the mid-1950s to the mid-1960s, continued to dominate the numbers from 1988 to 2010, both in decennial census data (when the census conducted shelter counts) and in data from the Department of Homeless Services in New York City, which has the longest, most complete records of shelter usage. The age at which a single man was at highest risk of being found in a shelter (relative to the numbers in the overall population), peaked at 34–36 in 1990, 37–42 in 2000, and 49–51 in 2010 (Culhane, Metraux, Byrne, Stino, & Bainbridge, 2013).

In the New York data, it is not the same people who continue to experience homelessness across the different decades, but newcomers to the homeless system are most often drawn from the same cohort of late baby-boomers (Culhane et al., 2013). In-depth interviews with homeless individuals sampled at a New York City drop-in center for older adults found that roughly half of the sample (42 of 79) had led conventional lives with long periods of residential stability and employment through middle age (e.g., a grocery store manager, an army colonel, a fundraiser for a nonprofit) until some event, and usually a cascade of events, pitched them into homelessness. The other 37 people had more long-standing patterns of housing instability, although not necessarily literal homelessness (Shinn et al., 2007).

Similarly, in San Francisco, successive groups of literally homeless adults found at shelters and free meal programs in San Francisco in each of four time periods, had a median age of 37 in 1990–1994 and a median of 46 in 2003. The earliest group had been homeless for 2 years on average, but the last group reported 6 years of literal homelessness (Hahn, Kushel, Bangsberg, Riley, & Moss, 2006).

The national data reported by HUD show a similar aging trend. Among people experiencing homelessness as individuals, the percentage 62 years and older grew from 4% in 2007 to 8% in 2018, and the percentage between 51 and 61 years old grew from 20 to 26% (Henry, Bishop, et al., 2018).

The story for families with children is different. In the New York City data, from 1988 to 2005, the modal age of heads of families remained 21–23 (Culhane et al., 2013). More recent national data on families suggest an older typical age, as only 23% of adults in families using shelters at some time during 2017 were between the ages of 18 and 23. There was only a very small aging trend between 2007 and 2017 (Henry, Bishop, et al., 2018). Because infants and preschool children are common in families experiencing homelessness, it may be the age of children rather than the age of their parents that is critical for families. About half of the children in families using shelters over the course of a year are under the age of 6, and 11% are infants less than 1 year old (Henry, Bishop, et al., 2018). The slight increase in age of mothers may be because the mean age of U.S. mothers generally at the time their first child was born increased from 24.1 in 1988 to 26.8 in 2017 (Martin et al., 2018; Mathews & Hamilton, 2002). The number of adult men in homeless families is increasing (Henry, Bishop, et al., 2018), but this may be a function of the increasing willingness of shelters to accommodate couples rather than the changing composition of the families themselves.

The last decade has seen important changes in the numbers of people experiencing homelessness—changes that are particularly marked for people with chronic patterns of homelessness and for veterans. Overall, the number of people counted nationally in PIT counts decreased almost 15% from about 647,000 in 2007 to about 553,000 in 2018. Most of the drop of close to 100,000 total people was among people who were unsheltered. The numbers of people in shelter (on a single night) stood at about 391,000 in 2007, rose a bit during the aftermath of the Great Recession, came back to 391,000 in 2015, and has dropped a bit—to 358,000—since then. The additional progress in the last 3 years has been partially offset by a smaller increase in the unsheltered population (Henry, Mahathey, et al., 2018).

The number of people with chronic patterns found on the night of the counts decreased 26% from about 120,000 to less than 89,000 over the same period (Henry, Mahathey, et al., 2018).[15] We think that decrease is real, not just a matter of reporting, because we do not think that systematic changes have taken place in

---

[15] This figure is based on estimates from point-in-time counts. Based on revised HMIS data standards and reporting protocols, HUD expects to start using administrative data to estimate the number of people homeless over the course of a year who have chronic patterns of homelessness.

the way communities nationwide count chronically homeless individuals. We also think the drop is consistent with the success of permanent supportive housing programs that combine housing with voluntary services, as we will discuss in Chapter 3, on ending homelessness for people who experience it.

The number of veterans experiencing homelessness nationally fell even more dramatically from about 73,000 in 2010 (the first year data were available), to about 38,000 in 2018 (Henry, Mahathey, et al., 2018). We believe that federal and local policy efforts that we will describe later, in Chapters 3 and 4, account for cutting veteran homelessness nearly in half. These decreases, especially for veterans, show what can be done with concerted effort.

Total Numbers Over a Day, a Year, or a Lifetime

We have HUD's estimate of 553,000 people on a single night in January, 2018. Given the likely undercounts of people staying in unsheltered locations, the total number of people experiencing homelessness in the U.S. nationwide on a particular night in January 2018 was probably more than 600,000.

But what about longer periods? Over the course of a year, we believe the number is closer to 1.6 million people. HUD's estimate of the number of different people who used a shelter at some point during the course of a year was just over 1.4 million in 2017, dropping from almost 1.6 million in 2007.[16] To get a total that includes people who were unsheltered, we might add another 200,000. That is the unsheltered PIT count, which as we have already pointed out, misses many people

---

[16] The way programs that serve homeless people are labeled may result in undercounts, both of people homeless on a particular night and of people homeless over the course of a year. HUD considers people homeless if they stay either in emergency shelters or in transitional housing programs, which do not provide permanent housing but instead temporary shelter for up to 2 years. There is no bright line between emergency shelters and transitional housing, either in actual lengths of stay or in the types of services provided. After some attempt to create definitions (Jill was involved), HUD gave up and accepts whatever programs choose to call themselves.

With encouragement from HUD and advocacy organizations, and based on evidence that transitional housing was not effective (see Chapter 4), many communities have shifted their emphasis from transitional housing beds, whose occupants are counted as homeless, to short-term rental subsidies ("rapid re-housing"), whose occupants are deemed permanently housed. The logic of considering people in rapid re-housing programs permanently housed is that, although the subsidy is short-term, people with the rapid re-housing form of assistance live in housing they control and in which they could remain if they could find a way to pay the rent after the subsidy ends. When reporting data to HUD, communities appear to have changed the labels of some programs from transitional housing to emergency shelter (which does not affect the counts of sheltered homeless people) and the labels of other programs from transitional housing to rapid re-housing (which does). Such relabeling may account for some of the drop in sheltered homelessness—e.g., the 3,700 fewer families counted in shelters and transitional housing programs in January 2018 compared to January 2017, at the same time the inventory of transitional housing dropped by about 20,000 units (Henry, Bishop, et al., 2018; Henry, Mahathey, et al., 2018). But we don't really know, so we do not make an adjustment to the number of people using shelters over the course of a year.

who were on the streets that night. It also misses people who were unsheltered on a different night during the year. But many people who experience unsheltered homelessness also use shelters at other times and are already in the 1.4 million. If about the same number who are missed also use shelters at any point over the year, then the total number of people experiencing literal homelessness over the course of a year may be 1.6 million.[17,18]

Thus far we have estimates of people homeless on a particular night (sheltered and unsheltered, about 600,000 people) and people homeless over the course of a year in shelters (about 1.6 million people). But a year is a short period of time. Much larger estimates of the number of people experiencing homelessness come from asking people who are living in conventional housing about homelessness they experienced at some time during their lives and not just in the past year or two.

Back in 1990, researchers led by Bruce Link undertook a study of public attitudes toward homelessness with a rigorous sample survey of adults in households with telephones in the continental United States. Because they thought that those attitudes might be influenced by people's personal experiences of homelessness, they decided to ask about those experiences and then to ask some follow-up questions to anyone who acknowledged having been homeless in the past. Survey organizations charge researchers by the minute for asking questions, thus the organization Link hired to do the survey had to come up with some sort of estimate of the number of people who would be asked the follow-up questions. Organizational representatives decided it would be such a small number that it would not be worth any charge. (After all, this was a household survey—anyone currently homeless or staying in a prison or mental hospital—who might be at higher risk of having been homeless in the past—would not be included.) They guessed wrong.

Fully 14.0% of the 1,507 survey respondents answered yes to the question "Have you ever had a time in your life when you considered yourself homeless?" and 4.6% said they had been homeless between 1985 and 1990 (Link et al., 1994, p. 1909). Respondents who classified themselves as having been homeless were asked three follow-up questions: "While you were homeless, did you ever (1) sleep in a park, in an abandoned building, in the street, or in a train or bus station?; (2) sleep in a shelter for homeless people or in another temporary residence because you did not have a place to stay?; (3) sleep in a friend's or relative's home because you were homeless?" (p. 1909). A little over half of the people who said

---

[17] In the point-in-time counts in Nashville in 2018 and 2019, about half of unsheltered people who were interviewed said that they had used a shelter at some time during the past year (Bernard, 2019).

[18] Broader definitions yield larger numbers. For example, HUD counted 270,301 children aged 6 to 17 in shelters and transitional housing programs from October, 2015 to September, 2016 (Solari, Shivji, de Sousa, Watt, & Silverbush, 2017). The U.S. Department of Education counted 1,300,957 children enrolled in public schools (including preschool programs) that met its broader definition of homelessness in the 2015–2016 school year (Henry, Bishop, et al., 2018).

they had been homeless at some time in their life, 7.4% of the survey respondents, said yes to one of the first two questions and were classified as literally homeless.[19] The other people, who said yes to only to the last question, were classified as precariously housed. The sequence of questions did not allow the researchers to determine definitively the percentage of people who had been literally homeless in the past 5 years, but 3.1% of the sample said they had been homeless in the past 5 years and also met the criteria for literal homelessness at some point in their lives.

The researchers asked about total duration of homelessness (including doubling up): the most frequent reply (46%) was between a month and a year. Only 8% had been homeless for less than a week, 33% between a week and a month, and 13% for over a year. In 1990 there were slightly over 185 million adults living in the United States, so the researchers estimated that 13.5 million adults had been literally homeless at some time in their lives, and nearly 26 million had considered themselves homeless if doubling up is included (p. 1910). The fact that many people are homeless for fairly short periods is also shown in later analyses of shelter records by Culhane et al. (2007; Kuhn & Culhane, 1998) and explains why the numbers for lifetime homelessness are so much larger than the numbers for any given night or year.

Estimates of people homeless or precariously housed at some time during a year show a substantial increase between the late 1980s and the early 2000s. The percentage of adult respondents to the national General Social Survey who replied yes to a combined question about whether the respondent "had to temporarily live with others or in a shelter or 'on the street'" during a single year increased from 2.57% when the survey was conducted in 1988–1991 to 4.13% when they survey was conducted in 2004,[20] almost as high as Link et al.'s (1994) estimate (4.6%) for a parallel measure over a five-year period. This, of course, is before the Annual Homelessness Assessment Reports that have shown more recent decreases.

Studies that were smaller than Link's (Toro, Tompsett, et al., 2007), more specialized (Rosenheck & Fontana, 1994) or more local (Culhane, Dejowski, Ibanez, Needham, & Macchia, 1994) have, like Link, found much higher rates when homelessness is measured over a period of time longer than 1 year. The rates are particularly high for young adults (Morton et al., 2018).

The Importance of Time Frames

The proportion of the population that becomes homeless over an extended period such as 5 years or a lifetime is vastly larger than the proportion homeless

---

[19] The margin of error for the estimate of 7.4% was from 5.7 to 9.1%. Estimates of the percentages of people with different characteristics have much greater uncertainty, so we do not report them here.

[20] Of 1,012 respondents who answered this question in 1988–1991 and 1,332 who answered in 2014—a significant increase (Smith, Davern, Freese, & Hout, 2017, p. 2833).

on any given night. As national telephone surveys and examination of shelter records for individuals and families have shown, most people who become homeless do not remain homeless forever. As the estimates of numbers of chronically homeless people show, only about a quarter of individuals and 5% of families remain homeless for as long as a year.

In this, homelessness differs from many other social statuses. The proportion of people in the United States who are immigrants does not vary much over a day or a year or a decade. Some people arrive, others leave or die, there are trends over time, but once an immigrant, always an immigrant. Homelessness is more like unemployment—many people experience it briefly, some have repeated bouts, some despair of finding jobs and leave the labor force entirely.

For homelessness, as for unemployment, it makes sense to ask how many people are in this status on a given day—what epidemiologists call *point prevalence*, to understand something about the need for services and to monitor trends. But the one-night estimate serves to minimize the scope of the problem. To truly understand the vastly larger number of people afflicted, estimates over a longer span of 5 years or a lifetime—what epidemiologists call *period prevalence*—are also important. Surveys of people living in ordinary housing miss anyone currently homeless, so they are not very good at estimating the effects of recent changes in policies to address homelessness. However, surveys do provide a window on the magnitude of the problem and the resources that will be needed to end it.

Phrases like "the homeless" suggest to the casual reader that people who are homeless are a species apart—just as the tiger does not change its stripes, "the homeless" will remain so—and maybe there is little anyone can do about it. Understanding that people move into and back out of homelessness provides more points of intervention. What policies and practices can prevent people from becoming homeless? What services can speed their exits and prevent them from returning to that state? The last four chapters of this book address these questions.

Challenges Faced by People Experiencing Homelessness

People who become homeless face many challenges. Among the most severe is high risk of mortality, a risk that is especially marked for younger adults. Excess mortality for younger adults comes from drug overdoses, along with excess suicide, homicide, and infectious disease. Older adults tend to die from the same causes (such as cancer and heart disease) as older adults more generally—but 10–15 years sooner (Baggett et al., 2013; Fazel, Geddes, & Kushel, 2014). Unsurprisingly, people who are unsheltered have higher mortality than people who use shelters, and in a study in Massachusetts that followed the same group of people over 10 years (known as a cohort sample), they had 10 times higher mortality than the overall population (Roncarati et al., 2018). People studied while homeless have high rates of infectious diseases, chronic diseases, psychiatric and substance use disorders, and injuries, some due to victimization (Fazel et al., 2014). Across diagnostic categories, they get sick and are admitted to hospitals at earlier ages (Adams, Rosenheck, Gee, Seibyl, & Kushel, 2007).

Rates of disability among people who experience homelessness are also extremely high. HUD reports rates of disability from all causes, including physical and cognitive disabilities and those due to substance abuse and mental illness. In 2017, the share of sheltered individuals with disabilities was 49%. This is greater than the share of people with disabilities in the U.S. population with incomes below poverty, 32% (Henry, Bishop, et al., 2018). Levels of disabilities are a bit higher for veterans (59%) and substantially lower for adults in families (22%). Both those figures are still higher than in the general population, or even the population in poverty (16% for families).

The data on disability (based on everyone who used shelter over the course of the year) do not distinguish between disabilities associated with mental illness, substance abuse, developmental disability, cognitive impairment, and physical causes.[21] Nor does HUD look carefully at the way disabilities are identified by the program staff that report data into the information system that is the basis for the HUD estimates. But we think the basic point is accurate: about half (51%) of adults who experience sheltered homelessness over the course of a year as individuals do not have any disability, and more than three quarters (78%) of those who are part of a family with children do not have a disability.

Studies of mental health and substance abuse problems among people experiencing homelessness find wildly different rates. For example, a systematic review of mental health diagnoses among homeless individuals (excluding families) in wealthy countries, primarily in Europe, found prevalence rates for psychotic illness ranging from 2.8 to 42.3% and of major depression ranging from 0.0 to 40.9%. The best estimates from this review, considering factors such as the size of samples, are that among unaccompanied adults experiencing homelessness, 12.7% currently have a psychotic illness, 11.4% major depression, 23.1% a personality disorder, 37.9% alcohol dependence, and 24.4% drug dependence. Slightly higher rates of alcohol dependence and slightly lower rates of major depression are found in mainland Europe compared to other wealthy countries (Fazel, Khosla, Doll, & Geddes, 2008).

Almost all of the studies were cross-sectional—that is, they sampled a group of people who are homeless at a particular point in time, rather than a sample of all people who become homeless over a period of time. We have already shown that studies describing people at a particular point in time provide a different picture from studies showing who becomes homeless over a longer time period. (For example, the proportion of families who are homeless on a given night is larger than the proportion homeless over the course of a year because families stay

---

[21] This detail is collected in the HMIS administrative data, but only for HUD-funded shelters and transitional housing programs, and not for the large number of shelter beds that are privately funded or funded by cities without using federal money.

longer, on average.) Why might that matter for understanding rates of disability among people experiencing homelessness?

Compared to all people who ever become homeless, those who are counted in a point-in-time survey include a higher proportion of people who remain homeless for a long time or return repeatedly to that state, that is, of people with chronic patterns of homelessness. People who became homeless a month or 6 months before the survey but who returned to housing quickly are not included; others who became homeless at the same time but remained so are counted. To the extent that problems such as mental illness or substance abuse make it difficult to extricate oneself from homelessness, estimates of those problems will be magnified in cross-sectional studies (Phelan & Link, 1999). A PIT count is an example of a cross-sectional study. It minimizes estimates of the number of people who experience homelessness but maximizes estimates of their problems.

To illustrate, we return to the typologies of homelessness for individuals and families and focus on Philadelphia, where researchers matched records of shelter use to records of treatment for substance abuse (Culhane et al., 2007; Kuhn & Culhane, 1998). For individuals, fewer than 10% of people who entered shelter were long stayers, but they used just over half of the shelter days. That means that, on any given day, one would be likely to find that just over half of the shelter residents were long-term users, and the long stayers and episodic users of shelters had more problems such as substance abuse than the transitional (short-stay) shelter users. Among all individuals who entered shelter over 28 months, 37% reported substance problems, and 29% had received substance abuse treatment from a publicly funded source. If a cross-sectional survey had used records for the same Philadelphia shelters, it would likely have found 54% with self-reports of substance problems and 33% with treatment records.

As we noted earlier, studies of people in the midst of an episode of homelessness arguably catch them at the worst point in their lives. Returning to housing can reduce mental health and substance problems. This point is illustrated by the Family Options Study of housing and service interventions for homeless families, which we will discuss more in Chapter 3 on how to end homelessness for people who experience it. That study found that as families began to stabilize, rates of serious psychological distress, alcohol dependence, and drug abuse went down (Shinn, Gubits, & Dunton, 2018). Further, giving families offers of ongoing rental subsidies that held their housing costs to 30% of their income not only ended homelessness for many but also reduced their rates of psychological distress, substance use, and experiences of domestic violence compared to families who received the usual care available in their communities (Gubits et al., 2015, 2016). Distress and substance abuse, like homelessness itself, are not permanent traits, but instead states that can be influenced by environmental circumstances. Just as hardship and shelter rules can shape family composition, hardship and homelessness can sometimes precipitate psychological distress or substance abuse. Although addictions lead some people into homelessness, others do not hit the bottle until they hit the street. And at least for families, housing is an important mental health "treatment."

Some observers consider the challenges faced by people experiencing homelessness as a sufficient explanation for that state. Often these observers focus on challenges they may consider moral failings such as substance abuse. But the logic is faulty. College students have high rates of substance abuse; as with homeless adults, the favored substance is alcohol. But observers rarely claim that young people become college students because of their substance abuse. Some college students do in fact become homeless, but it is poverty and food insecurity rather than substance abuse that distinguishes them from their peers (Broton & Goldrick-Rab, 2018). More nuanced explanations are necessary. Chapter 2 analyzes causes of homelessness.

Summary

In this book, we focus on literal homelessness—staying in a place not intended for people to sleep (unsheltered homelessness) or in a shelter or transitional housing program for homeless people (sheltered homelessness). Broader definitions would include more people.

Relying largely on two sources of information—point-in-time counts conducted by all communities across the country on a single night in January and data from shelter records from those same communities over the course of a year, we examine people in five overlapping groups developed to help governments and social service systems respond to homelessness: families with children, adults without children, youth, veterans, and people with chronic patterns of homelessness. We note that seemingly basic distinctions are often shaped by service systems, such as family shelters that do not admit men. More men than women experience homelessness in the U.S., infancy is the age at which a person is most likely to be found in a homeless shelter, and African Americans and Native Americans are at especially high risk.

The face of homelessness has changed over time, both in the run-up to the modern era of homelessness when younger people, including women and minorities, replaced older white men, and in the past decade when social policies have led to a reduction in homelessness, especially for veterans and people with chronic patterns. In the past decade we have also seen that single adults who experience homelessness are getting older.

We estimate the total number of people experiencing literal homelessness over a day (600,000), a year (1.6 million) and a lifetime (over 7.4% of the entire population, based on a telephone survey from 1990—and nearly twice that percentage if we include precarious housing). The numbers are much larger over longer time periods because most people who experience homelessness do so only briefly and then return to housing. Understanding this fact leads to multiple points of intervention to prevent people from becoming homeless and to help them return to housing.

Finally, we examine the challenges people who experience homelessness face. A PIT count may exaggerate those challenges, for several reasons. First, people with more challenges may have trouble extricating themselves from homelessness, so are more likely than those with fewer challenges to be surveyed on any particular date. Second, people's challenges depend in part on their circumstances and can be reduced by restoring them to housing.

2

What Causes Homelessness?

It is conventional to divide explanations for homelessness between societal or "structural" factors and individual vulnerabilities. As rising levels of homelessness began to capture the attention of researchers and social theorists in the 1980s and 1990s, proponents of individual and structural explanations clashed. Each argued to focus on "root causes" but defined those causes quite differently as residing in individual vulnerabilities or societal failures.

The proponents talked past one another because they were analyzing causes at different levels. An exercise one of us (Beth) sometimes uses in undergraduate classes may help to clarify. I pass out slips of paper of different colors with questions about the origins of several social problems and ask students to write down their thoughts. Unbeknownst to the class, there are two forms of each question, for example:

- Why do some people become homeless? (yellow slips)
- Why do so many people become homeless? (blue slips)

I ask for answers to the question about the origin of homelessness on the yellow slips of paper, and get replies such as mental illness, addiction, family conflict, and job loss. I then ask for responses to the question about origins on the blue slips, and get suggestions such as income inequality, housing costs, high unemployment, and deinstitutionalization. Before revealing the questions, I invite students to analyze the difference in the two sets of answers. The distinctions are rarely quite so neat—some people are predisposed to think in individual

In the Midst of Plenty: Homelessness and What to Do About It, First Edition.
Marybeth Shinn and Jill Khadduri.
© 2020 Marybeth Shinn and Jill Khadduri. Published 2020 by John Wiley & Sons Ltd.

terms even if prompted with a more structural question, and vice versa, but students can quickly distinguish the levels of analysis in the explanations.[1]

Explanations at both levels matter, but they matter differently. Homelessness is like the children's game of musical chairs—the chairs are inexpensive housing units; the players are poor individuals or families who need them. As the supply of cheap housing shrinks (chairs get removed from the game), some people double up (sit on each other's laps) when the music stops, while others are left homeless or find chairs outside the circle (housing they cannot afford) and eventually have those chairs pulled out from underneath them and become homeless (McChesney, 1990). Structural factors such as levels of poverty, inequality, social exclusion, and rents that outstrip incomes at the bottom of the income distribution determine the number of chairs and the number of players—and hence the rates of homelessness. Individual vulnerabilities such as mental illness, poverty, and domestic violence—plus simple bad luck (not being right in front of one of the chairs)—determine who isn't nimble enough to grab a chair, sit on someone's lap, or find a chair outside the circle.

In this chapter we argue for a nuanced version of the structural view that homelessness is a product of broken social policies: individual characteristics are risk factors for homelessness only because of social arrangements. For example, it is undeniable that people who experience serious and persistent mental illnesses are more likely than others in the U.S. to become homeless, but why should the penalty for mental illness be homelessness? We view that question as more than rhetorical. The answer is written in social policies that keep disability benefits below the poverty level and housing costs out of reach for poor households, compounded by social exclusion that makes it harder for people with mental illness to find employers willing to hire them and landlords willing to rent to them.

Our central argument in this book is that homelessness arises primarily because poor people do not have access to housing they can afford. Housing affordability is a joint function of incomes and the cost of housing. Incomes below levels that cover basic needs put even the lowest-cost housing out of reach for many. Landlords cannot afford to operate housing that meets the minimum standard required by society at prices people at the bottom can afford to pay without public income or rent subsidies, and public subsidies have not kept up with the need.

---

[1] The exercise works less well when the social issue—such as college dropout—is closer to home. Social psychologists have shown in countless laboratory studies that observers attribute causation to individual volition even when the individuals' behavior has been manipulated by experimental conditions. As we mentioned in Chapter 1, the erroneous tendency both inside and outside the laboratory to ascribe causation to individual agency rather than environmental causes is so widespread as to be dubbed the fundamental attribution error. There is also a difference between actors in the experiments, who understand the contingencies affecting their behavior, and observers who, even when aware of the contingencies, attribute causation to individual choice. College students who themselves have experienced the financial and familial pressures that can lead to dropout may be closer to actors than observers and often offer structural explanations even when give an individual ("some students") prompt.

Households with just one low-wage earner—whether a single adult or a single parent—struggle to find housing they can afford. Increasing income volatility is hard to weather for people already struggling to make ends meet and with little or no wealth to fall back on. People are resourceful and get help from family and friends, so most who have just one source of risk in addition to poverty manage, somehow, to get by. Some groups of people are at special risk of homelessness due to social exclusion. Racial segregation and ongoing as well as past discrimination in housing and employment put some minorities, especially African Americans, at heightened risk. People leaving prisons and jails are at high risk because a criminal record makes it harder to find employment and excludes some people from housing subsidies, and the United States has the highest incarceration rates in the industrialized world. The disability benefits that people with mental illnesses or physical disabilities receive are too low to allow them to rent market-rate housing, and social stigma can add to risk. Families sometimes exclude lesbian, gay, bisexual, transgender, and queer or questioning (LGBTQ) young people from their homes, and former foster children too often have no family connections. Others have bad luck or face cascading risks, often compounded by the fragile economic situation of their relatives and social networks. When people lose housing and find nothing available that they can afford, they "double up" with other households in the same dwelling unit or, when that fails, take to the streets or to public or private shelters for people experiencing homelessness.

In the remainder of this chapter, we elaborate the argument that homelessness is caused, essentially, by lack of affordable housing. We begin by suggesting that the rate of homelessness in the United States is higher than in other wealthy countries because of high rates of poverty and inequality. Then we examine the growth in extreme or "deep" poverty and the crisis of housing affordability that began in the 1970s, showing that both result from policy choices. We suggest that those policy choices are associated with sociocultural attitudes, including patterns of social exclusion and an unwillingness to fund an adequate social safety net. We then illustrate the parallel ways that social exclusion of minorities and people with serious mental illnesses and other disabilities has affected income, accumulation of wealth, access to housing, and incarceration, leading to heightened risk of homelessness. We end by showing how individual factors, some of them related to social exclusion, can augment risk.

Homelessness, Poverty, and Inequality in an International Context

The United States is among the wealthiest countries in the world but also has very high rates of homelessness. As noted in this book's first chapter, a nationally representative telephone survey in 1990 found that 4.6% of adults in the United States reported that they had been homeless (including doubling up) in the past 5 years (Link et al., 1994). A large representative survey in England in 1994/1995 found that a slightly smaller share—4.3%—said they had been homeless over a 10-year period (Burrows, 1997).[2] A series of smaller telephone surveys in multiple developed countries done in the early 2000s examined literal homelessness—although in Europe, the questions asked not about homelessness per se, but whether the respondent had "ever been in a difficult situation, such as …" followed by examples such as sleeping in a shelter or a park. That is, the Europeans did not have to endorse the stigmatized term, "homeless." In those surveys, lifetime rates of literal homelessness in the United States and United Kingdom (6.2 and 7.7%) were substantially higher than in Germany, Italy, or Belgium (2.0–4.0%; Toro, Tompsett, et al., 2007). Results in these surveys have larger margins of error than those by Link et al. and Burrows, because of both the smaller samples and the lower response rates, and they were conducted later, when homelessness was on the rise. Rates of homelessness clearly differ between the two Anglophone countries and the Continental Europeans. Another line of evidence suggests that large-scale homelessness arose earlier in the United States than on Continental Europe. Among European countries, only the UK and France had much research on homelessness prior to 1996, whereas the research literature in the U.S. burgeoned a decade earlier (Philippot, Lecocq, Sempoux, Nachtergael, & Galand, 2007).

Anglophone countries generally and the United States in particular have more poverty (Gornick & Jäntti, 2016) and less generous social programs (Alesina & Glaeser, 2004; Smeeding, 2005) than other wealthy developed nations, facts that help to explain the higher levels of homelessness in Anglophone countries. The usual way of comparing poverty across countries is to examine the proportion of a county's population that receives less than half of the median household income for that country—a measure known as relative poverty.[3] Further, one can look at just money income from all sources, known as market income, or one can calculate disposable income by adjusting for the taxes that households pay out and the transfer programs they receive—that is, cash and "near cash" benefits such as food stamps, cash housing allowances,[4] and refundable tax credits.[5] When just earnings and income from assets are taken into account, the percentage of people in the United States in households with income below half of the national median is high but not off the charts. The percentage in most of Europe, aside from the Nordic countries, is higher. However, in the United States, taxes, cash grants, and other transfer programs do less than similar programs in other high-income

---

[2] Lifetime (rather than 5-year) homelessness, including doubling up, was 14.0% in the U.S., and lifetime literal homelessness in a public place or shelter was 7.4%. We use the 4.6% figure for 5-year homelessness from Link et al. (1994) for comparability with the English results. The English study (Burrows, 1997), did not ask questions allowing either a lifetime estimate or an estimate of literal homelessness.

[3] If all the households in a country are lined up in order of income, median income is that held by the household halfway down the line. Half of households have higher income, half lower.

[4] Cash income does not include housing vouchers paid to landlords, as in the Housing Choice Voucher program.

[5] All calculations of poverty rates adjust for household size.

countries, and even than those in lower income countries in southern and eastern Europe, to reduce the percentage of people in households with few resources (Gornick & Jäntti, 2016).[6] And this comparison does not even count health insurance or child care, two social benefits where most European countries are far more generous than the United States. These facts mean that high levels of relative poverty in the United States reflect policy choices, not the inexorable consequences of the private market. We could choose differently.

Largely as a result of these policy choices, the proportion of the population in households with disposable incomes below half of the country's median income is higher in the English-speaking countries of Australia, Canada, Ireland, and the United Kingdom, in addition to the United States (an average of 12.3% of the population) than in France, Germany, Luxembourg, and the Netherlands (an average of 7.6% of the population) or in Nordic countries of (6.5%). At 16.2%, the United States tops other Anglophone countries and every country in Western Europe in the percentage of households who are poor by this international standard.

Homelessness among families with children is largely an American phenomenon. Most other countries do not report separately on homelessness among families because it is rare.[7] Both rates of homelessness for families and the large proportion of homeless parents who are separated from their children in the U.S. (Burt et al., 1999; Cowal, Shinn, Weitzman, Stojanovic, & Labay, 2002; Walton, Wood, & Dunton, 2018) are likely consequences of American social policies that do too little to alleviate hardship among the poorest families with children. One in five American children under the age of 18 (21.1%) lives in in a household with disposable income less than half of the median, compared to an average of 13.9% in Anglophone countries generally and 11.6% in continental Europe[8] (Gornick & Jäntti, 2016, Table 2). The poverty rate for families with single mothers is higher than for two-parent families everywhere, but the percentage living with disposable income that is less than half the country's median is much higher in the U.S.: 36.5% of all people in families of single mothers in the United States compared to 24.0% in all English-speaking countries (Gornick & Jäntti, 2016, p. Table 3).[9]

---

[6] The average reduction in relative poverty due to tax and transfer policies in the U.S. (15.1 percentage points) is lower than the average for all Anglophone countries, that is Australia, Canada, Ireland, the United Kingdom, and the U.S. (21.8). It also is lower than the average reduction in France, Germany, Luxembourg, the Netherlands (28.6 percentage points), Nordic countries (Denmark, Finland, Iceland, and Norway, 23.3 percentage points), Southern Europe (Greece, Italy, and Spain, 24.4 percentage points) and Eastern Europe (the Czech Republic, Estonia, Georgia, Hungary, Poland, Russia, Serbia, the Slovak Republic, and Slovenia, 28 percentage points).

[7] For example, an international literature review on mental disorders among people experiencing homelessness included both men and women but excluded the only study of mothers in families that it found (from the U.S.) as a "selected population." Family homelessness appears to be on the rise in the last decade in Australia and Ireland, based on Beth's visits and conversations with the homeless sectors there.

[8] See footnote 6 for countries.

[9] By the official U.S. poverty measure, 40.8% of people in families with a single mother were poor in 2017, and 48.4% when children were under the age of 6 (Fontenot, Semega, & Kollar, 2018 Table 4).

Although more childless adults than children are homeless in the U.S., the previous chapter showed (Figure 1.1) that the age at which a person is most likely to become homeless is infancy. Rates remain high in the preschool years and drop when children are old enough for free child care in the form of public school. In the United States, poverty is especially high among families with very young children. One quarter of all episodes of poverty in America begin with the birth of a child (Waldfogel, 2001). In one respect, this is a mechanical consequence of the way poverty thresholds are adjusted for family size: the same income is less adequate when spread across more people. But the expenses associated with young children are very real. Children are a joy, but especially in poor families, they are also a financial burden. Infants require food, diapers, laundry, and equipment, and they outgrow their clothing every time one turns around.

Most importantly, infants require care that either keeps the mother or another unpaid caregiver out of the labor force or requires expenditures that eat up a poor parent's wages. Subsidized child care becomes somewhat more available as children grow a little older, but, with limited funding, only 6% of children under 3 who are eligible for Early Head Start by reason of incomes have access to a slot, and only 31% of children ages 3–5 who are eligible for Head Start have access (National Head Start Association, 2016). Other kinds of child care subsidies also exist, but across all forms, estimates of enrollment among eligible families range from 7% to 34%, with the most disadvantaged families least likely to use the subsidies (Forry, Daneri, & Howarth, 2013). Reasons include funding limitations, lack of awareness, and the difficulty of applying and recertifying eligibility (Adams, Snyder, & Sandfort, 2002; Shlay, Weinraub, & Harmon, 2010).

Cross-national comparisons also show the United States to have not only high levels of poverty but also high levels of inequality of both income and wealth compared with other wealthy countries (McFate, Lawson, & Wilson, 1995; Piketty, 2014; Smeeding, 2005). For example, in the U.S. the ratio between the income of people at the 90th percentile[10] of the income distribution and that of people at the 10th percentile is much greater than in other wealthy countries (Fisher & Smeeding, 2016). That ratio in 2016 or 2017 (the most recent year available) is 6.3 for the U.S., 3.8 for German, 3.4 for France, and 3.3 for Sweden (OECD, 2019). Why does this matter? Isn't just the lack of resources of people at the bottom of the income distribution relevant to homelessness? Probably not, because people with higher incomes compete with poor people for use of the same land (O'Flaherty, 1996). The competition is perhaps most visible (and most closely related to homelessness) in the case of gentrification, urban renewal, and the replacement of Single Room Occupancy (SRO) "hotels" (single rooms units, typically with a bathroom down the hall) by luxury apartments and condos.

A recent study by Carliner and Marya (2016) demonstrates the relationship between income inequality and the affordability of rental housing in the U.S.,

---

[10] 90% of people have incomes below the 90th percentile.

Canada, and 10 countries in Western Europe.[11] As already noted, the U.S., by several different measures, has the greatest level of income inequality. The U.S. also has the largest fraction of cash renters[12] paying more than half their income for housing. The only country that comes close to the U.S. is Spain, where a very small share of its population rents rather than owns their housing. In the bottom income quintile in the U.S., the median cash renter pays 74.8% of income on rent, higher than for any other country.

Increasing "Deep Poverty" in the United States

Examinations of poverty within the United States generally use a measure that assesses how income relates to needs, rather than showing how well people at the bottom of the income distribution are doing in comparison to others in the society (the basis for the international comparisons of poverty levels we've just shown). The measure was set in 1963 as three times the cost of a subsistence food budget, on the basis that poor families spent about a third of their income on food. The measure is adjusted for household size and composition (so there are multiple poverty thresholds) and compares a household's pretax cash income, including cash benefits, to the relevant threshold (adjusted for changes in the Consumer Price Index) to determine whether the household is poor. When first developed, the poverty "line" was about half of median income, so comparable to the international standard. By the early 2000s the official line was less than 30% of median income, so a household labeled "poor" was much less well-off relative to others in society (Haveman, Blank, Moffitt, Smeeding, & Wallace, 2015).

Particularly pertinent to homelessness is "deep poverty," which is defined as having a cash income below half of the relevant poverty threshold. People who are deeply poor have essentially no ability to trim other expenses to pay for housing. For a single parent with one child, deep poverty meant an annual cash income, in 2018, of less than $8,654; for a married couple family with two children, less than $12,733; and for a single adult less than $6,532 (U.S. Census Bureau, 2019). In 2017, 5.7% of Americans, including 5.9 million children (8.0%), were living in deep poverty. The majority of these desperately poor people are white, because the majority of Americans are white, but minority group members, especially African Americans, are at higher risk. For example, 10.4% of African Americans were living in deep poverty as of 2017, compared to 4.2% of Americans identifying themselves as white and non-Hispanic (Fontenot, Semega, & Kollar, 2018).

---

[11] Austria, Belgium, France, Germany, Italy, the Netherlands, Spain, Sweden, Switzerland, and the United Kingdom. The study uses the 2013 European Union Statistics on Income and Living Conditions, the 2011 Canadian National Household Survey, and the 2013 U.S. American Housing Survey, supplemented by other data in some cases.

[12] Cash renters exclude people who live rent-free in housing they don't own, typically housing supplied by an employer (e.g., some farm workers, clergy, resident managers) or a relative. These exclusions make up less than 2% of the U.S. population.

Poor people are getting poorer over time. The percentage of all poor people living with incomes that are less than half the official poverty threshold has increased substantially since the 1960s, with the largest changes occurring between 1960 and 1990. In particular, the fraction of all people living in poverty who are deeply poor increased from 29% in 1968 to 44% in 2012 (Haveman et al., 2015) and stood at 47% in 2017 (Fontenot et al., 2018).[13] This is the same period that saw the beginning of "modern" homelessness.

Family Poverty and Antipoverty Programs

The restructuring of federal poverty programs in the late 1990s tilted means-tested benefits away from the poorest families and toward those with greater labor market engagement (Haveman et al., 2015). The Personal Responsibility and Work Opportunity Reconciliation Act of 1996, dubbed "welfare reform," replaced Aid to Families with Dependent Children (AFDC) with Temporary Aid to Needy Families (TANF), with time limits and work requirements. An expansion of the Earned Income Tax Credit (EITC) that took place around the same time supplemented the wages of low-income workers with children. The EITC is credited with lifting substantial numbers of families out of poverty and even extreme poverty but may not be available to parents with multiple barriers to working (Haveman et al., 2015; Shaefer & Edin, 2013).

At the same time, cash assistance to households who do not work plummeted. Often families who are eligible for TANF benefits fail to receive them. In the first half of the 1990s, participation rates in AFDC among eligible families exceeded 80%; by 2002, TANF participation among eligible families was 48% (Parrot & Sherman, 2007); whereas by 2016 only 23% percent of children in poor families received TANF cash assistance (Hoynes & Schanzenbach, 2018). Edin and Shaefer (2015) describe both the barriers that states erect to make applications difficult and the frequent belief among impoverished families that assistance is no longer available. The amount of help provided by welfare benefits has also shrunk. In constant 2012 dollars, the maximum cash assistance benefit for a single parent with two children in the median state had dropped from $763 per month in 1981 to $550 in 1996 (under AFDC) to $427 in 2012 (under TANF), a total reduction

---

[13] Rossi (1989, pp. 78–79) shows a doubling of the number of people living in extreme poverty between 1969 and 1987, using a more expansive measure, 75% of the official poverty threshold, based on Current Population Survey data adjusted to 1987 dollars. An alternative measure of poverty called the supplemental poverty measure, takes account of various noncash benefits including housing assistance, SNAP, WIC (Special Supplemental Nutrition Program for Women, Infants and Children) and tax credits such as the EITC, and subtracts income and payroll taxes, and some expenses including child care, medical, and work expenses; it also adjusts the poverty line for local housing costs, among other changes. By the supplemental poverty measure, slightly more people are poor (13.9% of Americans in 2017 compared with 12.3% by the official measure), but children under 18 are slightly less likely to be poor 15.6% vs. 17.5%, and poverty has fallen much more over the last half century, reflecting the importance of government assistance not included in the official measure. Deep poverty is reduced to 4.9% overall and 4.8% among children (Fox, 2018; Stone, 2018).

of 44% (Falk, 2014). As of 2019, after a few states increased benefits, TANF benefits still do not exceed 60% of the poverty level even in the relatively generous states; in 33 states, benefits leave a family at or below 30% of poverty (Burnside & Floyd, 2019).

The Supplemental Nutrition Assistance Program (SNAP, formerly and still informally called food stamps) partially compensated for the shrinkage in cash benefits. SNAP is the closest thing to a universal income support program in the U.S., at least for families, with no time limits and most poor households with children continuously eligible for assistance. About 14% of the U.S. population received benefits as of 2016; 84% of those participants had cash incomes placing them in poverty and 43% in deep poverty (Oliveira, Prell, Tiehan, & Smallwood, 2018).

In addition to the deep poverty now tracked by the U.S. Census Bureau, analysts have used the World Bank's standard for the poorest countries in the world of $2 or less per person per day to measure extreme poverty. Shaefer and Edin (2013) use the Survey of Income and Program Participation (SIPP) to show that, in the U.S., 4.3% of all nonelderly households with children had this level of deprivation in 2011 (based on total monthly cash income) and that the prevalence of extreme poverty rose sharply after 1996, especially for those most affected by the drop in welfare reform caseloads. During the same period, the increase in the SNAP caseload protected many families with children from this level of destitution. EITC helped as well, perhaps because some people save the refund to protect against short periods of no income. However, even after counting noncash transfer programs like SNAP, some 600,000 households with children were living on $2 per person per day in 2011 (Shaefer & Edin, 2013). Is it any wonder that over half a million people in families with children (about 173,000 families) experienced homelessness at some time during that year (Henry, Bishop, de Sousa, Shivji, & Watt, 2018)?

How do families cope with such Dickensian hardship in twenty-first century America? Edin and Shaefer (2015) use ethnographic approaches to learn things that surveys cannot and show the stratagems deeply poor mothers use to survive, including supplementing intermittent employment with work in the informal economy or selling plasma, relying on private charity, and stretching meager resources. A common way of making do with less is doubling up in the same housing unit with family or friends. Such arrangements are usually unstable, often "perilous … ending in sexual, physical, or verbal abuse" (p. 73). All of these coping strategies are tenuous and cannot always protect families from plunging into homelessness.

Poverty for Childless Adults and Antipoverty Programs

Much less analysis has been done of poverty and trends in poverty for childless adults. The poverty rates for single men and women were 18.2 and 23.2% in 2017 (Fontenot et al., 2018). Some of the poverty of households without children may be ephemeral or not reflect real hardship—for example, some young people studying or starting their careers may have family support that does not show up in household income statistics.[14] However, childless adults with incomes below the poverty level are even more likely than families with children to be deeply poor, 11% of single adults in 2017 (Fontenot et al., 2018 Table 5).[15] As the Social Security retirement system became more generous, poverty dropped for older adults—from 25% in 1968 to 12.1% in 1990 to 9.1% in 2012 (Haveman et al., 2015). "Traditional" homelessness was concentrated among older men (Rossi, 1989), but since the beginning of the "new homelessness" in the 1970s a very small percentage of people who become homeless are elderly (Henry, Bishop, et al., 2018; Rossi, 1989). This reflects the relative strength of the safety net for older Americans, a major and popular policy achievement.

Creators of U.S. social policies often consider adults who are not living with children and are not yet elderly to be unworthy of public support unless they have the level and type of documented disability that qualifies them for disability benefits. For example, since the restructuring of welfare in 1996, food stamps are available to nonworking "able bodied adults without dependents" for only 3 months in any 3-year period—a time limit that can be waived in some circumstances (Oliveira et al., 2018). But many unattached adults living in poverty have health conditions that make it difficult for them to work. Even when unemployment rates overall are low, they remain stubbornly high for people who have not graduated from high school and for groups who face ongoing discrimination, including racial minorities and people who have been incarcerated (as documented later in this chapter). When it exists, work is often intermittent (Edin & Shaefer, 2015).

State programs known as General Assistance are the only cash assistance programs for which most nonelderly childless adults who are not working qualify. As of 2015, only 26 states still had such programs, and only 11 provided benefits to people without disabilities. Benefit levels shrank as well, with many states providing only a quarter of a poverty-level income (Schott & Hill, 2015). For some adults without children who are able to work (those between the ages of 25 and 64), the EITC is available to supplement earnings but provides a much smaller supplement than received by a worker with a qualifying child. Non-custodial parents are not eligible for the higher amount (Holzer, 2015a; Marr, Huang, Murray, & Sherman, 2016).

---

[14] Jill participated in the creation of several allocation formulae for the U.S. Department of Housing and Urban Development (HUD) programs that included measures of poverty across locations. When results were puzzling, it was noticed that towns with large university populations such as Bloomington, IN have very high poverty rates, so the analysists switched to using family rather than overall poverty.

[15] Technically, thes are "unrelated individuals" not living in a household with others. Rates of deep poverty in 2017 were 5.7% for all Americans, 8.0% for children, 11.0% for unrelated individuals, and 22.9% for people in "unrelated subfamilies." An unrelated subfamily is a married couple with or without children or a single parent with children doubled up with a primary householder but not related to the householder by birth, marriage, or adoption.

Income Volatility

Households along the spectrum of the income distribution need to cope with fluctuations in income, but a disruption in income can pitch a household living on the margin into homelessness. Year-to-year volatility in household income increased after 1970, particularly for people with low incomes or little education—precisely those with the least ability to weather such changes (Gosselin & Zimmerman, 2008; Morris, Hill, Gennetian, Rodrigues, & Wolf, 2015). For example, the chance that a family would experience a 50% drop in income over a given 2-year period increased from 4.6% in the decade beginning in 1974 to 7.8% in the decade beginning in 1994. The destabilizing events most commonly associated with a household's losing half its income were fall in work hours of the wife, unemployment of the household head, and birth of a child (Gosselin & Zimmerman, 2008).

Kalleberg (2011) summarizes a large body of literature on the increase since the 1970s in the number of U.S. workers, particularly women and minorities, who have jobs that are precarious as well as low-paying. This is not a cyclical pattern but instead reflects structural changes in the economy that are unlikely to disappear, including the declining role of unions, weak enforcement of labor laws, globalization of the economy (Kalleberg, 2011), and the increasing role of gig labor.

For families with children, variability in income from month to month is larger than variation from year to year (Morris et al., 2015). Low-wage employment is often inherently unstable because workers with low skills can easily be replaced and have to accept whatever work schedules they are offered (Kalleberg, 2011). For parents, low-wage work often combines with inflexible or unreliable child care to create additional instability: the boss requires a mother to work unanticipated overtime; if she complies, she angers her child care provider and may lose care; if she refuses, she loses her job. Or when her child (or child care provider) is sick and she misses work to care for her child, she loses the job (Chaudry, 2004).

At the bottom end of the distribution where variability is highest, changes in transfer income can contribute to this volatility rather than offsetting it (Morris et al., 2015). Some of this is an intentional feature of social policy that makes income transfers conditional on work. TANF benefits require work, and families that fail to meet the work requirements may be sanctioned and lose benefits, creating a drop in income. Because the EITC is intended to reward work among families with children, each additional dollar earned (at the bottom of the income distribution) is supplemented by the tax credit, so that a reduction in earnings also causes a larger drop in income. Thus programs that are intended to help poor households—and do help lift many families out of poverty—can also contribute to income volatility at the bottom, where connections to the workforce are particularly fragile.

Historically, economic cycles are also associated with cycles in homelessness (e.g., Hopper, 2003), and O'Flaherty and colleagues showed that two recent recessions were associated with increases in homelessness in New York City (before good national data were available) (Cragg & O'Flaherty, 1999; O'Flaherty & Wu, 2006). The national data used for the Annual Homeless Assessment Reports since 2007 show a small increase in family homelessness following the start of the Great Recession but not perhaps as much as might have been expected. There was even less effect on homelessness among individuals (Henry, Bishop, et al., 2018). One explanation is that programs such as SNAP helped cushion job loss. Another is that the job loss during the recession was concentrated among people with incomes somewhat greater than the deeply poor families and individuals most likely to become homeless—that is, people who may have had savings or family and friends able to help out.

Wealth

Wealth, that is assets minus liabilities, is even more unevenly distributed than income. The Federal Reserve Board has developed a new tool to track the distribution of wealth held by different American households. Although the total net worth of U.S. households more than quadrupled in nominal terms from 1989 to 2018, essentially none of that increase went to the bottom half of the wealth distribution, whose share fell from 4 to 1% of the total over the last three decades. Meanwhile, the share held by the top 1% of the income distribution increased from 23% to nearly 32%. The next 9% held fairly steady in terms of relative wealth. Thus, the rise in wealth of the top 1% came largely at the expense of those from the 50th to the 90th percentile in the wealth distribution, whose share decreased from 36 to 29% over this period, sometimes called the hollowing out of the middle class (Batty et al., 2019).

Poverty, Housing, and Homelessness

So far, we have shown that the U.S. has great inequality of income and wealth, leaving many people at the bottom of the income distribution with too little to pay for basic necessities and little reserve to fall back on. In *Down and Out in America: The Origins of Homelessness* (1989), Peter Rossi demonstrated that people who fell into homelessness in the late twentieth century were a subset of people in deep poverty, but he paid scant attention to what had happened to the housing market that drove poor people out of housing units and onto the street or into shelters. Here we make the link between poverty and housing, providing three types of evidence at the core of our argument that homelessness is essentially a lack of access to affordable housing. First we show that the onset of "new homelessness" in the 1980s followed closely on a period in which the quality of housing in the U.S. improved but poor people could no longer afford it. Then we review the evidence that homelessness is most prevalent in places where housing costs are highest. Finally, we show that policies that make housing affordable for individual low-income households prevent them from becoming homeless.

Evidence from Time Trends

In the decades that followed World War II, the U.S. housing stock changed radically. Housing without complete plumbing dropped from 47% of the housing stock in 1940 to 6% in 1970. This was in part a result of the U.S. becoming a more urban society, but even in urban areas 23% of housing units were without complete plumbing in 1940 compared with only 3% in 1970. The quality of the housing stock has continued to improve since then. A measure of "severely inadequate" housing, a complex measure that uses the detailed questions on housing conditions in the American Housing Survey (AHS)[16] shows a drop from 4.2% of all units in 1974 to 1.7% in 1989 (Weicher, 2012).[17] Overcrowding of housing units dropped as well, with 4.2% of all households in the U.S. living with more than one person per room, not counting kitchens and bathrooms in 1978, down to 1.5% in 2015 (Nelson, Vandenbroucke, Lubell, Schroder, & Rieger, 2003; Watson, Steffan, Martin, & Vandenbroucke, 2017).

These improvements in housing quality largely reflected overall income growth in the 1950s and 1960s, although the systematic destruction of older neighborhoods in pursuit of "urban renewal" played some role as well (Anderson, 1964). As the poorest quality housing disappeared, families and individuals with poverty-level incomes could no longer find housing units they could afford. In 1960, 35.3% of all renters (regardless of income) were paying more than a quarter of their income for housing; by 2009, 72.5% were doing so. Some of this may reflect a willingness of people at all income levels to devote a larger share of their income to housing, but the percentage paying more than *half* their income for housing climbed as well, reaching a quarter of all renters in 2009 (Weicher, 2012). Not surprisingly, most households with "severe rent burdens," paying more than half their income for rent and utilities, have poverty-level incomes. In 2015, 75.8% of

---

[16] The AHS was originally called the Annual Housing Survey. The name changed in 1985 when the national AHS began to be conducted only in odd-numbered years.

[17] Severely inadequate is a strict standard (Eggers & Moumen, 2013a). A housing unit qualifies if it lacks complete plumbing facilities including hot and cold running water or electricity, or if it experiences certain heat failures or electrical problems or it has at least five of six structural conditions, namely outside water leaks or inside water leaks in the past 12 months, holes in the floor, cracks wider than a dime, areas of peeling paint larger than 8 by 11 in., and rats. We see no reason to question the trend of improvement in these serious inadequacies over time but note that much of the housing visited by Desmond (2016) in *Evicted* and by Edin and Shaefer (2015) in *$2.00 a Day*, had serious deficiencies that (typically) fell short of the official standard. In 1991 in New York City, Beth passed torn-out mailboxes, broken windows, vacant lots, and piles of garbage to interview previously homeless families and their poor but never-homeless counterparts in their homes. An interviewer for the study (Shinn et al., 1998) requested a flashlight to negotiate a dark urine-soaked stairway to get to the upper floor of an apartment building where a family lived. Tenants complained of a promised oven that never arrived, safety issues (seeing someone murdered in front of her), and "rats bigger than cats" (Stojanovic et al., 1999). None of these problems would have made their units "seriously inadequate," unless the rats were accompanied by at least four other deficiencies.

renters with incomes below 30% of area median[18] and no housing assistance were paying more than half their income for rent (Watson et al., 2017).

How can people pay so much of their income for housing? The answer in part is that poor people's income is volatile, so a measurement taken at a single point in time may overstate the extent of this phenomenon. However, severe rent burdens persisted for at least 3 years for about half of very-low income households with this problem (Hardiman, Lynch, Martin, Vandenbroucke, & Yao, 2010; U.S. Department of Housing and Urban Development, 2007). In his study of poverty and housing in Milwaukee, Matthew Desmond (2016) illustrates a pattern in which people agree to rents they cannot pay because they have no other choice. When the landlord loses patience they move or get evicted. At times they end up in shelters or sleeping in public spaces.

Earlier in this chapter, following McChesney (1990), we used an analogy to the game of musical chairs that implies that the size of the housing stock is fixed. In reality, units are constantly added to the housing stock in response to growth in demand as people form households or move from place to place (Khadduri, Burnett, & Rodda, 2003). However, the housing stock does not expand by adding units for people with the lowest incomes. Mobile homes are an exception, but they are affordable for people with poverty-level incomes only when they can be placed on land that is also affordable. They do not make up a large portion of the U.S. housing stock (only 6.6% in 2017), especially not in urban areas (U.S. Census Bureau, 2017).

In wealthy countries like the U.S. that no longer permit construction of homes with insubstantial materials or without heating, ventilation, and indoor plumbing,[19] most housing occupied by people with poverty-level income is older housing that was built for better-off households and has changed occupants over time, "filtering down" in the income distribution (Rosenthal, 2014).[20] But in terms of the rents people can afford, the housing stock does not filter down far enough. The filtering process stops at a rent level that is more than the lowest income households can afford to pay. There is a floor on the rental income a landlord can receive and have enough to keep maintaining the housing and the utilities costs that are a major portion of total rent (economists call this "gross rent") for the lowest cost units.

What happened starting in the late 1970s and early 1980s is that poor people could no longer afford to pay for the housing that was available through either

---

[18] Thirty percent of area median income, the "extremely low income" threshold, varies by location but is roughly similar to the federal poverty level.

[19] In poorer countries such as India, occupancy of housing not made of permanent materials is part of the definition of homelessness. In the U.S., the recent growth of "encampments" made up of tents or other insubstantial materials is counted as homelessness and may represent a response to the failure of the market to provide housing that deeply poor individuals can afford.

[20] In urban areas, trailer parks probably also go through a filtering process, with progressively poorer people occupying the aging mobile homes. Desmond (2016) describes the filtering down and, ultimately, removal from the housing stock of a mobile home park in Milwaukee.

filtering or new production, and modern homelessness arose. The U.S. Department of Housing and Urban Development produces biennial reports to Congress, based on AHS data, that estimate the number of renters with incomes below half the local median income who do not have government-assisted housing and either have severe rent burdens, with more than half of their income going to rent and utilities, or live in severely inadequate housing. Over the 1978–2015 period for which comparable data exist, these problems have increasingly been only a severe rent burden, so these reports essentially track that indicator. The number of households with these "worst case needs" more than doubled from 4 million in 1978 to 8.5 million after the 2008 financial crisis and stood at 8.3 million in 2015 (Nelson et al., 2003; U.S. Department of Housing and Urban Development, 1994; Watson et al., 2017).

Increases in numbers of renters with worst case needs reflect both overall population increases and lagging incomes (so more renters have incomes below 50% of the area median). At the same time, the number of rental affordable units has failed to keep up (Watson et al., 2017).

Since 1996, the worst case needs reports also track how many housing units are affordable and available for poor renters compared to the number of poor renters. For example, in 2015, for every 100 renters with extremely low incomes (below 30% of the area median or the poverty line), there were only 38 units that a household right at that income cut-off could afford[21] and that were not occupied by a household with a higher income. A larger number of units are technically affordable (66 units for every 100 extremely low-income renters), but unavailable because those units were occupied by households with relatively higher incomes (Watson et al., 2017). Those households may have been happy to find housing that would not require a high portion of their income or may have had reasons for staying where they were when their incomes grew. Even these rates of available affordable units understate the problem for people at the very bottom of the income distribution—nothing on the private market is affordable for people living on $2 per person per day.

During the 1990s there was a large decline in the number of affordable and available units from 52 per 100 extremely low-income renters in 1991 to 42 per 100 in 1999 (Nelson et al., 2003). Using a conceptually similar measure, Cushing Dolbeare traced the origin of the affordability crisis to the 1970s. At the start of that decade, there was a slight surplus in units that were affordable to households at the top of the poorest quartile (quarter) of renters, but by 1975 the number of lowest-quartile renters exceeded the number of units even those at the top of the bottom quartile could afford. By 1980 there were 6.4 million such households but only 3.5 million affordable units. (Dolbeare, 1991, 1992).[22]

---

[21] Affordability here is the HUD standard of paying no more than 30% of income for housing.

[22] Calculations compared households with incomes in the bottom quartile of renters to affordable units, whether available or occupied by higher income families.

Evidence from Locations where Homelessness is more Prevalent

Since the 1970s, the market has not produced housing that poor families and individuals can afford in any part of the U.S., because rents cannot filter down far enough and still allow owners to cover maintenance costs, so housing drops out of the stock rather than being operated at lower rents.[23] However, housing is less affordable in some parts of the country than in others, and an extensive body of research, summarized by Hanratty (2017), shows that variations in homelessness are related to high rents and high poverty rates. Hanratty reviews nine studies that date back to the first efforts to count people experiencing homelessness in the 1980s and 1990s and include more recent use of the point-in-time counts to model relationships between homelessness and rent levels, vacancy rates, unemployment rates, and poverty. The preponderance of the evidence, as well as Hanratty's estimates that use a time series of point-in-time counts, indicates that places with high rents have high rates of homelessness. A simpler illustration of the relationship is shown in Figure 2.1. Homelessness rate is the point-in-time count of homeless people, both sheltered and unsheltered, divided by the metropolitan statistical area (MSA) total population.

Some parts of the country and particular cities have high rents and upward pressure on rents. This does not seem to be a temporary pattern in which the market is simply slow to build new housing in response to increased demand. For example, the mismatch between numbers of poor people and numbers of affordable and available units is greatest in the western census region, with only 30 rental units affordable and available per 100 renters with extremely low incomes in the West in 2015, compared to 38–43 units in the other regions (Watson et al., 2017). That has been a consistent pattern, and the growth over time in the numbers and percentages of renters with worst case needs also has been greatest in the West (Nelson et al., 2003; U.S. Department of Housing and Urban Development, 1994). The high housing costs in the West are also reflected in a higher percentage of the population living in poverty in that region, when the Supplemental Poverty Measure, which takes into account regional housing costs in addition to noncash benefits, is used to measure poverty (Haveman et al., 2015). A study of the filtering process by Nelson and colleagues used AHS data for 41 metropolitan areas surveyed twice between 1985 and 1992 and found that some metropolitan areas had both low rates of

---

[23] This does not happen immediately. Desmond (2016) describes an "eviction mill" in Milwaukee, where owners let their units deteriorate below levels of basic habitability, charge rents they know tenants will not be able to afford, and take advantage of institutional weaknesses in enforcement of occupancy rules to make short-term profits before abandoning the housing. A landlord in Cleveland reported keeping rents affordable by buying cheap housing units, minimizing maintenance, and when even that becomes too expensive, abandoning the housing (Edin & Shaefer, 2015). In the 1970s landlords in New York abandoned over 100,000 units, some torched in arson fires, and the rest acquired by the City through tax foreclosure (Furman Center for Real Estate and Urban Policy, 2006).

Homelessness rate (Percent)

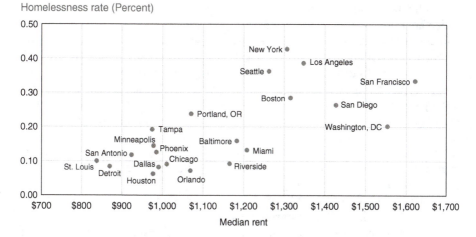

Figure 2.1 Homelessness is Especially Common in More Expensive Rental Markets. *Source*: Harvard Joint Center for Housing Studies, *America's Rental Housing* (2017a), www.jchs.harvard.edu. All rights reserved. *Notes*: Included metros are the 21 metropolitan statistical areas (MSAs) among the 25 largest MSAs by total population for which at least 80% of population falls within one or more metro Continuums of Care (CoCs). Metro CoCs have at least 90% of their population falling within one MSA. Median rent is median gross rent including utilities. Homelessness rate is the point-in-time count of homeless people, both sheltered and unsheltered, divided by the MSA total population. *Sources*: U.S. Department of Housing and Urban Development 2016 Point-in-Time Count of Homelessness; U.S. Census Bureau, 2015 American Community Survey 1-year Estimates. Reproduced by permission.

construction and high rates of loss of affordable units: Anaheim, Boston, Los Angeles, New York, Newark, Philadelphia, San Francisco, and Washington DC (Nelson, Burns, Khadduri, & Vandenbroucke, 1998).

The pattern in which new housing is built in response to demand and subsequently filters down is interrupted by phenomena that are not completely understood but that appear to have to do with income inequality at both ends of the income distribution and with the influence of land use and other regulations that increase the costs of housing construction. O'Flaherty (1996) argues that the filtering process has not recently produced as much housing affordable for poor families and individuals as it did in the past, because the hollowing out of the middle class means that fewer new housing units are produced for middle income households, and those units (rather than luxury housing) are the units that filter down as they age. This does not seem to be the case nationally. Analysis that uses the AHS to track the creation and disappearance of rental units affordable to households with incomes at half the local median income shows that older units continued to become affordable at about the same pace over the period between 1985 and 2013 (Weicher, Eggers, & Moumen, 2017). It may, however, explain the high rates of homelessness in New York City and the coastal California cities, which are home to both large numbers of poor people and large numbers of very affluent people. Cites with very broad income distributions (a bloodless term for inequality) often also have constraints on the total amount of housing that is produced. Rafael shows that housing affordable to the lowest income households is in shorter supply in the most heavily regulated housing markets, with more heavily regulated geographic areas experiencing fewer additions to the housing stock and greater increases in prices and a direct correlation between high rent-to-income ratios and homelessness (Raphael, 2010). Malpezzi and Green (1996) show that, in some cities, rents for low-quality units are very close to the rents of standard quality units and "take this as prima facie evidence of imperfections at the bottom of these housing markets." They point to differences in the extent to which land use is constrained by zoning and other regulations as an explanation of the relative lack of filtering in some places.

Cross-national comparisons are again relevant. The share of rental housing made up of single-family, detached homes is larger in the U.S. than in other countries, a fact that contributes to rental units being somewhat larger and costlier, on average, and one that may limit the extent of rent reductions as housing filters down to lower-income renters. The size of units reflects preferences to some extent, but also zoning requirements that limit construction of less expensive multifamily housing leading to high levels of unaffordability in the U.S. Regulations in other countries may require rather than constrain density (Carliner & Marya, 2016).

A particular type of affordable housing that began to disappear in the 1970s was SRO hotels. Rossi describes the occupants of these units as part of an older wave of homelessness dominated by men who supplied casual labor in U.S. cities, had weak or nonexistent family ties, and typically were older than the "new homeless." These men may have spent some time on the street, but generally they were not homeless by current definitions, because they lived in the SROs or worse "cage hotels." Some SROs were converted to luxury apartments, while in other cases the land was used for something other than housing. For example in New York City in the middle of the twentieth century, there were more than 200,000 SRO units that made up over 10% of the City's total rental housing stock; 175,000 of those units have been lost, with City policies exacerbating market forces (Sullivan & Burke, 2013). Other U.S. cities—Los Angeles and Chicago, for example—also had large losses in SRO housing during the 1970s and 1980s (Rossi, 1989).

Government has not made up for the loss of affordable units in the private sector. The number of households receiving federal rental subsidies continued to rise, modestly, through the 1980s but was essentially flat for the next two decades, while need soared. Between 1993 and 2013, the number of very low-income renter households eligible for assistance rose by 3.8 million, while the number of assisted renters increased by 0.5 million. As of 2013, only a quarter (26%) of renter households with incomes low enough to receive assistance (no more than half of area median) actually received it (Joint Center for Housing Studies of Harvard University, 2016, pp. 33–34).

The cross-national study that showed a relationship between income inequality and the proportion of citizens living in unaffordable housing (Carliner & Marya, 2016) identified lower levels of government rental assistance as a major driver of housing unaffordability in the U.S. The authors conclude that the extent to which countries provide housing allowances (the type of subsidy that in the U.S. is called a Housing Choice Voucher) is related to renters' cost burdens. In the U.S., only 6% of all cash renters receive assistance, compared with figures as high as 46% in the United Kingdom and 55% in France, where the government devotes roughly 10 times as large a proportion of Gross Domestic Product (GDP) to housing allowances. Although assistance is more widespread in other countries, the amount of assistance per household is generally smaller.

Without housing assistance, many renters struggle. Nowhere in the United States can a minimum-wage worker who works 40 hours per week, year around, afford the fair market rent (FMR)[24] for a two-bedroom apartment. In only 28 of more than 3,000 counties can that minimum wage worker afford even a one-bedroom, and all of those 28 counties are in places where the prevailing minimum wage is higher than the federal level of $7.25/hour (Aurand, Cooper, Emmanuel, Rafi, & Yentel, 2019). Figure 2.2 shows the hourly wage actually required to pay the FMR, on average, across states.

Evidence from Housing Policies

Further evidence that the unaffordability of housing is at the root of homelessness, at least for families in the United States, comes from the fact that housing subsidies virtually eliminate it. These subsidies typically hold costs for housing, including utilities, to approximately 30% of a household's income. The strongest evidence comes from two recent national experiments, one that showed that housing subsidies prevented homelessness for families receiving welfare (Wood, Turnham, & Mills, 2008) and a second that showed that they ended it for families recruited in homeless shelters (Gubits et al., 2018). Housing subsidies with voluntary supportive services also end homelessness for individuals with serious mental illnesses (e.g., Aubry et al., 2015, 2016; Stergiopoulos et al., 2015; Tsemberis, Gulcur, & Nakae, 2004). We will return to these studies in the chapters on ending and preventing homelessness.

---

[24] FMRs are a widely used index of rental costs. They are set at about the middle of the rental market for each metropolitan area or group of state nonmetropolitan areas and control the subsidy levels used by public housing authorities for housing vouchers. Affordable here is the HUD standard that a household should spend no more than 30% of income on rent and utilities.

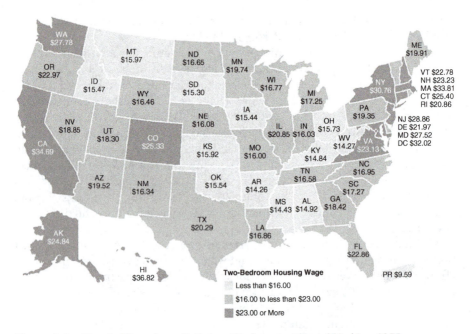

Figure 2.2   Hourly Wage that a Full-time Worker must Earn (Working 40 Hours a Week, 52 Weeks a Year) in Order to Afford the Fair Market Rent for a Two-bedroom Rental Home Without Paying More than 30% of Income. *Source: Out of Reach*. National Low Income Housing Coalition nlihc.org/oor (Aurand et al., 2019, p. 13). Reproduced by permission.

Cultural Attitudes, Social Welfare Policy, and Social Exclusion

We have argued that the central cause of homelessness in the United States is lack of affordable housing. Housing affordability is a joint function of incomes and housing costs, both factors that are influenced by social policies. National tax and welfare policies shape income distributions, and a variety of national and local policies contribute to the unaffordability of housing. In Chapter 6 we will consider alternative policies that would prevent homelessness. In the remainder of this chapter, we consider why American policies are less generous than those in many other countries and the ways that multiple forms of social exclusion often embedded in policy choices shape who becomes homeless in the United States. We argue that these forms of social exclusion turn individual characteristics into vulnerabilities for homelessness.

Tax and transfer policies that shape income inequality and fail to alleviate poverty do not arise in a vacuum but instead reflect underlying cultural beliefs about the causes of poverty and the people deemed worthy of help. For example, in a sample of 30 nations, Alesina and Glaeser (2004) found that the average extent to which survey respondents in a country believed that poverty is society's fault was highly associated with the proportion of GDP devoted to social welfare spending. Among nations with per capita GDP of more than \$15,000 in 1998 (so the wherewithal to offer generous benefits), the association was still stronger.[25] Specific to homelessness, Toro et al. (2007) found less compassionate public attitudes toward homelessness in the same English-speaking countries that have less equal income distributions and less generous social programs than other nations.

Alesina and Glaeser (2004) also found that social welfare spending as a proportion of GDP is an inverse function of ethnic fractionalization in different societies.[26] They argue that ethnic fractionalization shapes social welfare policy directly, because majorities are unwilling to pay for redistributive policies that favor minority groups, and indirectly, because it interferes with the formation of a unified labor movement. The greater racial heterogeneity of the United States accounted for two thirds of the gap in social spending between the United States and Europe. Within the United States, where the generosity of welfare benefits is decided by individual states, there was an inverse correlation between maximum welfare benefits and the percentage of the state population that is black. Alesina and Glaser do not discuss homelessness, but their analysis suggests that social exclusion of racial and linguistic minorities leads to homelessness indirectly, by reducing the generosity of social welfare programs. Other effects of racism and social exclusion are more direct.

Racism, Social Exclusion, and Homelessness

As Chapter 1 noted, some racial and ethnic minorities are more likely than others to experience homelessness. The United States is not alone here. Minority groups are at heightened risk of homelessness throughout the industrialized world (Philippot et al., 2007) but the particular groups at risk vary from one country to the next. In the United States, the percentage of African Americans found in homeless shelters is almost three and a half times the proportion in the general population and the percentage of Native Americans is twice as high (Henry, Bishop, et al., 2018). These patterns are long-standing (Burt et al., 1999; Hopper & Milburn, 1996). Yet they likely underestimate the housing insecurity of Native populations, who often return to reservations where they continue to experience high rates of homelessness rather than staying in metropolitan shelters (Olivet, Dones, & Richard, 2018). In Canada, 28–34% of the shelter population is indigenous or about five times their representation in the Canadian population

---

[25] This belief explained 43% of the variance in spending across the 30 nations and a whopping 82% of the variance among the wealthier countries.

[26] They found that racial heterogeneity explained 66% of the variance and linguistic heterogeneity (taken separately) explained 41% of the variance in countries' social welfare spending as a proportion of GDP. They do not report the correlation of these measures with each other or with the belief that poverty is society's fault, but these sizable associations suggest that ethnic fractionalization is also associated with that belief.

(Gaetz, Dej, Richter, & Redman, 2016). In Australia, it is Aboriginals and Torres Strait Islanders who are at special risk (Homelessness Task Force, 2008). The pattern is also prevalent outside of Anglophone countries. In France, Africans and people from overseas departments in the Caribbean and Africa are at higher risk than others (Firdion & Marpsat, 2003). In Japan, ethnic minorities such as the Ainu, Koreans, Okinawans, and groups such as the Eta and Hinin who fall outside of the main social classes face discrimination and segregation in poor residential districts and hence, presumably, heightened risk of homelessness (Okamoto, 2007). The great variety of groups affected makes it hard to point to cultural characteristics as contributors to homelessness (although stereotypes abound). Instead they point to social processes at play across nations and continents that put some groups, everywhere, at a disadvantage.

Four forms of social exclusion seem particularly important in explaining links between minority status and homelessness. These are in the areas of income, wealth, housing, and imprisonment. While we focus on the United States, cross-national research suggests that the structure of prejudice is very similar in Western Europe (Pettigrew et al., 1998; Pettigrew & Meertens, 1995), and it is plausible that links to homelessness are also similar.

Income

The first form of exclusion is in access to adequate income, whether from employ-ment or from social benefits. In the United States, the earnings and employment of black Americans relative to white Americans eroded in the 1980s, as homelessness began to rise, and by 1997 the median income of black families was only 55% that of white families (Conley, 1999). Over the last three decades, the unemployment rate among people seeking jobs has been roughly twice as high for blacks as for whites, with only minor fluctuations despite large changes in the overall rates (U.S. Department of Labor, 2019b). By late 2018 unemployment was relatively low for both groups but was still nearly twice as high for blacks as for whites, 6.1 vs. 3.2% (U.S. Department of Labor, 2019a). Among full-time wage and salary workers black men earned 75.5% as much as white men; black women earned 81.5% as much as white women (U.S. Department of Labor, 2019c).

Differential outcomes do not by themselves prove discrimination, if differ-ent groups bring different qualifications to the labor market. Bertrand and Mullainathan (2004) tested discrimination directly. The researchers sent out up to four resumes in applications for each of over 1,300 jobs listed in newspapers in two American cities (Boston and Chicago). Resumes met the minimum require-ments for jobs but were of higher or lower quality based on experience, gaps in work history, and additional credentials. Within each resume pair (high quality or low quality), the researchers randomly assigned one a "black" name (e.g., Lakisha or Jamal) and the other a "white" name (e.g., Emily or Greg), with the designa-tion based on both the proportions of black and white children actually given the names and perceptions of the names in survey data. The researchers then counted how often the employer called to invite the supposed applicant for an interview. Putative white applicants got an interview invitation for every 10 resumes sent out, black applicants for every 15, a difference that held across occupational categories tested. The white advantage was equivalent to that conferred by 8 additional years of experience on the resume. Further, the advantage of having better credentials was greater for white than for black applicants, suggesting that even skills and experience do not overcome employers' racial biases. A 2017 review of a number of similar studies conducted since 1989 concludes that there has been no change in levels of hiring discrimination against African Americans since that time (Quillian, Pager, Hexel, & Midtbøen, 2017). Thus current, ongoing discrimination in employment is an important mechanism linking race to social exclusion on a dimension related to homelessness.

Wealth

A second form of social exclusion is inability to accumulate wealth. In the case of race, historical discrimination in jobs, housing, and credit markets affects the distribution of wealth, which is even more strongly associated with race in the United States than is the distribution of income (Kochhar & Fry, 2014).

For example, in 1994 the median net worth of white families in the United States was nearly eight times that of African American families (Conley, 1999, p. 25). By 2013, white median wealth was 13 times greater than that of black households, with the Great Recession having reduced the wealth of the median black household from $19,200 in 2007 to $11,000 in 2013 (Matthew, Rodrigue, & Reeves, 2016). The median white household with less than a high school education has more wealth ($82,968 in 2014) than the median black household with a college degree ($70,219; Darity et al., 2018). Thus, minority families have less cushion to fall back on, in the event of a loss in income or other housing crisis. Furthermore, African Americans' informal social networks of friends and relatives are also less likely to have assets, in the form of cash or housing, with which to help out a family or individual at risk of falling into homelessness (Heflin & Pattillo, 2006).

Among households with moderate incomes, most wealth takes the form of pensions and housing, net of mortgages (Saez & Zucman, 2016). Home equity accounted for 56% of the wealth in households in the bottom quintile (fifth of all households) by income in 2000 relative to 32% for all households (Herbert & Belsky, 2008). The Great Recession wiped out much of that home equity, and African American homeowners were particularly hard hit, losing much of their net worth (Garriga, Ricketts, & Schlagenhauf, 2017). After a decade of increases peaking in 2005, the national rate of homeownership declined sharply, reaching a low of 63.4% in 2016, slightly below its rate in 1994 (Joint Center for Housing Studies of Harvard University, 2017b, pp. 19–20). The foreclosure crisis that led to this drop in homeownership was not the result of just another business cycle. Financial deregulation led to a spike in subprime loans for both purchasing and refinancing homes, and households were unable to sustain these high-cost loans in the economic downturn. Black Americans were targeted for these loans (Immergluck, 2009). For example, in 2006, nearly 45% of loans to purchase homes in low-income minority communities were high-priced "subprime" loans, compared to 15% of loans in high-income, predominantly white areas (Joint Center for Housing Studies of Harvard University, 2008).

Lack of wealth can affect homelessness across generations. Firdion and Marpsat (2007) note that homeless adults often grow up in poor families or those with low social status, circumstances disproportionately affecting African American children. The relationship between childhood poverty and adult homelessness suggests three different underlying mechanisms. One, based on a "culture" of poverty, suggests that children who grow up poor lack motivation to extricate themselves from that state as adults. "Culture" here is often taken to mean race. However, associations between race and educational attainment, unemployment, and premarital childbearing in the United States are all greatly diminished and sometimes reversed by taking social class of the family of origin (parents' education and various forms of assets) into account (Conley, 1999). A more economic theory suggests that adults from poor backgrounds have less individual or family wealth to draw on when they encounter difficult times. The fact that in a New York study of families receiving public assistance, childhood poverty predicted shelter entry but had no effect on long-term housing stability after families received housing subsidies suggests that the economic explanation may be more important (Shinn et al., 1998). Any psychological factors lost potency when economic resources were provided. Firdion and Marpsat (2007) suggest a third mechanism, whereby growing up in poverty is related to poor physical and mental health in adulthood, which may make it harder to sustain employment. Childhood poverty is also related to the opportunity to acquire human capital (education and skills) that provide income in adulthood (Conley, 1999). In all of these ways, racial disparities in wealth based on historical and contemporary discrimination are carried forward. In his systematic review of the intersection of inequality and race, Shapiro (2017) describes differences in inheritance as "a lynchpin of toxic inequality, for it is a phenomenon in which America's history of racism collides with the indisputable reality of inequality today."

We argue that one way in which that history plays out is in racial disparities in rates of homelessness.

Housing

Discrimination in the housing market is a third form of social exclusion relevant to homelessness. One widely used measure of residential segregation is the dissimilarity index, which measures the difference in the distributions of two groups across some geographic area. Across all metropolitan areas in the United States, the dissimilarity index for African Americans relative to whites in 2010 was 59.1, meaning that 59% of African Americans would have to move from heavily black to less-segregated areas to obtain the same distribution as whites. Dissimilarity was lower for Hispanics 48.5, and for Asians and Pacific Islanders 40.9. These figures represent some improvement for African Americans and Hispanics since 1980 (when comparable numbers were 72.8, 50.3, and 40.8), but the decline is slow, and even affluent blacks live in neighborhoods with higher poverty rates than those lived in by poor whites (Logan, 2013).[27] Of course, residential segregation is also associated with segregation in schooling (Pettigrew, 2004) and proximity to jobs (Kain, 1968; Wilson, 1996), both of which feed into economic disadvantage. But as in the case of jobs, differential distributions don't prove active discrimination. Experiments do.

The U.S. Department of Housing and Urban Development assesses racial discrimination via systematic paired tests, in which two otherwise comparable renters or buyers, one minority and one white, visit rental or real estate agents to ask about advertised housing units. The test partners are matched on income, asset and debt levels, family circumstances, job characteristics, education levels, and housing preferences. Discrimination is observed when only one member of the pair is offered the unit or gets some other form of favorable treatment such as a lower rent. Although it is illegal, housing discrimination remained common in the latest round of national tests in 2012, with whites receiving more favorable treatment than African Americans. For example, when seeking to rent, blacks were told about 11.4% fewer units and were shown 4.2% fewer units. Blacks seeking to buy homes were told about 17.0% fewer units and were shown 17.7% fewer units. The authors suggest that although the most blatant "door-slamming" forms of discrimination are much less frequent today than in earlier decades, "minorities still face significant barriers to housing search, even when they are well-qualified as renters or homebuyers" (Turner et al., 2013, p. xxiii). In addition to making fewer units available, real estate agents also frequently steer white homebuyers into neighborhoods that are overwhelmingly white, and black home-buyers into areas where minorities are overrepresented (Galster & Godfrey, 2005). Such steering of African Americans into areas where homes are less likely to appreciate in value contributes to racial disparities in wealth. The study commissioned by HUD is likely to underestimate overall levels of discrimination, both because the study examined only advertised units and because the minority members of testing pairs were assigned higher income levels and assets than typical minority home seekers. Discrimination is likely to be greater for those with less income and wealth (Turner et al., 2013).

HUD's testing of discrimination against Native Americans is less extensive— examining only eight metropolitan areas in three states in 2002. However the findings suggested that American Indians may be "more likely than [any other

---

[27] Affluent is defined as having an income over 350% of the poverty line for a family of four; poor is defined as having an income below 175% of that poverty line. In 2005–2009, the average neighborhood poverty rate for affluent non-Hispanic blacks was 13.9%; the average for poor non-Hispanic whites was 12.9% (Logan, 2013, Table 2 and footnote 2).

racial or ethnic group] to be denied access to available rental housing in metro-politan areas" (Turner & Ross, 2003, p. 4-1).

Contemporary housing discrimination contributes to homelessness in at least two ways: by reducing opportunities for minorities to accumulate wealth and by reducing their opportunities to live in neighborhoods rich in assets such as high-performing schools. Past discrimination also takes its toll, as disadvantage crosses generations from the era when racial segregation was not simply a *de facto* pattern of private discrimination but *de jure*, not merely ignored but actually abetted by federal, state, and local laws and policies. In the 1990s, in *American Apartheid*, Massey and Denton described the patterns of social exclusion that led to the creation of black ghettos in the twentieth century and the role of those ghettos in role in perpetuating African American poverty (Massey & Denton, 1993). More recently, in *The Color of Law*, Rothstein (2017) provided extensive documentation of government policies and practices that have fostered residential segregation and limited the ability of African Americans to accumulate wealth and pass it on to their children. For example, the first housing developed by the government for civilian defense workers near shipyards and munitions plants was restricted to whites, even in areas where African Americans were a significant part of the workforce. Public housing followed, starting in the Great Depression, and separate projects were built for black and white families as late as the 1950s, even when built in neighborhoods that had previously been integrated. Also in the 1930s, the federal government began to provide mortgage insurance for loans with long payment schedules, to make homeownership more attainable and less risky. While this may have been good social policy, it was implemented in a way that exacerbated residential segregation and reduced the ability of African American families to accumulate wealth. To protect against risk of default, the Federal Housing Administration (FHA) created color-coded maps with red codes if any African Americans lived in the area—the origin of the term "redlining." Appraisal standards in the underwriting manual sought "protection against some adverse influences" such as "infiltration of inharmonious racial or nationality groups" (Rothstein, 2017, p. 69). Following World War II, the FHA and the Veteran's Administration often refused to insure or guarantee mortgages to African Americans, or even to whites in neighborhoods with African Americans present. The percentage of FHA-insured loans that went to African Americans remained tiny as late as 1967 (Pritchett, 2008). When FHA guaranteed loans for mass-production of entire suburbs like Levittown's 17,500 homes, the agency approved plans that required the homebuyers to be all white and may even have compelled such restrictions.

De jure segregation by states and localities may have been even more important than the federal government role. The first segregation ordinance was passed by Baltimore in 1910. The Supreme Court overturned one such ordinance in Louisville in 1917, but localities found various ways to circumvent the decision (Rothstein, 2017).

By the time racial segregation in housing was finally outlawed in the Fair Housing Act of 1968, the suburban housing that white families bought with government mortgage insurance or loan guarantees had appreciated substantially, accounting in large part for racial differences in wealth that persist today. African Americans more often remained renters or bought homes that appreciated at far lower rates in less desirable neighborhoods.

The consequences of housing discrimination and residential segregation for homelessness go beyond their effects on the prospects of individual households. Studies have found that families who experience homelessness in two American cities were disproportionately likely to come from neighborhoods with high concentrations of poor, African American households headed by women with young children. The neighborhoods that generated homelessness also had higher rates of unemployment and a number of difficult housing conditions—higher rent burdens, more abandonment, more crowding (Culhane, Lee, & Watcher, 1996).[28] Furthermore, differences in house price appreciation across neighborhoods account for the diminished ability of African Americans to accumulate wealth through homeownership (Shapiro, 2017).

De jure displacement of Native Americans from ancestral lands to steadily shrinking reservations dates back to before the Civil War. For example, the 1830 federal Indian Removal Act forced the Cherokee, Chickasaw, Choctaw, Creek, and Seminole nations to migrate to Oklahoma on the "Trail of Tears." States also passed laws facilitating removal of Native lands and assaulting Native culture. Many analysts trace current high rates of homelessness and poverty among Native Americans to these historical forms of trauma (Olivet et al., 2018).

Incarceration

Imprisonment is another form of social exclusion that disproportionately affects African Americans. The United States has the highest incarceration rates in the world, according to the Institute for Criminal Policy Research at the University of London, four and a half times as high as the nearest contender in western Europe and 10 times as high as in Scandinavia (Walmsley, 2018). Although rates of incarceration in prisons and jails and correctional supervision (probation and parole) have decreased in the past decade, one in 38 adults 18 or older in the United States was under some form of correctional supervision at the end of 2016 (Kaeble & Cowhig, 2018). Cross-national studies suggest that in every country, incarceration rates are higher for at least some minority groups than for

---

[28] The study did not control for individual characteristics such as income, so it is not clear to what extent impoverished neighborhoods sent large numbers of people to shelter simply because a lot of poor people lived there, or to what extent people with similar incomes are more likely to go to shelters if they live in a poor neighborhood, perhaps because there are fewer neighbors in a position to help, or fewer opportunities for employment, or simply more information about how to access shelters. The neighborhoods also had higher vacancy rates, which the authors interpret as showing the undesirability of neighborhoods and the risk of under maintenance and abandonment of buildings.

the majority (Tonry, 1997), and this pattern in the United States is stark. Among adult men, aged 20–34, 11.5% of non-Hispanic blacks were incarcerated in 2000, compared to 1.5% of non-Hispanic whites. Both the totals and the disparities were down a bit by 2015, but still 9.1% of black men 20–34—one out of every eleven—was incarcerated, compared to 1.6% of their white counterparts (Pettit & Sykes, 2017).[29]

The war on drugs was responsible for much of the increase in the U.S. prison rate at a time that most forms of crime, and violent crime, were falling. But the war targeted black Americans disproportionally. A range of data suggests that use of drugs is similar across racial groups. If anything whites, especially white youths are more likely to sell drugs and to end up in emergency rooms for drug use than African Americans, yet blacks are vastly more likely to be imprisoned (Alexander, 2011). Because prisoners are more likely than others to become homeless (e.g., Firdion & Marpsat, 2007; Philippot et al., 2007), and because individuals who are incarcerated are missed in telephone surveys, the far higher rate of imprisonment in the United States than in Europe may create a differential bias in telephone survey estimates of homelessness described in Chapter 1.

There is strong reason to believe that imprisonment leads to homelessness in the United States, both for the individuals incarcerated and for their families. Approximately 1 in 10 black children aged 0–17 had a parent in prison or jail in 2015 (Pettit & Sykes, 2017), and a larger number had a parent with a history of incarceration. Families lose income while a wage earner is imprisoned, and the offender's employment prospects are diminished after release. A felony conviction also entails a range of civil disabilities that often last long after completion of a sentence. Depending on state laws, people convicted of felonies, especially drug offenses, can be denied welfare benefits, food stamps, and financial aid for higher education (Mauer & Chesney-Lind, 2002). When a released convict returns to live with family, the entire family is barred from many forms of subsidized housing, regardless of need.[30] Similarly, families can be evicted from public housing if any member is found using an illegal drug (Rubinstein & Mukamal, 2002).

Former offenders also find it difficult to gain employment. Pager (2003) used a variant of the audit methodology used in housing tests to examine this phenomenon. She sent paired testers of the same race (both black or both white) to visit employers and apply for advertised entry-level jobs on successive days. One member of the pair claimed to have a criminal record: a nonviolent felony drug conviction for possession with intent to distribute cocaine, with a consequent 18-month prison sentence. Members of the pair rotated who portrayed the offender and were equated in other ways. The criminal offense was disclosed on applications, where requested (74% of application forms asked) and listed work experience in the correctional facility and offered the parole officer as a reference.

---

[29] Rates for Hispanic men in the same age range were 3.7% in 2000 and 3.9% in 2015.

[30] Local public housing authorities often have more restrictive policies than those required by federal law (U.S. Department of Housing and Urban Development, 2013).

The researcher counted whether applicants were called back for an interview or offered a job on the spot. The study showed discrimination both against blacks and against people with criminal records. Applicants with a criminal record were only half to a third as likely to get a call-back as same-race applicants without a criminal record (17% vs. 34% for whites, 5% vs. 14% for blacks). Whites with a criminal record were actually more likely to get a call back than blacks without one.[31] African Americans with criminal records thus suffer two forms of social exclusion, which compound each other. The "prison penalty" in unemployment for black women is even worse than the penalty for black men.[32]

Mental Illnesses and Other Disabilities

Another group at universal risk for homelessness is people with serious mental illnesses (Philippot et al., 2007), although the relative visibility of people with mental illness may fuel exaggerated perceptions of the problem. At least before the advent of cell phones and Bluetooth, anyone poorly dressed, walking down the street, talking to himself, and gesticulating in the air was deemed to be homeless and mentally ill. The person sitting quietly on a park bench was more likely to be missed. As shown in Chapter 1, even cross-sectional studies, which overemphasize people experiencing chronic homelessness, suggest that only about a quarter of adults experiencing homelessness have a serious mental illness, if we do not count alcohol and drug dependence, and only about an eighth have a psychotic illness. Alcohol and drug dependence, which often co-occur with other forms of mental illness, were the most common mental disorders, experienced by almost two fifths (alcohol) and one quarter (drugs) (Fazel, Khosla, Doll, & Geddes, 2008).[33] These studies do not include children or women in families, who may experience high rates of depression or anxiety, but who have lower levels of psychotic disorders and substance use disorders. A study of families found in emergency shelters found that 11% of parents (including some men) reported current alcohol dependence, and 13% reported current drug abuse. Serious psychological distress was fairly common among mothers at the time they were in shelter (22%), but fewer mothers reported those symptoms 21 months and 3 years

---

[31] This last difference was not statistically significant. Further, black and white applicants were not compared directly—the researcher always sent two white people or two black people to apply for a job, but the resumes they presented were identical, and all four testers were trained to approach employers in similar ways.

[32] In 2008, unemployment among 35–44-year-olds was 43.6% for black women who had been incarcerated, compared to 6.4% for black women in the general population. Comparable numbers were 35.2% vs. 7.7% for black men, 23.2% vs. 4.3% for white women, and 18.4% vs. 4.3% for white men. Further, formerly incarcerated black women were most likely to be relegated to part-time jobs (Couloute & Kopf, 2018).

[33] For comparison, 16–17% of full-time college students have illicit drug or alcohol dependence in the past year according to the National Survey on Drug Use and Health (U.S. Department of Health and Human Services, 2014, Table 6.93B).

after the shelter stay, suggesting lower rates of serious mental illness (Shinn, Gubits, & Dunton, 2018).

Some observers attribute the prevalence of mental illness among people experiencing homelessness to deinstitutionalization—the closure of many state mental hospitals. It is certainly the case that some people on the streets today would have been placed in mental hospitals in the 1950s. But attributing the rise in homelessness to deinstitutionalization is too simplistic—for one thing, the explanation is off by about a decade. The population of mental hospitals peaked at over half a million in 1955 and had declined by more than half by 1974. A 1977 report that documented the decline lamented that some former patients had gone to nursing homes and others were housed in substandard room and board facilities or SRO "welfare" hotels without adequate provision for their needs (General Accounting Office, 1977). These alternatives to mental institutions did not live up to the promise of community integration, but their residents were not homeless (Felton & Shinn, 1981; Scull, 1981). Homelessness in the United States arose later, when inexpensive housing for people both with and without mental health problems disappeared (O'Flaherty, 1996). As we will show in Chapter 3, affordable housing with voluntary services ends homelessness and provides dignity and independence for people with serious mental illnesses (Aubry et al., 2015, 2016; Kizer et al., 2018; Stergiopoulos et al., 2015; Tsemberis et al., 2004).

Social exclusion operates in similar ways for people with mental illnesses and other disabilities as for racial minorities—via income, inability to accumulate wealth, housing discrimination, and incarceration. The maximum federal Supplemental Security Income (SSI) benefit for the 4.8 million disabled adults between 18 and 64 is $750 a month (Social Security Administration, 2018a, 2018b), far too low to rent unsubsidized housing in almost any market. Social Security Disability Insurance or SSDI payments for people who have paid payroll taxes for 40 quarters of employment are higher, depending on work history. Twenty-one states supplement federal SSI benefits, often modestly ($10/month in Maine), three by more than $100/month, and one (Alaska) by $362/month. Even with these supplements, on average the Fair Market Rent for an efficiency apartment would consume 99% of the entire SSI benefit (Schaak, Sloane, Arienti, & Zovistoski, 2017).

People who experience mental illness also face discrimination in employment (Draine, Salzer, Culhane, & Hadley, 2002), although this is illegal under the Americans with Disabilities Act, just as racial discrimination is illegal. Further, despite several provisions of the law that are intended to encourage work, continuation of benefits depends both on continuing medical disability and on not earning too much. The law allows exclusion of some work income in the calculation of eligibility for benefits, but earnings while receiving disability benefits remain severely limited, and work involvement by recipients remains low. SSI recipients who are able to work keep the first $65–$85/month of income (depending on whether they have any income outside of their earnings). Half of any remainder is subtracted from the monthly benefit (Social Security

Administration, 2018a).[34] In states that have not expanded Medicaid under the Affordable Care Act, losing SSI benefits often means losing health insurance, which is particularly fraught for people with disabilities.[35] Since 1996, a substance use disorder no longer qualifies as a disability for Social Security programs.

Mental illness also impedes the accumulation of assets that could form a cushion in a crisis. SSI disability benefits cease if an individual accumulates more than $2,000 in assets ($3,000 for a couple), with some exclusions and special exceptions.[36] The most important such exclusion is for a home, so that people lucky enough to own a home are not turned out of it before they can receive disability benefits.

Like racial minorities, individuals with mental illnesses and other disabilities face housing discrimination. Indeed, almost three fifths of fair housing complaints filed with HUD in FY 2017 involved discrimination on the basis of disability (U.S. Departmentof Housing and Urban Development, 2017). HUD commissioned a study of rental housing discrimination on the basis of mental disabilities using paired testers, parallel to paired testing for racial discrimination, in multiple cities in 2013–2014 (Hammel, Smith, Scovill, Campbell, & Duan, 2017). Testers with a mental illness or an intellectual disability, paired with a person without either but matched on other characteristics, applied for the same advertised apartments by email, phone, or in person. The individual with a disability disclosed the issue and asked for a reasonable accommodation—either a service animal or a reminder when rent was due. In the email tests, individuals with a disability were less likely to receive any response and less likely to be invited to see the unit. In telephone tests, they were also less likely to be invited to see a unit and more likely to be steered to a different unit from the one advertised. During in-person tests they were less likely to be told that the advertised unit was still available. Regardless of modality, a large percentage were refused their reasonable accommodation. Rates of adverse treatment were higher for individuals with mental illnesses than for people with intellectual disabilities (although these groups were not directly compared). Similar paired tests showed housing discrimination against well-qualified home

---

[34] Benefits are more generous for people who are blind. There are also some exclusions, for example for impairment-related work expenses.

[35] Medicaid can be continued if the recipient was eligible for an SSI cash payment previously, would be eligible for continued payments except for earnings, remains disabled, meets all other eligibility rules including the limits on assets, needs Medicaid in order to work, and has gross earned income insufficient to replace SSI, Medicaid, and any publicly funded attendant care. SSDI is again more generous in eligibility for Medicare (Social Security Administration, 2018a).

[36] Under the Achieving a Better Life Experience Act of 2014 of ABLE Act, individuals who became disabled before turning 26 can also have savings accounts to pay costs associated with disabilities to which they or their families can contribute up to $15,000 per year to a total of $100,000 without affecting eligibility for SSI (ABLE National Resource Center, n.d.). And individuals who develop a specific, approved Plan to Achieve Self-Support (PASS) to pay expenses for education, vocational training, employment-related assistive technology, or starting a business in order to achieve an approved work goal can exclude earnings deposited in the PASS account from earnings used to calculate SSI benefits (Social Security Administration, 2018a).

seekers who were deaf or hard of hearing, compared to hearing applicants, and against wheelchair users compared to ambulatory applicants. Further, housing providers either failed to provide a clear response or denied more than a quarter of requests for modifications that would make housing more accessible to wheelchair users (Levy et al., 2015).

In the case of many people who receive SSI disability benefits for mental illness, low incomes are an additional barrier to renting on the private market. Although as already noted, supported housing programs that offer people private apartments and supportive services with respect for residents' choices have successfully housed many people with histories of both homelessness and mental illness, many individuals are shunted into far more restrictive settings. For example, a federal court ruled that New York State discriminated against thousands of mentally ill people in New York City by placing them in privately run "adult homes," where residents are segregated from other community members. Some even forced individuals to undergo unnecessary surgery to get money from federal insurance programs.

Incarceration is all too common. Studies of individuals with serious mental illness who are living in the community in the United States have found high lifetime rates of arrests (between 42% and 50%). A Bureau of Justice Statistics report found that almost half of people in prison and over three fifth of those in jails either met the threshold for serious psychological distress on a survey measure or had been told by a mental health professional that they had a mental health disorder (Bronson & Berzofsky, 2017). Rates of serious psychological distress (14% for prison inmates and 26% for jail inmates) were four to five times as high as in the general population (4–5%).[37] Because rates of serious psychological distress among people who had been arrested in the past year were also quite high (13–14%), distress or behaviors associated with that distress may put people at risk of arrest, as well as jail conditions having created distress. Although we know of no specific study of discrimination against people with mental disorders who have been incarcerated, it seems likely that the findings that employers are biased against former offenders apply here too. This would make it harder for people with arrest records to supplement disability benefits or to earn enough to avoid homelessness.

Homelessness puts people with mental illnesses at risk of incarceration. Fischer, Shinn, Shrout, and Tsemberis (2008) found that people with serious mental illnesses were not very likely to commit crimes, but the same individuals were more likely to do so during periods when they were homeless than during periods when they were housed. Offenses included "subsistence crimes" such as stealing food, failing to pay fares on transportation, and trespassing or breaking into a place to sleep, as well as more serious crimes, which may have been precipitated by stressful and sometimes dangerous living conditions in shelters or on the streets.

---

[37] The general population estimate was standardized to match the prison and jail populations on the basis of sex, age, race, and Hispanic origin.

Draine, Salzer, Culhane, and Hadley (2002) believe that the causal role of mental illness in relation to crime and homelessness is overestimated, because researchers fail to take account of poverty and disadvantage that people with mental illnesses often face. "Social problems become erroneously simplified as psychiatric problems" (p. 565). Members of minority groups who also experience mental illness likely face multiple forms of discrimination. The different forms of social exclusion described here are often intertwined with one another and with poverty to put people at risk for homelessness.[38]

Sexual Orientation and Gender Identity

We have suggested that discrimination in income, wealth, housing, and incarceration are central ways in which that social exclusion puts both racial minorities and people with disabilities such as mental illness at risk. Sexual orientation and gender identity are also sources of social exclusion that can lead to homelessness, particularly for youth, but the pathways are different. In addition to community-level discrimination, in some case youths face rejection by their own families. As noted in Chapter 1, children under 18 who experience homelessness over-whelmingly do so with their families. But families sometimes cast out LGBTQ children and youth at an age when they are not yet ready to make it on their own. Service providers in a national survey reported that two thirds of homeless LGBTQ youth had been rejected by families, and more than half had experienced abuse before leaving home (Durso & Gates, 2012). Disclosure of homosexuality may exacerbate preexisting family conflicts of the sort that also lead many hetero-sexual youths to leave home (Castellanos, 2016). LGBTQ youth face more family conflict, physical and sexual abuse by caretakers, and also victimization once they are on the street than their straight counterparts (Toro, Dworsky, & Fowler, 2007).

Less is known about LGBTQ adults. Most surveys of people experiencing homelessness do not ask about sexual orientation or gender identity. A few that do have found higher prevalence rates than in the local population, especially in San Francisco, but it is unclear whether that is due to greater risk overall or a tendency of LGBTQ individuals to migrate to relatively friendly urban areas (Ecker, Aubry, & Sylvestre, 2019). Nor have studies examined routes into home-lessness for individuals who identify as LGBTQ (Ecker et al., 2019). Thus, it is not clear to what extent LGBTQ youth who experience homelessness con-tinue to have episodes of homelessness as adults or whether homophobia, transphobia, or lack of support from families leads to heightened risk for home-lessness among LGBTQ adults relative to their heterosexual counterparts. It is known from the same sorts of paired testing studies that document discrimina-tion against racial minorities and individuals with mental illnesses or intellectual

---

[38] Social scientists refer to the multiple overlapping and intersecting forms of discrimination based on different social identities as "intersectionality," a term coined by Crenshaw (1989).

disabilities, that gay and lesbian couples also face discrimination relative to hetero-sexual couples across 50 major housing markets (Friedman et al., 2013).[39] Surprisingly, discrimination was actually a bit more likely in states with legislative protections against housing discrimination on the basis of sexual orientation.

Of course, LGBTQ individuals have multiple other identities, and there are economic and racial disparities among people who identify as LGBTQ just as there are among people who identify as heterosexual and among people with mental illnesses. People who experience "multiple layers of oppression" may be at special risk for homelessness, for the other forms of social exclusion we have described, and for other ills such as violent victimization or HIV. For example, in a sample of 569 young men aged 17–28 who have sex with men in New York City, Hispanics were at special risk of homelessness—with rates almost seven times as high as for whites (53% vs. 8.4%) and almost twice as high as for blacks (26.5%) (Clatts, Goldsamt, Huso, & Gwadz, 2005).

We turn now to other individual and social characteristics that may lead to homelessness in additional ways.

Other Individual Risk Factors for Homelessness

Our focus on poverty and social exclusion does not deny the role of individual vulnerabilities and bad luck in the path to homelessness. Two widely cited char-acteristics associated with homelessness in the research literature are domestic violence and social isolation. We consider these next.

Social Isolation

Some social scientists, largely before the rise of modern homelessness, deemed social isolation or "disaffiliation" as so central to homelessness that they consid-ered lack of affiliative bonds rather than lack of a roof as the central defining characteristic of homelessness (Bahr, 1968, 1970, 1973). Jencks argued that "the decline of marriage has played a major role in the more recent spread of homelessness among women and children" (1994, p. 58). We are not convinced. As we discussed in Chapter 1, shelter policies influence the characteristics of people found there, and Jenks based his understanding of the marital status of homeless women largely on studies conducted in shelters that excluded men. Far more recently, when shelters have gotten better about accommodating full fami-lies, the Family Options Study found that 27% of families recruited in 12 sites had a spouse or partner with them in shelter, and another 10% had a spouse or partner who was not with them (Gubits et al., 2015; Walton, Dunton, & Groves, 2017). Qualitative data suggested that most of those separations were due to shelter

---

[39] In this case discrimination was demonstrated via emailed inquiries for advertised units.

rules, which also excluded adult children, three-generational families, and sometimes older boys (Shinn, Gibbons-Benton, & Brown, 2015).

The same pattern holds for residents of shelters for single adults. For example, fewer than 3% of adults who do not have children with them are accompanied by someone else in shelters (Henry, Bishop, et al., 2018), but most shelters for adults do not allow couples, friends, or other family configurations to be housed together. By way of contrast, over 30% of the 236 individuals interviewed in unsheltered locations in Nashville's most recent point-in-time count were staying with others on the streets: half with a spouse or partner, 5% with other family members such as an adult child, and 9% with nonrelatives (Bernard, 2019).

Conflating individual characteristics with shelter rules is one problem; confusing consequences of homelessness with causes is another. When researchers look only at people in the midst of an episode of homelessness, they cannot tell causes and consequences apart. Because the people (mostly individuals) Rossi studied in Chicago had been jobless much longer than they had been homeless, he suggested that they had probably gotten help from families and friends until "the patience, forbearance, or resources of these benefactors eventually ran out" (Rossi, Wright, Fisher, & Willis, 1987, p. 1338). Similarly, although it is certainly the case that two-earner families are, on average, better off financially than single-parent families, studies that have looked for predictors of future homelessness among poor families have found that single-parent families are at no higher risk than families headed by a couple (Fertig & Reingold, 2008; Shinn, Greer, Bainbridge, Kwon, & Zuiderveen, 2013; Shinn et al., 1998; Smith, Flores, Lin, & Markovic, 2005).

In a study in New York City, Beth and colleagues compared mothers in families on the brink of a homeless episode with mothers randomly sampled from the public assistance (welfare) caseload (Shinn, Knickman, & Weitzman, 1991). The mothers on the brink, who had come to an intake center to request shelter, were *more* likely than their housed counterparts to report having a mother or grandmother, another close relative, and a close friend, and they were more likely to have been in touch with these members of their network in the past month. Only when it came to resources did the social networks of families on the brink of homelessness look inferior to the networks of housed families. Few mothers in either group thought that any of their relatives and friends had room to put them and their children up for more than a few nights or would allow them to stay if asked, but this was more true of mothers seeking shelter.[40] Nevertheless, over three quarters of families on the brink of homelessness had stayed with a family member or friend either on the night before requesting shelter or for the longest period in the past year (the only two times we asked about). Often they had

---

[40] Among housed mothers, 14.3% thought they could stay with their own mother or grandmother, 5.9% thought they could stay with another close relative, and 4.8% thought they could stay with a close friend. For the mothers requesting shelter the numbers were 3.2, 1.6, and 1.0%.

stayed with more than one other household. We conclude that families on the brink of homelessness did not lack social resources but had exhausted them, wearing out their welcomes like the individuals Rossi interviewed in Chicago. Five years later, when we interviewed both groups of families again, the size of their networks did not differ, but the formerly homeless families had slightly more strained ties. They also lived further away from their networks, probably because the city, paying no attention to where families had lived previously when offering them housing, frequently placed them in different boroughs from family and friends (Toohey, Shinn, & Weitzman, 2004).

Domestic Violence

Another explanation often offered for homelessness among families is domestic violence. For example, a recent book states (without citing any back-up research) that domestic violence "is the direct cause of homelessness for more than half our homeless women and is overall the third leading cause of homelessness in our country" (Snyder, 2019, p. 15). It is certainly the case that a lot of women who experience homelessness, with or without children, have been subjected to appalling violence by intimate partners, and the first stop for many women fleeing violent relationships is a domestic violence or homeless shelter (Jasinski, Wesely, Wright, & Mustaine, 2010). It is also the case that a lot of poor women experience domestic violence without becoming homeless. Without a comparison group of poor women who are housed, it is impossible to show that women who experience homelessness face differential levels of violence.

Studies that do include comparison groups have an odd pattern (cf. Shinn, 2011). When studies do a cursory job of measuring violence, they find that women who experience homelessness report more childhood abuse and adult victimization than other poor women who remain housed (e.g., Bassuk & Rosenberg, 1988; Ingram, Corning, & Schmidt, 1996; Shinn et al., 1991; Wood, Valdez, Hayashi, & Shen, 1990). Studies that do a more detailed job of measurement and focus on behavior rather than summary statements find that violence is near universal among poor women, whether housed or homeless, with little in frequency or seriousness to differentiate between them (Bassuk et al., 1996; Browne & Bassuk, 1997; Goodman, 1991). The high level of violence among poor women generally suggests the importance of providing "trauma-informed" services that are sensitive to the often horrific experiences that many women encounter. But they cast doubt on the idea that violence has a central causal role in homelessness. The fact that housing subsidies not only prevent and end homelessness for families (as described in detail in the next two chapters, but also reduce domestic violence (Gubits et al., 2018), suggests that, when it comes to homelessness, affordable housing is more important. Domestic violence and homelessness are both scourges that should be eliminated, but the connection between them should not be exaggerated.

Bad Luck

O'Flaherty (2010) suggests that much homelessness is the result of unpredictable events—bad luck. This is not simply a "there-but-for-fortune" argument. Many people are insulated from transient forms of bad luck by social insurance programs (health insurance, unemployment insurance), by their social networks, and by their own resources, although O'Flaherty suggests multiple ways of enhancing the social safety net. But an episode of bad luck can pitch someone already living on the margins over the edge into homelessness, perhaps exhausting social networks along the way.

Some kinds of bad luck are more likely than others to lead to homelessness. In a study of older homeless adults (Shinn et al., 2007), Beth and colleagues looked at the stressful life events respondents experienced in the year leading up to their (most recent) homeless episode. The study had a comparison sample of stably housed older adults. Overall, the number of events did not differentiate the two groups, after controlling for other demographic factors. Some events (bereavement, physical disability) were actually more common among the stably housed group.[41] But two types of events were more common among the group that experienced homelessness: job loss and being evicted or asked to leave a home. For example, José (not his real name) was 77 when we met him. He sold his furniture business and retired at age 72, thinking he would live on his pension. He was soon unable to afford the rent for his long-time apartment and was evicted. He said he was close to his children but did not want to be a burden to them, so took to the streets.

Even the eviction question (in our stressful life inventory) did not capture the multiple ways people lost access to housing: a fire, a flood, the death of a primary tenant, a shooting, a move that did not work out. For example, James owned a grocery store, which he sold at age 67, planning to live on the proceeds and some savings. A year later he lost his apartment in a fire. The city found him a place in a single-room occupancy hotel, but he complained that it was dirty and roach-infested and decamped to a drop-in center where we found him shortly afterwards. James was looking for a new place. He had two children, and said he could stay with either but wanted to live on his own.

Health problems were important largely when they restricted ability to work. Bill lived in the same apartment for 50 years until he was disabled by a physical illness at age 68. Unable to work, he lost the construction job that he had held for 15 years. When he could not afford the rent he stayed with relatives (a nephew, a sister) for 3 years, but eventually exhausted these resources and became homeless.

---

[41] This may be a consequence of the fact that the housed group was older than the group experiencing homelessness. Further, we asked the housed group to tell us about events in the last year, and the homeless group to tell us about events in the year before they became homeless, often several years back, exacerbating the groups' age difference in the year in question.

The stories our respondents recounted often suggested not just a single episode of bad luck but a cascade of events on top of a cornucopia of risk factors. Susan was employed in a series of jobs throughout her adult life and lived in the same apartment for 29 years. After an injury limited the work she could do, she got a job managing a thrift shop, and brought home so many items that her landlord declared it a fire hazard and evicted her for hoarding at the age of 74. We coded Susan as having both physical and mental health problems in her last year in conventional housing, no child, friend, or relative who could take her in, and a relatively short period of 5 years in the longest of the many jobs she had held, all factors that contributed, statistically, to homelessness.

Sometimes bad choices compounded underlying risk. Bob, a Vietnam veteran, was diagnosed with posttraumatic stress disorder, generalized anxiety disorder, and bipolar disorder, but he nevertheless made good money in a middle-management position at a bank. However his life fell apart when his long-term girlfriend left. He left his job and got in trouble with alcohol and gambling, so that he no longer had money to pay rent. His slide into homelessness at age 56 included a trip to detox and hospitalizations for both medical and psychiatric problems.

Although each story of how someone fell into homelessness was unique, supporting O'Flaherty's (2010) emphasis on bad luck, the predominance of events involving housing and the jobs to pay for it reinforces the idea that lack of affordable housing is the key driver of homelessness. In the New York study, the comparison sample was drawn from a public housing development, so that their access to affordable housing was secure and allowed them to weather bereavement and health problems.

Summary

Structural factors, including poverty, inequality, lack of affordable housing, and the lack of a strong social safety net—and in particular a safety net for housing—place many people in the United States at risk of homelessness. Social exclusion augments risk for minorities and others who face stigma on the basis of sexual orientation, mental illness, or a history of incarceration. Not all people at high risk actually experience homelessness. It also takes bad luck or sometimes a bad choice to propel an individual or a family who is already at risk into a shelter or onto the street (O'Flaherty, 2010). We have argued that social policies can augment or counteract individual risk. Just as individuals sometimes make choices that may lead them to homelessness, nations make choices that can lead to high rates of homelessness for their citizens.

3

Ending Homelessness for People Who Experience It

The last chapter was a discouraging account of the forces that continue to generate homelessness. The next two chapters are more upbeat. Rigorous research, much of it published in the last decade, provides a clear map for ending homelessness for families with children and for individuals who can benefit from intensive services. In this chapter, we present the strong research evidence for specific programs that work: long-term housing subsidies for families and supportive housing for individuals with high needs. In the Chapter 4, we turn to coordinated or comprehensive efforts to reduce and end homelessness for everyone experiencing it.

Long-Term Rental Subsidies for Families

Chapter 2 suggested that, for most people, homelessness is primarily a problem of housing affordability. If so, rental subsidies that make housing affordable should fix the problem. That is indeed the case. In the United States, the evidence is strongest for families with children.

Multiple studies show that that long-term rental subsidies that hold families' payments for rent and utilities to about 30% of their income end homelessness and promote residential stability. Providing permanent housing to families leaving homeless shelters lowered rates of return in Philadelphia (Culhane, 1992) and New York (Wong, Culhane, & Kuhn, 1997). A study in New York City found that, 5 years after entering a homeless shelter, 80% of families who received rental subsidies, compared to 18% who did not, had stable housing, defined as a place of their own where they had lived for at least a year without a move (the average was 3 years) (Shinn et al., 1998). A study in Alameda County, California found that, in a mixed sample of families and adults, both housing subsidies and entitlement income (two ways of attacking the problem of housing affordability) were associated with exits from homelessness into stable housing (Zlotnick, Robertson,

In the Midst of Plenty: Homelessness and What to Do About It, First Edition.
Marybeth Shinn and Jill Khadduri.
© 2020 Marybeth Shinn and Jill Khadduri. Published 2020 by John Wiley & Sons Ltd.

& Lahiff, 1999). These studies were not experiments, meaning that people who got the subsidies may have differed from those who did not, and these differences, rather than the subsidies, might have contributed to the better outcomes.

Much stronger evidence that long-term rental subsidies end homelessness for families comes from the Family Options experiment, in which both of us were centrally involved (Gubits et al., 2015, 2016, 2018). Our team recruited nearly 2,300 families staying in emergency shelters in 12 sites across the United States[1] and offered them one of four housing and service packages. Nearly 150 programs operating in the 12 communities delivered the services. Thus, we examined what was actually being implemented in communities across the country, rather than whether some theoretically valuable (but perhaps hard-to-implement) program cooked up by researchers could potentially work under ideal conditions. The families had all stayed in shelters for at least a week before joining the study, so those who could resolve homelessness quickly on their own were not included. National data suggest that 16% of families leave shelter this quickly (Henry, Bishop, de Sousa, Shivji, & Watt, 2018; Solari, Shivji, de Sousa, Watt, & Silverbush, 2017).

Some of the families were assigned at random to receive either offers of long-term rental subsidies, in most cases Housing Choice Vouchers, with no additional services or "usual care"—that is, no special help with housing beyond whatever the staff of the emergency shelter ordinarily provided. This random assignment— essentially a coin toss—created two well-matched groups at the outset. (We will describe results for two other programs to which some families were randomly assigned, transitional housing and rapid re-housing, in Chapter 4.)

Follow-up surveys 20 months and again 37 months later showed that families offered the housing vouchers were far less likely to be homeless or to be doubled up with another household in the same dwelling unit because they could not find or afford a place of their own. According to shelter records, 18.8% of the usual care group, but only 4.4% of those offered subsidies, had spent at least one night in an emergency shelter in the third year of the study, (Gubits et al., 2016, Exhibit 3–5, p. 36, 2018).[2]

In the Family Options experiment, families who were *offered* housing vouchers were compared with families who were eligible for the subsidies but did not get any special offer of assistance. Families in the subsidy group who actually leased a unit with the subsidy (84% of those with offers) did even better: only 1.4% spent a night in shelter in year 3, compared to 20.7% of those who were assigned by the

---

[1] The sites were Alameda County, CA; Atlanta, GA; Baltimore, MD; Boston, MA; Bridgeport and New Haven, CT; Denver, CO; Honolulu, HI; Kansas City, MO; Louisville, KY; Minneapolis, MN; Phoenix, AZ; and Salt Lake City, UT.

[2] Shelter records were supplemented by additional tracking data. The resulting "program use file" was updated slightly as described in (Gubits, McCall, Brown, & Wood, 2017), and this is reflected in the 2018 article and the numbers reported here; the earlier report has more detailed information about survey responses.

study to get subsidies but did not use them to rent a unit (Gubits et al., 2016, Exhibit H–7, p. H4).[3]

To use subsidies, families first had to pass screening (including criminal background checks) conducted by public housing authorities. The vast majority passed.[4] Then they had to find a unit that passed inspection within the time allotted by the housing authority (Solari & Khadduri, 2017). Previous studies have documented families' difficulty in using housing vouchers within the prescribed time limits, finding units that will pass inspections, and finding landlords willing to lease to voucher holders (e.g., Edin, DeLuca, & Owens, 2012). A recent study by the Urban Institute in five sites shows how daunting the process can be. Study personnel had to screen 39 ads, on average, to find one unit that appeared to meet the program rental cap and then make 1.5–2 calls on average to contact the landlord, only to be turned down outright by between 15 and 78% of landlords (depending on the city), who refused to rent to voucher holders. Even landlords who said over the phone that they accepted vouchers were more likely to stand up voucher holders who made an appointment to see a unit than other potential tenants of the same race (Cunningham et al., 2018).[5] Lease-up rates among the desperately poor families in the Family Options Study were higher than in any previous study of voucher rental subsidies, which usually are offered to people who already have places to live (Finkel & Buron, 2001).[6] Some Family Options families also encountered landlords who would not accept vouchers, and they sometimes settled for housing they found less than ideal, but most persevered, like this mother in Phoenix:

> Anybody who can't do it, I don't believe them. Without a car. Without a job. I don't believe them. Because I have four kids and no job and no car, and I did it. Yeah, so it's awesome. (Fisher, Mayberry, Shinn, & Khadduri, 2014)

---

[3] These findings about people who did or did not use the subsidy they were offered are suggestive, but they are not from a random comparison—families who used the subsidies may have differed from families who did not in their characteristics and resourcefulness, and that same variation could have led to different outcomes had they not received offers of subsidies.

[4] Interviewers did preliminary screening to assure that families in both groups appeared eligible for the subsidies, but did not do criminal background checks or check financial records for eligibility. Most families (98%) passed this initial screening; but 11% of these were subsequently screened out by the public housing authorities. Statutory reasons for ineligibility include lack of US citizenship or legal status, a drug-related criminal conviction, a past eviction from a federally funded housing program, or owing arrearages to a housing authority. Some authorities added local criteria for a consistent source of income or ability to pay security deposits (Solari & Khadduri, 2017).

[5] The study found higher acceptance rates by landlords in areas with source-of-income protection, meaning that landlords cannot legally discriminate based on the source the potential tenant will use to pay the rent. Thus legislation helps but does not completely resolve the problem.

[6] The lease-up rate among families issued vouchers (excluding the small number given subsidized public housing at the Honolulu site) was 82.3%. In some cases, families may have received help in locating units from shelter staff (Solari & Khadduri, 2017).

Less stringent screening of families, laws prohibiting discrimination against voucher holders, and more aid in finding housing might have led to even better results than those we observed.

In interviews conducted with some participants, families expressed a palpable sense of relief at having their own place. For example, a mother in Phoenix said:

> Since we just moved here we're still trying to settle in, and can't believe that we're actually waking up in our own house. [Laughter] We're just like, "Whoa, is this a dream?"

In response to a question about the best things about the living situation, a mother in Alameda County, California said,

> Just not having to worry about where am I going to lay my head, what are we going to eat tonight, and just able to be in the comfort of your own home.

And a mother in Phoenix echoed:

> Everything. Me and my kids are together. We have a roof over our head. We have food on the table. There's buses; there's schools. That's basically it. There's utilities; there's water.

In response to a similar question in the earlier study, a New York City child said simply:

> I have my own bed.

Gratitude for having a place to lay one's head, running water, and a bed of one's own gives some sense of the hardship entailed in homelessness. Annual incomes of families in the Family Options study averaged only $7,410 at the point they entered homeless shelters—far too little to lease a unit on the private market without help.

A more expansive theory behind rental subsidies suggests that affordable housing not only ends homelessness but also gives families a platform to solve other problems on their own. Results support that theory. The long-term subsidies in the Family Options Study had radiating benefits in all the other domains of outcomes we considered: self-sufficiency, family preservation, and adult and child well-being. Compared to families who got no special offer of assistance (i.e., families who received usual care), families offered rental subsidies were less likely to report food-insecurity (based on a list of questions such as whether, because of lack of money to buy food, adults cut the size of meals, ate less than they thought they should, were hungry but didn't eat, or went an entire day without food).[7]

---

[7] Among families assigned to usual care, almost half of parents reported yes to two or more of six questions in this widely used scale developed by the U.S. Department of Agriculture at both 20 months (46%) and 37 months (47%) after entering emergency homeless shelters.

Children were less likely to be separated from their parents or go into foster care—findings of particular importance because children who experience either event are more likely to become homeless as adults (Cutuli, Montgomery, Evans-Chase, & Culhane, 2017; Lee et al., 2017; Shinn et al., 1998; Shinn, Greer, Bainbridge, Kwon, & Zuiderveen, 2013). Children also moved schools less often and had lower absenteeism and lower behavior problems at the 3-year follow-up. Adults reported lower levels of psychological distress, substance abuse, and domestic violence. That is, problems that can sometimes lead to homelessness were reduced when families got housing subsidies. Other studies have also shown that adult and child well-being improve over time when families who have been homeless regain housing (Samuels, Fowler, Ault-Brutus, Tang, & Marcal, 2015; Shinn et al., 2008; Shinn, Samuels, Fischer, Thompkins, & Fowler, 2015).

Interviews with Family Options families shed light on how housing with rental subsidies provided a platform for improvements in other aspects of life. A mother in Phoenix described the improvements in her children's behavior:

> My youngest son, Jason, had a big problem adjusting [in the shelter]. He always had an attitude, he was always getting into trouble, he was always mouthing back to his teacher. I guess he thought, "Well I'm not going to be here for long, so what the heck?" But now it's different. He's been getting a lot of As in school, doing reading one up, math one up. Before he was going grades low from moving school-to-school. Now his situation, he's at the top of his class, and my daughter, too. She was getting Fs, she was failing big-time, and since we've been moved here and since they've settled down in one spot, the grades have improved so much.

A mother in Kansas City described how housing reduced worries and permitted families to get on with their lives:

> So for me to actually have a nice house for our children without having to be completely worried about rent, rent, rent for this month because my husband is trying to go back to school full-time and so am I ... that way we know we're supported and we don't have to worry about losing the house because we are trying to go to school and work and we're safe, we're okay and we'll get things back on track.[8]

The overwhelmingly positive results for subsidies were tempered by one negative effect and one ambiguous one. Adults in families who received subsidies were slightly less likely to be employed, although their incomes were not lower. Because subsidies peg families' housing costs to 30% of their income, they effectively create

---

[8] Most of the quotations in this chapter from Families who participated in the Family Options Study have not been published previously. Some have also been reported in Fisher et al. (2014) and Shinn, Gibbons-Benton, and Brown (2015). The earlier quotation from a child in New York is from a study by Shinn et al. (1998).

a 30% marginal tax (on top of payroll taxes) on each additional dollar earned.[9] Housing subsidies also permit people to make reasonable decisions to reduce their hours—for example, to care for a sick child or to complete a training course.[10] More research is under way about designing subsidies in ways that do not dampen work effort.[11]

Also, at the longer-term follow-up, couples who had been together in the emergency shelters were more likely to have separated. We deem this an ambiguous finding, because the housing subsidies led to lower levels of domestic violence, and domestic violence was correlated with couple separations. Thus, subsidies may have helped some women to escape abusive relationships. On the other hand, restriction of housing subsidies to people who pass criminal background checks mean that some families had to separate in order to take advantage of the subsidy. One respondent in Phoenix who chose a housing voucher (often referred to as "Section 8," because the voucher program is authorized by Section 8 of the U.S. Housing Act) over her partner lamented:

> I do think it would be easier if Section 8 allowed my fiancé to live here. That definitely would make it easier, you know?… Especially since, I mean, if he was a violent criminal or something like that I could understand. But I mean, he's a shoplifter. So it's like they're protecting people from big, bad shoplifters.[12]

The Family Options study also looked at the costs of housing and service programs used by families assigned to the different groups. The cost data make clear that "usual care" was far from nothing. Families who were eligible for subsidies but received no special offer of assistance nevertheless used housing and service programs with a total cost averaging $42,134 over 37 months. The largest share of that cost went to extended stays in emergency shelter, followed by transitional housing and various forms of subsidized housing. Families assigned to rental subsidies cost only 9% more: an average of $45,902 over the same period.

---

[9] This is on top of taxes such as social security that even the poorest people pay, but the combined effect is mitigated somewhat by the Earned Income Tax credit.

[10] Economists call these two reasons that safety net programs may induce families to work less the "tax effect" and the "income effect."

[11] For example, the Department of Housing and Urban Development (HUD) has commissioned a study of "rent reform" that will show whether fairly modest changes to the subsidy formula and its application mitigate or reverse the tendency of housing subsidies to depress work effort (Riccio, Deitch, & Verma, 2017). As of this writing, results were not published, but we have heard informally that changes to the subsidy formula had modest positive effects in two of the four housing authorities participating in the study. HUD also plans to test the effect of adding explicit work requirements to subsidy rules. One of us (Jill) serves on the federal advisory committee that recommended such a test.

[12] Although the particular criminal offenses that lead to exclusion form housing assistance vary from place to place, misdemeanors would not be a likely reason for exclusion anywhere. Quotation reported previously in Fisher et al. (2014).

Perverse Incentives

Advocates often argue that that it would be cheaper to give a rental subsidy to everyone who becomes homeless rather than to maintain a costly shelter system. The cost data from Family Options study suggests that they are not completely right, although if additional costs associated with foster care or psychological distress and domestic violence were factored in, the balance might tip. Administrators, on the other hand, often worry that a policy of providing subsidies to people experiencing homelessness would create a perverse incentive, drawing more people into shelters in order to access this benefit (Jencks, 1994; Main, 1993). Since 1996, New York (where both families and single individuals have a legal right to shelter) has required shelter requesters to prove that they are truly homeless, resulting in many being turned away. "I can't screw the front door any tighter," said the City's Commissioner of Homeless Services (Bernstein, 2001, February 7). Some voice similar concerns about opening up shelters or improving their condition. For example, in 1985 New York's Mayor Ed Koch said "We are going to, whenever we can, put people into congregate housing like the Roberto Clemente shelter—which is not something people might rush into, as opposed to seeking to go into a hotel" (Basler, 1985, December 17). New York City has long since abandoned congregate shelters for families in favor of modest apartments, but many administrators still share the concern that the availability of shelters draws people into them.

O'Flaherty and colleagues tested these claims against the data in two eras in New York City and found them overblown. The first period spanned 1986–1993 (Cragg & O'Flaherty, 1999), the second 1997–2003 (O'Flaherty & Wu, 2006). Not surprisingly, the researchers found that economic conditions mattered, with a bit of a lag, and in the earlier period reductions in welfare benefits also contributed to a rise in the shelter population. But, perhaps counter to intuition, when placements into subsidized housing were *reduced*, the numbers of families using shelters *increased*. In the earlier period, a policy of placing more families in subsidized housing did draw a few more families into the shelter system but not nearly enough to offset placements out of the system. The authors calculated that it took placing seven families into subsidized apartments to draw one family into shelter. In the latter period, the authors found no effect of housing placements on luring families into shelter (although the number of applicants whom the City found ineligible did increase). Increases in placements into subsidized housing did slow "natural" exits from the shelter system, in which families leave on their own without assistance—that is, some families stayed in shelter in hopes of getting a subsidy. Nonetheless, the researchers clearly found that placing families in subsidized housing reduced rather than increased the number of families in the homeless service system.[13] In Chapter 6 on countering social conditions

---

[13] Further analysis suggested that it took about three placements in subsidized housing to reduce the shelter census by one family.

that generate homelessness, we discuss a broader policy to expand availability of rental subsidies to people who are deeply poor, with funding allocations that are national but emphasize geographic regions with the highest rates of homelessness. Expanded availability of rental subsidies would reduce any perverse incentive to declare oneself homeless in order to obtain one.

We believe concerns that rental subsidies will entice families into shelter to be misplaced in another way. Most readers of this book would not give up their homes and rush down to a new shelter that opened up down the block in hopes of securing a rental subsidy for a modest apartment at the other end of a homeless spell. It is a mark of both deprivation and desperation that a shelter stay looks more attractive than what people have now.

Psychosocial Services

Subsidized housing resolves homelessness for most families. However, to attain enough income to thrive without ongoing subsidies, many families may need some additional help. For families with high needs, Rog and Gutman (1997) suggest that mental health services to deal with ongoing stresses may be especially useful, although the Family Options study found that simply supplying housing subsidies reduced psychological distress. Most providers agree that services should be "trauma-informed"—that is, they should be sensitive to the high rates of adverse childhood experiences and intimate partner violence experienced by parents who become homeless, as well as the traumatic experiences of both parents and children during the immediate crisis that sends them into homelessness (e.g., Hopper, Bassuk, & Olivet, 2010).

The field has produced good evidence about the impact of housing subsidies in reducing family homelessness, but little evidence about services. A six-city study in which families deemed at high risk were given both subsidies for renting in the private market and social services to address their problems found that 86% of families were still in the same subsidized housing 18 months later. This study had no comparison group who did not receive housing subsidies, but cities with more intensive social services did not have better housing retention rates, suggesting the central importance of the housing subsidies (Rog, Holupka, & McCombs-Thorton, 1995).[14]

A study of 20 programs in Washington State that gave high needs families both subsidized housing (either housing vouchers or units in housing projects) and intensive case management, with services addressing domestic violence, mental health, chemical dependency, and children's mental health and education found the families in the programs had increased access to behavioral health services, higher rates of family reunification, and lower rates of criminal justice involvement than similar families found in emergency shelter; however, it is not clear to

---

[14] This is despite the enormous variability in the intensity of case management from an average of 52 hrs in the first year at one site to less than an hour a month at two others (Rog & Gutman, 1997).

what extent it was the housing that mattered or the services that mattered. A second comparison group of families in public housing fared just as well on all but one outcome (access to behavioral health services). As in the Family Options study, the authors concluded that "housing itself is a powerful intervention and may help foster improvements for families even without special services" (Rog, Henderson, Wagner, & Greer, 2017, p. 8).

Because most families who become homeless have young children, affordable child care may be the single most important service for families. Recall from Chapter 1 that rates of homelessness among children drop sharply when children reach school age, freeing parents to work. Quality child care is also important for children's cognitive development, and this is especially true for poor children (Yoshikawa et al., 2013). Among young children of families in the Family Options experiment, those who attended Head Start or center-based child care programs had stronger prereading and premath skills than their counterparts who received only parental care (Brown, Shinn, & Khadduri, 2017).

Federal policy gives priority access to Head Start to children who experience homelessness, and indeed, 20 months after entering homeless shelters with their families, children in the Family Options study enrolled in Head Start at rates comparable to other poor children. Access to other forms of center-based care was more problematic, especially for families who experienced ongoing housing instability (Brown et al., 2017). Understandably, families may give priority to finding secure housing over finding child care. And although families experiencing homelessness may be eligible for child care subsidies, they may not be able to lay out money before getting reimbursed (Taylor, Gibson, & Hurd, 2015). Further, requirements that parents have a job before receiving child care creates a Catch 22 (Mayberry, 2016) as described by this mother in Phoenix:

> They did have child care, but you had to be working a certain amount of hours. And I'm like—well, I don't have a job at all. It doesn't exactly look right taking your kids to interviews.

Access to good jobs would also help. In the Family Options Study, 40% of those families who were not working at the time they were in shelter gave inability to find a job as the reason (Walton, Dastrup, & Khadduri, 2018). Stabilizing jobs and child care, along with stabilizing housing, might allow more formerly homeless parents to raise their incomes to the point that ongoing subsidies are unnecessary.

Subsidies Plus Voluntary Services for High Needs Individuals

Even without additional services, ongoing rental subsidies that make housing affordable are sufficient to end homelessness for most families. Families may be the easy case. Although levels of psychological distress are high when families enter shelter, distress and substance use dissipate as families receive housing (Gubits et al., 2018; Samuels et al., 2015). People with long histories of homelessness compounded by severe and persistent mental illnesses and co-occurring substance use disorders make up the other end of the spectrum of need. They usually experience homelessness as individuals: they have no children, their children have grown up, or their children are with someone else. It turns out that affordable housing is key to ending homelessness for these individuals as well, but more extensive services are likely to be needed. We say "likely" because no studies have examined what happens when such high-needs individuals are given rental vouchers without services. The evidence shows that supportive housing[15]— affordable housing where clients have leases and services are voluntary—works to end homelessness (with follow-up periods of 2 years), increases tenure in housing, and increases consumer satisfaction compared to other housing models and usual care (Kizer et al., 2018; Munthe-Kaas, Berg, & Blaasvaer, 2018; Rog et al., 2014). We view a particular model of supportive housing—the Pathways Housing First model—as especially successful. We review some of the evidence, giving weight to strong experimental studies.

An early experiment in San Diego randomized to four groups individuals experiencing homelessness with mental illnesses and often substance abuse problems: some received access to rental subsidies; others did not. In both groups some were additionally chosen at random to receive intensive case management, and the others received normal case management services. The intensity of case management made no difference to housing outcomes; housing subsidies did. Individuals who received the rental subsidies were more likely to be independently housed in their own house or apartment over the next 2 years than those who did not. People who did not get the subsidies were more likely to be in residential programs, board and care homes, or staying with relatives, although they were not more likely to be literally homeless (Hurlburt, Hough, & Wood, 1996).

Another study randomized homeless veterans with mental illnesses across four sites to three groups. One group received housing vouchers provided by the Department of Housing and Urban Development (HUD) paired with intensive case management services provided by the Veterans Administration (VA) under the HUD-VA Supportive Housing or HUD-VASH program. A second group got the intensive case management without the housing vouchers, and a third got only standard VA care. The HUD-VASH group had many more days

[15] The label "supported housing" was initially used in contradistinction to a more dominant model dubbed *supportive* housing with mandatory services and requirements that consumers be housing-ready prior to entry. As evidence accumulated that low-barrier programs with voluntary services are more successful in ending homelessness, "supportive" housing has adopted many of the principles of "supported housing" and is the term in wider use in the United States. "Supported housing" is used in Europe. The Washington State programs for families described earlier are also considered supportive housing.

housed and fewer days homeless, especially in the first year. Differences between the groups were somewhat smaller at the 3-year follow-up point. The HUD-VASH group also reported fewer housing problems, had larger social networks, and reported better quality of life, but did not differ from the other groups on measures of mental health or substance use (Rosenheck, Kasprow, Frisman, & Liu-Mares, 2003).

It is not clear to what extent services were voluntary in these studied programs. In the San Diego study, people were excluded if they had "substance abuse problems with which they [were] not willing to deal" (Hurlburt et al., 1996). In the HUD-VASH study, participants were identified as eligible by professional staff from the Health Care for Homeless Veterans program and were three times more likely than other veterans served by the program to have been in residential treatment. Further "each veteran had to agree to a treatment plan involving further participation in case management and other specified services," although once they were housed retention of housing vouchers did not depend on treatment (Rosenheck et al., 2003).

The dominant model of treatment for homeless people with mental illnesses at the time these studies were conducted—and to some extent continuing today—is variously labeled "treatment first," "housing readiness," or "the staircase model." The idea is that, in order to succeed in housing, individuals with mental illnesses and substance use problems need to be clean and sober and participate in psychiatric or substance abuse programs. (Wags call this taking the drugs doctors want them to take and not the ones they prefer.) By abiding by rules, maintaining sobriety, working to achieve housing "readiness," and succeeding in treatment, clients can earn their way up the staircase from fairly regimented emergency shelters to supervised transitional housing facilities (where clients typically share rooms with assigned roommates), to more independent permanent supportive housing programs, still with ongoing supervision. Independent housing at the last step is reserved for people who have demonstrated success in treatment. Consumers who relapse are bounced back to a lower step.

Clinicians at the time talked explicitly about using housing as leverage to induce consumers to comply with a treatment regimen that they saw as needed in order for the consumers to sustain that housing (Susser & Roche, 1996). Consumers, on the other hand, overwhelmingly prefer independent housing with services that they control (Ridgway & Zipple, 1990; Tanzman, 1993). As Howie the Harp, who was homeless after being released from a mental hospital but who went on to serve as program coordinator for the Oakland Independence Support Center wrote (in a scientific journal):

> I tried living in a residential facility but could not tolerate the regimentation, abuses, and lack of freedom. I could not follow the rules of those who neither gave nor earned respect, and thus the streets became my only alternative. (Howie the Harp, 1990)

Pathways to Housing

The Pathways to Housing program revolutionized this approach. It skipped over the intermediate steps in the standard treatment model, offering consumers found on the streets housing first, without prerequisites, and with voluntary services under their control, as shown in Figure 3.1.

The origins of the model are instructive. Shortly after graduate school, Pathways' founder, Sam Tsemberis, drove the van that pulled homeless people off the streets of New York City when temperatures dropped to the point that City officials feared they would die of exposure. The City had a "right to shelter" at the time, so Tsemberis asked his passengers why they chose to stay on the frigid streets. Answers paralleled those voiced by Howie the Harp. Listening to his passengers, Tsemberis developed a consumer-run drop-in center, Choices Unlimited, which welcomed consumers without prerequisites. Staff followed rehabilitation principles, and consumers had a direct voice in Center operations. For example, consumers developed a system of banking for managing their money, chose to employ a formerly homeless individual as a manager in lieu of a security guard, and determined the Center's hours of operation. Arguably, the drop-in center empowered consumers, but they did not have the resource they wanted most, namely housing (Tsemberis, Moran, Shinn, Asmussen, & Shern, 2003). So Tsemberis founded Pathways to Housing, using funds from the New York/New York agreement—a fund created jointly by the City and the State to provide housing to people with serious and persistent mental illnesses and long histories of homelessness.

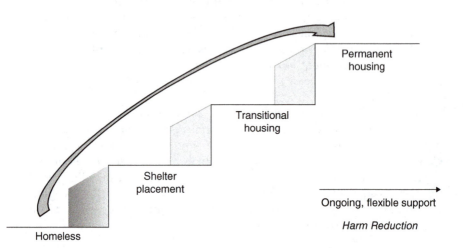

Figure 3.1 Housing First Bypasses the Steps in the Staircase Model of Care and Gives Consumers Immediate Access to Independent, Permanent Housing with Support Services that They Choose. Padgett, Henwood, and Tsemberis (2016, p. 13). Used by permission.

Pathways to Housing provides consumers living on the street with immediate access to apartments with private landlords, without prerequisites for sobriety or participation in treatment. Wrap-around services, offered 24-7 by multidisciplinary "Assertive Community Treatment" (ACT) teams consisting of peer counselors, nurse practitioners, vocational rehabilitation specialists, and psychiatrists, are voluntary. In a requirement that was later dropped, consumers had to allow the agency to become a representative payee, receiving whatever disability or other income the consumer was due, taking 30% to match with a New York/New York housing subsidy to pay the landlord, and turning over the remainder to the client on an agreed-upon schedule. Most consumers avail themselves of services, but they receive no bonuses for doing so (Tsemberis, 2010).

The Pathways to Housing model views housing as a human right, not a privilege to be earned. The program's most fundamental tenet is to honor consumer choice. Indeed, Tsemberis initially labeled the program "a consumer-preference independent living model," a phrase that comes less trippingly off the tongue than "housing first" but succeeds in focusing the lens on choice (Tsemberis, 2013). Because consumers are deemed the best judges of what they need, they choose the type and sequence of services they want. Independent housing is key because that is what consumers overwhelmingly ask for, and what they want first. Once housed, they may choose other services to help them reach other goals. Goals reported by 20 Pathways tenants in an experiment described below included work, education, painting, and writing poetry, whereas 19 out of 20 control group participants, even those in housing programs, had the single goal of getting an apartment of their own (Barr, 2004).

Another key feature of the program is separation of housing from services. This contrasts with single-site residential programs, where the service provider often doubles as an enforcement agent for program rules. In the Pathways program, tenants hold leases in buildings dominated by tenants without any special needs and are subject to the same discipline as other leaseholders. People who drink quietly behind closed doors are not a problem; people who deal drugs from an apartment or make a ruckus in the middle of the night are likely to be evicted. If that happens, the Pathways program sticks with consumers, helps them to find another apartment, and advises them on how to avoid being evicted again. This is an example of the program's "harm reduction" approach to substance use. The point is not to enforce sobriety but to ensure that substance use does not interfere with consumers' other goals, such as maintenance of housing, employment, or reconnecting with family. Recovery consists of attaining the consumer's own goals and dealing with mental health and substance problems that hinder them. The program also continues to work with people who may need a respite in a psychiatric hospital, rehab center, or even a jail, preserving their apartment if the stay is brief. As Peter described in an interview:

> Sam [Tsemberis] doesn't give up on you when you fail. I went to jail and figured Sam and his mother-hen crew couldn't get me (I was still fighting him). But two

weeks before I got out he sent a letter: "Call us, we have an apartment." I relapsed again and I was really ashamed. I was in a substance treatment program, and it dawned on me that I want to do the right thing, but now I won't have a chance. Then my worker called and came to get me. Now I'm in a 2-bedroom apartment. I'm living with my [adult] son. My daughters and grandchildren come to visit. I have a good job. I'm an addict, it's a week from payday, and I have money in my wallet.

The stories of Pathways' tenants explain why the program is able to get people with long histories of homelessness and serious mental illnesses who have rejected other programs to come indoors. Prior to moving into Pathways, one tenant slept in the stairwell of an apartment building rather than give up her beloved cat. A friend in the building kept the cat, and after the friend's husband left in the morning, the future Pathways resident was allowed into the apartment to shower and spend time with her cat. She declined shelters, but when offered an apartment where she could keep the cat, the woman was glad to move in. Conversations with residents of homelessness encampments in other cities suggest that the requirement to separate from loved ones or pets is a major deterrent to entering shelters and housing programs.

Pathways tenants make their modest apartments into homes that not merely reflect but assert their personalities. The couch one tenant sat on looked worn, but his lamp had a scalloped shade that would have complemented a Victorian antimacassar. "Other programs seek to control you," he said. "Pathways is not like that." Another tenant had every windowsill lined with pots of flourishing plants. A third had turned his small living room into a weight room—the only furniture was a weight bench, along with some impressive barbells. Visiting, one gets the sense that tenants are rebelling against more institutional settings.

Tsemberis compared the results of his program with those attained by all the other housing programs for people with serious mental illnesses funded under the New York/New York agreement and found that 88% of the Pathways tenants remained housed after 5 years compared to 47% of individuals in the other programs (Tsemberis, 1999; Tsemberis & Eisenberg, 2000). However, consumers had not been randomly assigned to the different programs, and people administering the more traditional programs argued that their clients could not possibly function with the freedoms of the Pathways model: without requirements for sobriety, the program would simply enable substance abuse, and clients would quickly fall out of housing.

It was time for an experiment. At that point one of us (Beth) who had been one of Tsemberis's graduate school professors, got involved. We randomly assigned consumers with documented diagnoses of mental illnesses and an average of 6.5 years of homelessness and 4.9 psychiatric hospitalizations to either Pathways to Housing or usual care, which meant working with outreach workers to become housing-ready for traditional programs. The study targeted unsheltered individuals. Participants had to have spent at least 15 of the prior 30 days on the street. Because of the need for documentation of homelessness and mental illness to secure New York/New York funding, referrals to the study came largely from outreach workers. (A subset of participants was recruited from mental hospitals, but met the homeless criterion immediately before their hospitalization.)

At the time, the approach was radical, and recruitment to the study lagged because we were not getting enough referrals. We held a breakfast for outreach workers at New York University (where Beth taught at the time) to ask for their help. One worker ate our bagels but argued that referring her clients to the study would violate her ethics. If they got randomly assigned to Pathways to Housing and received their own apartments without close supervision, she would be setting them up for failure. Things changed a couple weeks later when a Pathways tenant proudly invited his family and his outreach worker to dinner in his new apartment. The outreach worker, amazed at the transformation of this formerly disheveled street-dweller into a gracious host, returned to his agency where he and his colleagues referred dozens of clients to the study (Shinn, 2010).

Results showed that Pathways to Housing was far more successful than traditional treatment-first programs in reducing homelessness in the short term and over the next 2 years. After the first 6 months, the experimental group spent about 3% of days homeless, whereas the percentage of time homeless among control group members never dropped below 20% in any 6-month period (Tsemberis et al., 2003; Tsemberis, Gulcur, & Nakae, 2004).

Substance use did not differ between the two groups. How could it be that programs that required sobriety did not produce more of it than a program that did not? People who succeeded in getting in and staying in treatment-first programs did indeed use fewer substances, but people randomized to usual care who did not get into those programs used more. That is, the data seem to show that the treatment-first programs did not change people so much as they sorted them into those permitted to come indoors and those relegated to the streets. The initial promising results and promotion of the approach by the Federal Interagency Council on Homelessness in its strategic plan (2010) led to more widespread adoption.

At Home/Chez Soi

For a long time the program had been studied rigorously in only one site, New York City, in a study with a relatively modest sample (225 people) in which the program's founder was also the principal investigator. Although programs elsewhere continued to get good housing results, they lacked comparison groups. This problem was overcome more recently by the five-city At Home/Chez Soi experiment in Canada, which replicated the initial success. All of the more than 2,000 participants were either literally homeless (82%) or precariously housed with two or more episodes of homelessness in the past year (18%). All had a serious mental illness, and a majority had co-occurring substance problems

(Goering et al., 2014). Prior to random assignment, the participants were strat-ified into high need and moderate need groups. Those with high needs had a bipolar or psychotic disorder, low community functioning, and histories of either substance abuse, repeat hospitalizations, or incarceration.

Participants were randomized to Housing First based on the Pathways model, with wrap-around services provided by ACT teams or to treatment as usual with housing and support services such as group homes, congregate supportive housing, and mental health services. Participants judged to have moderate needs in four of the five cities were randomized to Housing First with intensive case management services, which was cheaper than ACT teams, or to usual care. The fifth city, Moncton, was too small to allow for two different treatment groups, so all Housing First participants were assigned to ACT teams. Across sites, both Housing First groups had substantially more time in stable housing than their respective control groups. As in New York, the Housing First and control groups did not differ on substance use—that is allowing choice about treatment did not lead to increases in use (Aubry et al., 2015, 2016; Stergiopoulos et al., 2015). Additional differences between the high-need Housing First and its control group included getting housed faster, and in the first year, improvements in community functioning and quality of life. The groups converged on these two measures by the end of the second year.[16] Mental health symptoms decreased for all high-need participants but slightly more for the control group (Aubry et al., 2016).

Although we have emphasized tenants' rights to select and refuse services, Housing First, especially for people with serious mental illnesses, is not housing only. The original Pathways to Housing model provides an array of health, mental health, vocational, and recreational services under tenant control, and also hous-ing services: help in locating housing, providing a resource to landlords, and responding quickly to their complaints to make them more willing to rent to ten-ants. The program might even plaster and paint over the hole when a tenant claws into the wall trying to locate the source of the voices he hears (Tsemberis, 2010).

In response to a proliferation of programs calling themselves "Housing First" but not necessarily following the model developed by Tsemberis, Pathways to Housing rebranded itself as "Pathways Housing First," and researchers devel-oped a measure of fidelity to the model. Across several studies, participants did better when their programs adhered most closely to the Pathways to Housing model of permanent supportive housing. In 12 programs in the Canadian At Home/Chez Soi study, participants in programs with greater fidelity had greater improvements in housing stability, community functioning, and quality of life (Goering et al., 2016). Housing outcomes were better across 86 programs in

---

[16] Initial improvement on the quality of life measure (dubbed "condition-specific quality of life") was similar across the two groups, but neither group improved on a health measure that the authors described as "generic quality of life." The measure that showed changes asked participants to rate aspects of their life in the domains of family, leisure, living situation, safety, social and overall, on a scale from delighted to terrible (Stergiopoulos et al., 2015).

California when programs had higher fidelity scores especially with respect to participants' rights to choose or reject services and separation of housing from services (Gilmer et al., 2014). And in nine programs in New York, programs with higher fidelity on consumer choice in service plans and lack of requirements for substance abuse treatment had better retention in housing; despite the lack of requirements for treatment, participants reported less use of opiates and stimulants (Davidson et al., 2014).[17]

It is less clear that the scattered-site nature of the program with housing in independent apartments with private landlords is critical. A comparison of people randomized to scattered-site and congregate versions of the Pathways Housing First model in the Vancouver site of the At Home/Chez Soi study found no differences in housing stability (although both groups were far more stable than a group assigned to usual treatment). Further, individuals with mental illness and often co-occurring substance disorders who were assigned to the congregate program had better psychological community integration—a subjective report of community belonging—and recovery—a subjective appraisal of psychiatric and physical health. A limitation is that the comparison involved only one congregate program, which offered tenants who had private suites common kitchens, common dining, recreation, and health care facilities, and opportunities for part-time work (Somers et al., 2017). Although housing tenants in a single building or complex makes provision of services more efficient, it can also create difficulties when one tenant is struggling to maintain sobriety while the tenant next door is freely using substances. If the same agency provides both housing and services, workers are often expected to police rules, rather than serving as advocates for tenants (McGrath & Pistrang, 2007), leaving little room for second chances if tenants are evicted for failing to follow rules.

Although Housing First following the Pathways model ends homelessness for people with long histories of homelessness, mental illnesses, and often co-occurring substance use disorders, success depends on good implementation. Two efforts at widespread adoption of the model show both similar successes and similar challenges. In the United States, the Veterans' Administration transitioned to using Housing First in their supportive housing program serving 85,000 people. In Canada, after the success of Pathways Housing First in the large-scale At Home/Chez Soi experiment, the Mental Health Commission of Canada sought to repurpose funds from the federal Homelessness Partnering Strategy to use this model.

Similar factors supported successful implementation in both cases: leadership, training and technical assistance, and program champions (Kertesz et al., 2014; Nelson et al., 2017). Although practitioners sometimes doubted that the program would work in their communities, many underwent conversion experiences like that of the outreach worker in New York once they saw that "people you

---

[17] Although self-reports of substance use may be suspect, it seems unlikely that participants in programs without requirements for treatment would hide their use more than participants in programs that had such requirements.

might think, oh my gosh they could never [live in their own apartment], were absolutely successful on their own" (quotation from a federal official interviewed in the Canadian study, Macnaughton et al., 2018, p. 9).

The Veteran's Administration and Canadian studies also showed similar challenges. In both cases, studied programs attained reasonably high fidelity and were able to provide housing with low barriers but struggled to provide sufficient supports for tenants. Canadian programs, where no new funds were available, also strained to provide rent subsidies (Kertesz et al., 2017; Macnaughton et al., 2018). The uneven implementation of services in both may be one reason that Housing First's success in ending homelessness does not generally extend to clinical outcomes. In particular, substance use is not enabled, but it is also not generally reduced (Kertesz & Johnson, 2017).

Proponents of Housing First have often claimed that it saves money. A recent review suggests the evidence for this claim is inadequate (Kizer et al., 2018).[18] Cost savings may depend on client needs. For example, in the At Home/Chez Soi project, $10 invested in Housing First for high-need participants was largely offset by reductions of $9.60 in other costs, but for moderate-need participants, the offset was only $3.42 (Goering et al., 2014). But society does not ordinarily expect that social and health interventions save money. We treat cancer to save lives, not to save money. Kertesz, Baggett, O'Connell, Buck, and Kushel (2016) note that Housing First programs often cost $8,000–18,000 per year of housing, amounts that are partially offset by reductions in costs elsewhere and that benefit not only the individuals involved but the community. "If we can countenance figures of $100,000 to $150,000 per quality-adjusted life-year for selected medical interventions, then the cost of successfully housing vulnerable people escaping chronic homelessness should be within reach" (Kertesz et al., 2016, p. 2116). As is the case for medical interventions, it is reasonable to ask whether the same results can be attained at less cost and whether services should continue to be offered by specialized providers (as in Housing First) or by community providers. Answers may depend on the quality and comprehensiveness of services available in communities.

Other Approaches for High-Needs Individuals

We consider two alternative approaches to housing with services for high-needs individuals that also have some research evidence to support their use: sober housing and the Critical Time Intervention [CTI].

Housing programs that require sobriety have at best modest impacts on homelessness but may have better clinical outcomes than Housing First

---

[18] Gulcur and colleagues (Gulcur, Stefancic, Shinn, Tsemberis, & Fischer, 2003) found lower residential costs for tenants randomized to the Pathways program, largely because tenants spent fewer days in psychiatric hospitals, but did not examine other costs, for example for other services.

(Kertesz, Crouch, Milby, Cusimano, & Schumacher, 2009; Munthe-Kaas et al., 2018).[19] Overcoming an addiction is tough, even for people who are highly motivated and who get excellent treatment, and randomized studies are not generally restricted to such people. Having the support of others can help. It seems reasonable for sober housing to be part of a homeless service system if it is truly freely chosen, meaning that other equally attractive, low-barrier options are available at the outset, and that those options remain available if people chose to use them later. Repeated demonstrations over half a century show that people are more likely to embrace choices as their own when coercion is minimal; further people rate choices they make freely as more desirable after they have chosen them, suggesting that the act of choosing to engage in treatment may enhance commitment (e.g., Brehm, 1956; Festinger & Carlsmith, 1959).

The CTI is a structured 9-month program of case management for people leaving institutions. The program is divided into three phases. In the first phase, transition to the community, the worker meets with the client in the institutional setting and identifies community providers who offer critical resources. In phase two, the worker links the client to supports, tests the system of support in action, and adjusts it as necessary. The final phase, transfer of care, completes the transfer of responsibility to community resources that will continue to provide support. Two small randomized experiments in the United States showed better housing retention for people with serious mental illnesses transitioning from institutional settings—a psychiatric section of a shelter or transitional housing for former inpatients on mental hospital grounds. In both cases, housing arrangements were already in place when CTI was added to the usual supports available (Herman et al., 2011; Susser et al., 1997).

An experimental study that supplemented rental subsidies with either time-limited services, following the CTI approach, or usual case management found few differences for high-need families in which the mother had mental health problems. CTI families exited shelter more quickly than control families required to be housing-ready, but both groups received subsidized long-term transitional or permanent housing and remained housed at high rates. Mothers in both groups had significant and clinically meaningful reductions in mental distress over time as they moved from shelter to community but the groups did not differ (Samuels et al., 2015). Both groups of children also improved over time across multiple measures of well-being, with modestly better outcomes for the CTI group (Samuels et al., 2015; Shinn, Samuels et al., 2015).

A randomized control trial in the Netherlands found that people moving from shelters to social housing remained housed at high rates whether they received CTI services or usual care, but the CTI group reported more family support and, among those with low social support, less psychological distress (de Vet et al., 2017). In these cases, CTI was an adjunct to, not a substitute for, housing. It can

---

[19] We do not consider evidence about sober housing programs that are not targeted to people becoming re-housed after an episode of homelessness.

succeed in linking people to community services that may help them to stay housed or improve quality of life after specialized services cease. We consider CTI as an approach to preventing homelessness for people leaving institutions in Chapter 5.

Summary

We find the evidence compelling that long-term housing subsidies end homelessness for families with children and that supportive housing with voluntary services ends it for most high-needs individuals. These programs keep people housed, without requiring that they first become housing-ready.

Research on different models of psychosocial services is sparser. In several studies the intensity of services did not seem to matter when housing was secure. The CTI model is helpful as an adjunct to housing for individuals leaving psychiatric facilities; its value for other groups is less clear.

The homeless services system in the United States, to which we turn in Chapter 4, has embraced the concept of supportive housing for individuals with chronic patterns of homelessness. However, in the absence of other housing resources, supportive housing has often been given to people with fewer needs for psychosocial services.

With the possible exception of military veterans, the level of resources for permanent supportive housing for high-needs individuals falls short of what is needed. Long-term housing subsidies for families with children are provided almost entirely outside of the homeless services system, as part of a woefully inadequate system of housing subsidies directed to a broader population. We consider the expansion of long-term housing subsidies in the final chapter of this book, on ending the conditions that generate homelessness.

4

Comprehensive Efforts to End Homelessness

In this chapter, we turn to comprehensive efforts to end homelessness. We introduce the homeless services system in the United States and review its components, including the evidence (in some cases, lack of evidence) on how well those components work. We then describe efforts to make the system more effective, including planning, reallocation of resources, and efforts to rationalize the system through coordinated entry to better match people experiencing homelessness to programs suited for them. Next, we turn to focused efforts to end homelessness for two particular groups: individuals with chronic patterns of homelessness and military veterans. We describe a national campaign to find and serve the most vulnerable people experiencing homelessness, and we focus on how that effort has worked in two very different places: Nashville and Los Angeles.

We chronicle some successes. The number of people with chronic patterns of homelessness is down, and many cities in the United States have ended homelessness for veterans. Finland has largely ended literal homelessness for all groups, and we discuss how that happened and its relevance for the United States. We conclude that homelessness can be ended for all people who experience it, if society is willing to devote the resources to do so.

The Homeless Services System

Since the late 1980s, a "homeless services system" has emerged in the United States, discrete from the broader "mainstream" systems of income support, housing subsidies, and social services that are intended to help people move out of poverty and mitigate its effects. The emergence of a homeless services system was in part driven by the responses to homelessness of particular cities and in part by a requirement by the U.S. Department of Housing and Urban Development (HUD) that requests for funding explicitly targeted to ending homelessness go through a single planning

In the Midst of Plenty: Homelessness and What to Do About It, First Edition.
Marybeth Shinn and Jill Khadduri.
© 2020 Marybeth Shinn and Jill Khadduri. Published 2020 by John Wiley & Sons Ltd.

organization in each community, the Continuum of Care. That organization also has responsibility for the data collection on people experiencing homelessness and the inventory of programs serving homeless people described in Chapter 1 as the basis for what we know about how many people experience homelessness in the United States.

In most communities, the homeless services system is a combination of local government, faith-based organizations, and other nonprofits that address home-lessness. As of 2018, the components of the system were emergency shelters, transitional housing, a relatively new program type called "rapid re-housing," and supportive housing for people leaving homelessness, called "permanent supportive housing" to distinguish it from time-limited, transitional housing. In some com-munities, services programs that help homeless people find jobs or send outreach workers to try to bring people on the street into shelter or housing are part of the homeless services system and also participate in the Continuum of Care.

Generally, mainstream housing assistance such as the long-term housing subsidies for families that we described in the Chapter 3 are not part of the system. However, housing authorities administer special allocations from the federal government of vouchers for Veterans Administration supportive housing (the HUD-VASH program), and some housing authorities have chosen to provide set-asides for permanent supportive housing from their general funding for vouchers.

Emergency Shelters

Cities produced modern homeless shelters, the heirs to eighteenth-century almshouses and poor houses, nineteenth-century police station houses, and late nineteenth- to twentieth-century municipal lodging houses, starting in the late 1970s and early 1980s in response to the rise of the "new homeless" at that time (see Chapter 1).[1] Rossi described these shelters as resembling "minimum security prisons whose gates are open during the day" (Rossi, 1989, p. 35). Although they have since evolved in most cities beyond "three hots and a cot," emergency shelters, as the very name suggests, have always been considered a short-term response to immediate crises in their clients' lives. Shelters range from barracks style rooms to cots in church basements that are open only on cold winter nights to modest apartments for families in some cities. Researchers have documented abysmal conditions in some shelters (Hopper, 2003; Kozol, 1988), and advocates have pushed cities and nonprofits to move from large-scale barracks to smaller, friendlier spaces with a modicum of privacy, caring staff, and an array of services.

The U.S. Conference of Mayors notes that shelters often separate families (indeed in congregate shelters, one family's husband and father is the next family's strange, potentially threatening male) and that people are frequently turned away

---

[1] For brief histories see Hopper (1990, 2003) and Rossi (1989). Police stations housed anyone who applied, with no presumption of criminality. In New York City in 1856 they housed 1,000 people a night – and turned away many more for lack of space (Hopper, 2003, p. 31).

from shelters for lack of space.[2] Both factors—lack of capacity and restrictive rules—are cited as explanations for the growing appearance of "encampments" or "tent cities" in many U.S. cities (Cohen, Yetvin, & Khadduri, 2019). Evaluations have tended to describe the case management and other services that shelters often provide (sometimes measuring their costs and patterns of use), but they have not examined whether they help individuals or families get back on their feet (e.g., Burt et al., 1999; Feins, Fosburg, & Locke, 1994; Spellman, Khadduri, Sokol, & Leopold, 2010). As noted in Chapter 1, the majority of users stay fairly briefly and do not return (Culhane, Metraux, Park, Schretzman, & Valente, 2007; Kuhn & Culhane, 1998).

Transitional Housing

When shelters do not suffice to help people return to housing, the next step is often transitional housing—programs that offer subsidized (sometimes free) housing for up to 2 years accompanied by intensive services. Most programs are in congregate, supervised settings, although some are scattered site—programs in which clients live in rental housing in the community rather than in a facility— to allow residents to assume the lease if they can afford to stay at the end of the program.

Services may include case management, employment, life skills training, and substance abuse and mental health services. These are "treatment first" programs designed to help people become ready to thrive in the private rental market after they graduate.

Until recently, transitional housing was the dominant alternative to shelters and permanent supportive housing (Burt et al., 1999). Surprisingly little research has been conducted on a program that has consumed so many public dollars. Most work on transitional housing for individuals is descriptive, examining patterns of use rather than measuring outcomes or comparing people who get the program to people who get something else (Khadduri et al., 2010). Some studies include transitional housing as part of the staircase model that has been found less successful for individuals with mental illnesses when compared with housing first.

Other work focuses on families. For example, "The Life After Transitional Housing for Homeless Families study" examined 195 mothers who left transitional housing programs over the course of the next year (Burt, 2010). Families were drawn from 36 programs in five communities, and the researchers made no claim that they were a representative group. Although the families certainly experienced

---

[2] For years, the Conference of Mayors reports gave both statistics. For example, in 2006, the report stated that in 55% of participating cities, families sometimes had to break up to be accommodated in shelter. Since then, the reports have included only the percentage of people turned away entirely. For example, in 2015, the report stated that 76% of surveyed cities sometimes had to turn away families with children and 61% sometimes had to turn away unaccompanied individuals due to lack of shelter capacity (US Conference of Mayors, 2006, 2015). All these are percentages of cities, not the percentage of people denied shelter.

hardship, many had never been literally homeless. Only 36% had spent any time in an emergency shelter in the 12 months before entering transitional housing, with (an overlapping) 15% in a domestic violence shelter, 9% in a vehicle, and 4% in a place not intended for habitation (with the last situations lasting no more than a few days). More commonly families spent time living doubled up with friends or relatives (65%) or in their own place (57%), but presumably threatened with eviction.[3]

The Life After Transitional Housing study and a review of other studies of transitional housing (Bassuk, DeCandia, Tsertsvadze, & Richard, 2014) suggest some positive outcomes for families. However, the review also notes the selectivity of many programs and the substantial rates at which programs asked families to leave, often for substance abuse. Only one study (Hayes, Zonneville, & Bassuk, 2013) had a comparison group of families found in emergency shelters, and even here, the families were not well matched at the outset. The review (prior to results from the Family Options Study) decries "the lack of evidence on which to build sound policy" (Bassuk et al., 2014, p. 472). But many of the individual studies that show positive outcomes for program graduates come to a more optimistic conclusion. For example, summarizing the results of the Life After Transitional Housing study, Martha Burt (2010, p. 151) suggests: "We cannot tell with the data available whether the families would have achieved these same goals without the programs—surely some of them would have done so. But equally surely some of them would not." The Family Options Study, which did have well-matched comparison families, drew a different conclusion.

In the Family Options Study, families who were randomly assigned to offers of transitional housing were less likely to use emergency shelters during the 2 years that they could still be in transitional housing, but they did not differ from families who got no special offer of assistance in other respects at either 20 months or 37 months after entering shelters. In particular, they fared no better with respect to all the housing readiness indicators that transitional housing is supposed to bolster: psychological distress, substance use, domestic violence, food security, work effort, income, child separations, or child well-being. Long-term housing subsidies improved many of these indicators; transitional housing did not. Transitional housing also cost 4% more than usual care without providing much additional benefit (Gubits et al., 2018).

The Family Options study also confirmed previous evidence that transitional housing often does not serve the families that, hypothetically, would be the most likely to benefit from a "treatment first" approach. This was observed by Dennis Culhane and colleagues when they used administrative data from several cities to study family use of emergency shelter and transitional housing.[4] The highest

---

[3] Numbers add up to more than 100% because families could stay in more than one place over the course of the year.

[4] There is no "bright line" between emergency shelter and transitional housing, and the researchers did not try to distinguish the two types of "shelter."

needs families were not those with the longest stays (Culhane et al., 2007). As we were setting up the Family Options Study, we found that transitional housing (and other program types as well) had screening criteria they were unable or unwilling to drop in the context of the study. We wanted to assign families at random, but we did not want to send families to programs that were bound to reject them, and we did not want to compare groups of families that differed because of different screening criteria. In response to this dilemma, we decided to prescreen families with questions based on requirements the programs supplied. Then we randomized the prescreened families among the programs to which they appeared eligible and the "usual care" control group.[5] We compared families assigned to transitional housing with families who passed the screen but were assigned to usual care.

Once families were given a special offer of assistance, programs could (and did) conduct further screening. For example, the prescreening asked about criminal history, income, and substance abuse,[6] but programs could also do criminal background checks, contact banks, or conduct urinalysis. And families who passed this second round of screening might or might not enter the program. For example, a family offered transitional housing might decide not to move in.[7]

Fewer than a third of the families initially screened to determine whether they were eligible for transitional housing (a) passed that prescreening, (b) if randomly assigned to the program, passed whatever additional screening the program conducted, and (c) moved in within the next 9 months. (This contrasts with nearly three quarters who passed the much lighter screening and rented a unit with a long-term housing subsidy.) Because transitional housing was in units that the programs operated, families had to have the appropriate size and composition for the available units. A large family could not squeeze into a studio, for example, and many programs (like many emergency shelters) could not accommodate

---

[5] Questions were of the form, "some programs will only accept families in which the head of household is clean and sober and who can demonstrate at least 30 days of sobriety. Would you like to be considered for programs with this requirement" (Gubits et al., 2013). We urged families to answer honestly, so that we would not send them to a program that would reject them. To preserve the integrity of the experiment, in evaluating how families offered a specific intervention fared in comparison to those who got no special offer (usual care), we included only those usual care families who could have been assigned to that intervention but lost the lottery. Thus, the usual care groups for each intervention overlap but are not identical. The fact that programs did not always have openings when families showed up in shelters was an additional constraint. Half of the families who were willing to participate in the study lost access to at least one of the options because there were no openings, suggesting that the homeless services system is seriously underfunded relative to family needs. However, these constraints did not affect the integrity of the experiment: the usual care group for each program included only families who both passed the eligibility screening and had the program assignment available, so that nothing but a flip of the coin decided where they would go.

[6] The particular questions that were asked depended on the requirements of programs that had openings at the time families entered the study.

[7] It was not always possible to distinguish these last two phases. In interviews we found families and programs sometimes had different perspectives. For example, a program might tell a family to get some income and come back, and the family might perceive this as a rejection.

fathers. Fully a fifth of families failed income requirements, which ranged as high as $2,000 per month. Required sobriety or agreement to participate in substance treatment was rarely an issue—only one family in 40 failed this screening test (Shinn et al., 2017).

Family preferences also mattered. Even desperately poor families staying in homeless shelters turned down some offers of assistance. Families wanted a place that was close to parents' work, children's schools, or relatives who could provide child care or other supports. Whereas housing vouchers (the dominant form of long-term subsidy) could be used in a broad range of neighborhoods and even, in some cases, outside the housing authority's jurisdiction, families sometimes rejected transitional housing because of its location. Families also turned down transitional programs when not all family members could stay together.

Some families also left transitional housing early, because they felt the program was not supportive or not a good place to raise their children, but other families found (different) transitional housing programs a great help, as these contrasting quotations from Bridgeport, CT and Phoenix show:

> And they wasn't helping me. They get fundings for you to go back to school and do what you want to do, but she kept telling me she did not have the—"Well I don't know if we have the fundings for you to go back to school." If you're here to help me, I understand you go out there and do what I have to do; that's okay, but if I—I know ya'll pay for classes. I wanted to take phlebotomy. She did not want to pay for that. She did not want to give me the money to pay for that class.

> I mean, when you go down there, they help you. They already have the listings of work that you can go through. And everything was helpful as far as getting into the right agencies, finding work, making you feel like you are still a part of something, you know? They never downed you for any reason. So yeah, that was comforting. (Fisher, Mayberry, Shinn, & Khadduri, 2014).

In sum, the Family Options study shows that transitional housing for families, like services-first permanent supportive housing, attains many of its results by sorting people rather than by helping people. If we include everyone, not just those who pass entry requirements and continue to comply with program rules to the point of graduation, families who are offered transitional housing look very much the same as families who receive no special offer of assistance.

It is possible that transitional housing is valuable for other populations that are indeed transitioning, but research is scant. Some limited evidence suggests that halfway houses and other forms of transitional housing for people leaving incarceration have been effective (Metraux, Hunt, and Yetvin, forthcoming). We consider programs for people leaving institutions in the next chapter on preventing homelessness and find that rapid re-housing, transitional housing, and Critical Time Interventions may all have a role to play.

Domestic violence shelters similar to transitional housing may be an important resource for women fleeing abusive relationships. Interpersonal violence is common among families who become homeless, and the results of the Family

Options Study probably apply to many—those fleeing domestic violence who have poverty-level incomes need housing with a lease in their name, sooner rather than later and supported by a long-term subsidy. Other families may have more resources and need only temporary protection until they find a place and space to put lives back together. We are not aware of research comparing alternative approaches here.

Another group that is also in transition, in this case from adolescence to adulthood, might also benefit from a transitional approach. Gaetz (2014) suggests that the housing first approach might be modified for young people, consistent with their developmental stage and preferences, to include options for shared or even congregate accommodations as well as independent living. After all, middle-class youth do not suddenly become independent at age 18—many go off to group accommodations, whether in dormitories or off-campus, when they go to college. The Foyer model, essentially transitional housing for young people with developmentally focused supports for education and employment, began in France and has spread internationally (Gaetz & Scott, 2012). Unfortunately, most research is at best descriptive. A recent review of 15 reports found the quality of evidence so weak that it drew conclusions only about strengthening the research base, not about the impact of programs (Levin, Borlagdan, Mallett, & Ben, 2015). If society invested a small fraction of what is spent on all these services on research, it would be possible to draw firmer conclusions.

Time-Limited Subsidies: Rapid Re-Housing

Concerns about the cost of transitional housing, and less than stellar outcomes, led some communities like Hennepin County (Minneapolis), Minnesota, and Columbus, Ohio to experiment with a different approach—short-term rental subsidies coupled with short-term case management to get families out of the shelter system and into regular housing as quickly as possible. Some initial successes (in relatively benign rental markets) led HUD to fund "rapid re-housing" programs more broadly, first in a pilot study in 23 communities, described below, and almost simultaneously on a more massive scale as part of the American Recovery and Reinvestment Act of 2009 ("the stimulus" funding provided in response to the Great Recession).

Currently HUD encourages, but does not mandate, communities to use Continuum of Care funds for rapid re-housing or permanent supportive housing rather than transitional housing. The Veteran's Administration (VA) uses rapid re-housing as a core component of the Supportive Services for Veteran[s and their] Families program (SSVF).[8] HUD-funded programs provide rental assistance with a variety of time limits. The VA limits assistance to 12 months in a 2-year period, although typically the length of assistance is shorter. The programs provide housing identification, rent, and move-in assistance and case management designed to

---

[8] Despite the "families" name, the majority of participants in the SSVF program are single individuals without children who receive either prevention or rapid re-housing services.

help people get and keep housing and to link them to "mainstream" services, that is, those service available to everyone in the community, not just people experiencing homelessness. Some programs provide only one-time financial assistance or move-in assistance, without any ongoing rent subsidy (Gubits et al., 2017).

As experience with rapid re-housing grew, the National Alliance to End Homelessness (2016) specified that rapid re-housing programs should not screen out households on the basis of barriers such as lack of income, employment, motivation, or presence of criminal, mental health, or medical histories and offered a set of goals for the program and benchmarks for measuring performance:

- Households should move into permanent housing in 30 days or less, on average
- 80% who exit the program should exit to permanent housing
- 85% who exit to permanent housing should not become homeless again within 12 months.

HUD and the National Alliance to End Homelessness define "permanent housing" in this case as staying in a place that the household rents or owns (with or without rental subsidy) or staying with family or friends without a clear end date (Gubits et al., 2017, p. 11). This use of "permanent" means something quite different than in the case of "permanent" supportive housing. In that case, the rental subsidy that permits the tenant to afford the housing is ongoing, so tenants can stay as long as they wish, absent the sort of disruptive behavior that would get anyone evicted from rental housing anywhere. The permanent housing that is the goal of the rapid re-housing approach is permanent only in the sense that it is not transitional—it is not intended to prepare people to be ready for housing.[9] Although the individual or family is not required to move on at the end of the program, permanency depends on the tenants' ability to secure some *other* way of paying for the housing when the rental subsidy ends. Indeed, the evidence suggests that arrangements are often far from permanent. Terms like ordinary, regular, or normal might describe the housing better than "permanent" to distinguish it from specialized housing programs without implying illusive longevity.

So how well does rapid re-housing work? Most studies are descriptive—that is, we can compare results to benchmarks but not to what would have happened had participants been given some other intervention—or no intervention. The most extensive study examines the Veteran's Administration SSVF program (Silverbush, Albanese, McEvilley, Kuhn, & Southcott, 2015). The average length of time it took to obtain "permanent" housing among the nearly 50,000 veterans who exited from the program in fiscal year 2015 was 45 days from program enrollment; a third got housing within 2 weeks (p. 30). The VA reports that 71% exited

---

[9] Some transitional housing programs, called "transition-in-place," allow households to assume the lease if they can pay the rent at the end of the program, blurring the distinction between transitional housing and rapid re-housing. The Family Options study did not include this type of transitional housing.

the program to "permanent" housing (p. 24), although veterans in households with children did better (79%) (p. 25). In 31% of the exits, veterans received permanent supportive housing via the HUD-VASH program, a much larger proportion over such a short period than would be possible for nonveterans in rapid re-housing programs.[10] This study did not provide information on returns to homelessness, but an earlier study (Byrne, Treglia, Culhane, Kuhn, & Kane, 2015) examined whether veterans who exited from SSVF in fiscal years 2012 or 2013 subsequently returned to homelessness, based on whether the veteran had a contact with a VA-specialized homeless program. Among single adult veterans, 16.0 and 26.6% became homeless within one and 2 years from program exit. Results were better for families, with 9.4 and 15.5% becoming homeless within the first and second years. Among households that did not receive HUD-VASH housing vouchers upon exit from rapid re-housing, 18.4% of families and 31.3% of individuals became homeless. Many veterans are additionally served by homeless assistance programs outside the VA system, and the study could not track such contacts, so these results are underestimates (Byrne et al., 2015). Not counting people who got a permanent housing subsidy, the VA program thus came close but missed all three of the benchmarks.[11]

Another large study used grantee reports to HUD to examine rapid re-housing provided by the Homelessness Prevention and Rapid Re-Housing Program (HPRP) funded as a part of the stimulus (U.S. Department of Housing and Urban Development, 2016). Of the nearly 40,000 program participants who exited in the third and final year of the program,[12] 82.9% left for "permanent" housing, although programs classified only 67.2% of participants who were literally homeless at program entry as "stably housed" at exit, without defining that term (p. 24). The study did not report either time to housing or returns to homelessness.

The Rapid Re-Housing Demonstration Program was one of the first federal efforts to implement the rapid re-housing model. The evaluation of the pilot measured housing outcomes in the year after 490 families left the program in the 23 communities funded by the demonstration. The program targeted families (not individuals) who had at least one "moderate" barrier to housing stability, but who had "or [are] willing to obtain, employment that increases the income of the household to such a degree that it can independently sustain housing at the end of the short-term housing assistance" (Finkel, Henry, Matthews, & Spellman, 2016, p. 4). One year later, 10% had returned to sheltered or unsheltered homelessness

---

[10] Among families assigned to rapid re-housing in the family options study, 23% had found some form of long-term subsidy by the time of the 20-month survey and 35% by the time of the 37-month survey.

[11] On the other hand, the study followed people with all types of exits, not just those who exited to the types of permanent housing specified in the National Alliance benchmark.

[12] Number calculated: 134,900 households served in year three, of whom 29.4% got rapid re-housing rather than prevention services. We make the additional assumption that households exited the program in year 3, because this was the final year.

(Spellman, Henry, Finkel, Matthews, & McCall, 2014, p. 33).[13] This is likely an underestimate. The majority of families were not interviewed, so information on homelessness was confined to administrative records for the jurisdiction where they were served, and, based on survey and tracking efforts, at least 76% of families had moved at least once in the year after leaving the program (p. 33). At the 12-month follow-up, 31% of families had some form of rental subsidy. Of the 47% who rented their own housing without a subsidy, more than two in five paid over half of their income for rent (p. 35).

A review of 43 mostly smaller, single-site studies of rapid re-housing found that most met or came close to the benchmark of 80% exits to "permanent" (regular) housing but failed to meet the target of getting people out of shelter in 30 days. The review concluded that more evidence was needed about returns to homelessness but that the benchmark "appears to be attainable" (Gubits et al., 2017).

Most studies surveyed had no comparison groups. One published study used statistical methods to create comparison groups of people who exited transitional housing, rapid re-housing, or emergency shelters in Georgia. It found that in the matched sample, 10.1% of households with children and 13.7% of households without children who used rapid re-housing returned to shelter in 2 years—figures that did not differ from users of transitional housing but were only a third to half as large as households who used only shelters. The study also showed how selective both transitional housing and rapid re-housing providers are. For example, among households without children, 83.1% of those who used rapid re-housing had a source of cash income when they entered the program, compared to 29.7% of for households who used only emergency shelter (Rodriguez & Eidelman, 2017).[14]

The Family Options experiment that we have already described for long-term housing subsidies and transitional housing provides better evidence. In that study, some families were randomly assigned to either offers of rapid re-housing or usual care in their communities, providing well-matched groups at the start of the study. Twenty months later, more than a quarter of both groups had stayed in emergency shelter in the past year, with no difference between them (Gubits et al., 2018). This time period—20 months after random assignment—corresponds, roughly to the year after program exit in the descriptive studies, because the rapid rehousing subsidies lasted about 8 months on average.

Why might results for rapid re-housing be worse in the experiment than in the descriptive studies? As in the case of transitional housing, the enrollment phase of the study showed winnowing of the families who got into rapid re-housing.

---

[13] An earlier study of this sample and additional families in the same program found 6% returns to shelter within 12 months, based solely on administrative records (Spellman et al., 2014, p. 10).

[14] This income disparity was observed after excluding chronically homeless households, who would be unlikely to be referred to rapid re-housing, from the sample. Matching using a technique called "propensity scores" reduced the disparities in whether households had *any* cash income source, but data limitations did not allow matching on *the amount* of income. Thus matching probably leaves some important differences unaccounted for.

Requirements stated by the rapid re-housing programs and used for prescreening prior to randomization led to rejection of fewer families than for transitional housing programs (9% vs. 29%), but more than for the long-term rental subsidy programs (4%). The most common reason for rejection was failure to meet minimum standards for income or employment. As a combination of this prescreening, any additional screening by programs after assignment, and choices by families, just over half of families originally screened for an available slot leased a unit (Shinn et al., 2017). Only those families would have figured in the calculations of returns to shelter used by the studies we have reviewed. The Family Options study reported results for everyone who passed the initial screening and was assigned to rapid re-housing, not just those who succeeded in leasing a unit. At the 20-month follow-up, families who used the subsidy to rent a unit were less likely than those who did not to have returned to shelter in the past year (22.6% vs. 33.1%), although rates of homelessness reported by families in the past 6 months were similar (21.5% vs. 24.1%) (Gubits et al., 2015, p. 84).

Although 23% returns to shelter comes close to the National Alliance to End Homelessness 15% benchmark, it is substantially higher than the rates of return found in the SSVF and Rapid Re-Housing Demonstration programs. The additional returns found probably reflect the fact that the Family Options study followed participants with interviews as well as administrative records. Studies that rely exclusively on shelter records miss a lot of people. Nationally, in 2015, the average "coverage rate" for beds in the homeless service data system was only 71%, suggesting that 29% of shelter stays would be missed, even if an individual or family stayed in the same jurisdiction. For families who moved to a different locale, 100% of stays would be missed. Unsheltered homelessness would also be missed, although this is likely a larger problem for single individuals than for families.[15]

In Family Options, residential outcomes improved at similar rates for both the group assigned to rapid re-housing and comparable families assigned to usual care by the time of the 3-year follow-up. Households who did and did not lease units with rapid re-housing subsidies used shelters at the same rate (Gubits et al., 2016, Exhibit H-8). Three years out, more than a third of both families assigned to rapid re-housing and families given no special offer of assistance had secured some form of long-term housing subsidy (Gubits et al., 2018).

The Family Options Study found no evidence that rapid re-housing subsidies had the sort of radiating impacts on other outcomes that we saw for long-term subsidies. In most respects, families who received offers of rapid re-housing did not differ from comparable families who received usual care either 20 months or 37 months after random assignment. The few differences that emerged could have been due to chance, and none were replicated at the two follow-up time

---

[15] Only 9% of people experiencing unsheltered homelessness on a single night in January 2017 did so as part of a family (which means an even smaller percentage of unsheltered households were families) (Henry, Mahathey, et al., 2018; National Homeless Information Project, 2017).

points. Families offered rapid re-housing took an average of 2.9 months to leave shelter, more than the National Alliance to End Homelessness guideline and only about 1 week faster than comparable families offered usual care.[16] The big selling point for rapid re-housing is that it gets comparable outcomes to usual care at about 9% lower cost over 3 years (Gubits et al., 2018). This is not trivial. In a homeless services system that still turns away many people who seek emergency shelter, making the same dollars go further is important. But it is hard to argue that rapid re-housing is an unmitigated success.

The National Alliance to End Homelessness guidelines focus on returns to shelter and do not mention doubling up as a negative outcome. (Studies that rely on shelter records cannot measure this outcome.) In Family Options, more than a quarter of families who were assigned to rapid re-housing reported doubling up with another household in the same unit because they could not find or afford a place of their own at some time in the half-year leading up to the 20-month follow-up point. Families assigned to rapid re-housing and to usual care did not differ here; families who did and did not use rapid re-housing subsidies to rent units were also similar in this respect.

Reasonable people may disagree about whether doubling up is a problem. One perspective is that the homeless services system should simply be a crisis response. Its job is done if people exit the system and do not come back. People who never experience homelessness often share dwellings with others. The number of households containing an adult other than the householder and the householder's spouse, partner or children under the age of 21 increased dramatically in the Great Recession (Eggers & Moumen, 2013b; Mykyta & Macartney, 2011). Sharing homes can also reflect cultural preferences, (Koebel & Murray, 1999). Our view is less sanguine. Although people share homes for a variety of reasons, the types of doubled-up arrangements people have access to after an episode of homelessness are often unhappy ones (Bush & Shinn, 2017). After all, if people had access to stable living arrangements with others, they probably would not have gone to shelters in the first place. Families in the Family Options study returned to an abusive ex, an alcoholic father, and a mother who locked her daughter and the daughter's children in the basement—when they could get into the house at all. Even the more positive situations were often strikingly impermanent, as this mother in Kansas City explained:

> Because it's not my own, it's not mine. It's like, you're comfortable, but you can't get too comfortable, because it's not yours. You know that this is just temporary. And I'm tired, I am. I'm like, I'm frustrated, I'm tired, I'm stressed. And in the back of your mind you're still thinking, my journey is not done yet. I still have to keep going.

---

[16] The team initially reported a slightly larger difference (Gubits et al., 2015), but more precise estimates suggested that the difference was not significant. Families offered long-term subsidies left shelter faster than those offered rapid re-housing, although both groups had to find units (Gubits et al., 2016, Appendix I).

In some cases, families' literal homelessness may have ended, but they were far from stably housed. As another Kansas City mother put it:

> Well, like, if I go stay with my friend for a few days, I'll wait like a week, and then I'll go to my mother's house … then I'll go stay with my auntie. And I just—how do I go about this homelessness? (Quotations from Bush & Shinn, 2017, pp. 348–349).

Why do people who face such unhappy situations not return to the shelter system? Some do, of course, but many cannot. As already noted, shelters often turn people away or have restrictions on how quickly someone can return after leaving. Few jurisdictions in the country—Washington, DC, New York City, and the State of Massachusetts—have a "right to shelter," meaning that people who can prove they are homeless cannot be turned away, and in Massachusetts, people who leave shelters cannot come back for the next 12 months. Further, people who feel they have not been helped when they turned to a system (whether because they failed or because the system failed them) may be reluctant to go back to that same system. Lack of return to the initial shelter system should not, by itself, be taken as evidence of success.

Proponents of rapid re-housing often argue for a "progressive engagement" or "progressive assistance" approach, offering just enough support to help people stabilize in housing. Support can be individualized at the start, based on household needs and later adjusted if the household needs change or are better understood. Support is then discontinued when stability seems likely in the near term (Gubits et al., 2017).

By 2017, 97% of 1,377 rapid re-housing programs that responded to an email survey reported that they used a progressive engagement or progressive assistance approach (Dunton & Brown, 2019).[17] What that meant in practice varied a great deal, with many programs reporting that the amount of rental assistance did not vary over time or was based on a standard formula for relating the assistance to income and housing costs. However, 23% of programs reported that they paid the rent only for the first 3 months, 38% reported that they phased down assistance over time, and 28% reported that they reassessed the family's situation on a case-by-case basis. Meetings with caseworkers were frequent, usually at least once a month.

The ideas behind progressive engagement, including frequent reassessments of household needs, sound good in principle. However, from the perspective of Family Options families offered rapid re-housing, which may not have followed all of the progressive engagement principles, the process was stacked against them. If they did not maintain regular income, their money would be taken away.

---

[17] The question asked was: "Does your program use a progressive engagement or progressive assistance approach to rent and utility assistance (i.e., start by offering the minimum assistance necessary and increase or decrease assistance only when necessary?)"

If they made too much, their money would be reduced. When they got jobs quickly to pay for housing, they couldn't get better jobs that would sustain it. The whole process seemed unsustainable and anxiety provoking. As this respondent from Bridgeport put it:

> I've always had the mindset of getting out of the programs because I think that partly they're designed to keep you down, because the minute you make too much money they start taking everything away from you so you're always here. You can never go above. You can never save money. You can't ever do anything. So I felt like I'm always going to be here if I'm in a program.

Later she continued:

> Okay, we get out of a shelter, find a place for who knows really how long, and then what? Wind up back in a shelter? It seems kind of counter-productive to me. Although I appreciate the help, certainly, but ultimately it seems kind of failed in that aspect ... because if by the end of the year I don't have a way ... where do we go from there? Everything seems to be closed.

This mother in Phoenix also lamented:

> I felt like I had to get a job. Fine, I'll work, that's not the problem. It's just the type of job—I had to in such a hurry, I grabbed what I could. And basically, it ended up being a job that I wasn't happy with and a job that was a dead end and low-paying of course and physically working your butt off and tired ... I work at a daycare, I'm exhausted when I come home, I get $8.25 an hour, how am I supposed to survive off of that? I need a degree, that's what I would like and not only just for to get out there and to get a better job, a higher paying job, but just because I want it, I want to earn it, I want it and I want to set the example to my children ... So now I'm like there and what do I do, do I resign? Now you're there and it's not easy to get back out because of course [I'm] getting paid now, if I resign and I can't look for work, I can't, I got two days off I can't, it's impossible. (Fisher et al., 2014)

Short-term subsidies with services to connect people to employment or disability benefits may well have a role to play for people who need a place to stay while they get on their feet after leaving institutions such as mental hospitals, prisons, and jails. We discuss these more in the Chapter 5 where we look at preventing homelessness. Short-term subsidies could also be used as a stopgap for people on waiting lists for longer-term subsidies, at the cost of some anxiety over lack of permanence. But for people who become homeless because they lack the income to pay for housing, short-term rental subsidies are likely too short to allow them to build the educational credentials or find the jobs that will enable them to afford housing in all but the most benign rental markets.

Permanent Supportive Housing

By the late 1990s, the mounting research evidence on the effectiveness of supportive housing, together with a determination that ending chronic homelessness was a feasible goal, led policymakers at the federal level and in many communities to focus resources for addressing homelessness on permanent supportive housing targeted to individuals with disabilities.

The U.S. Interagency Council on Homelessness urged providers of permanent supportive housing to follow a "housing first" model. HUD used the process through which federal funds for programs serving homeless people are awarded to encourage communities to develop more permanent supportive housing (and less transitional housing) and also started to use rhetoric about housing first.

Most programs would say that their permanent supportive housing programs follow a housing first model. Whenever a program gets official blessing (and a link to government funding), everyone claims to be doing it, as we have also seen for the progressive engagement approach to rapid re-housing. The reality turns out to be somewhat different. Many permanent supportive housing programs require participation in services or otherwise fail to maximize consumer choice and thus are different from the Pathways Housing First approach reviewed in Chapter 3. A study commissioned by HUD to do a descriptive analysis of three housing first programs reflected the reality of the programs studied by stating: "The Housing First approach is not a single model..., but rather a set of general features that communities may interpret somewhat differently (Pearson, Locke, Montgomery, & Buron, 2007)." The report included one program where "many clients enter housing at a safe haven that has a number of occupancy rules, including a prohibition on drugs and alcohol, a curfew, and assigned chores for all residents p. 103)."

The most thoroughly studied versions of permanent supportive housing, the Pathways program and the At Home/Chez Soi program in Canada that adhered closely to its principles,[18] along with the HUD-VASH program that provides housing vouchers to homeless veterans, are scattered-site programs. The extent to which the strong evidence attained with these approaches applies to other versions of permanent supportive housing is not clear. Many permanent supportive housing programs are "project-based," with the housing produced explicitly to expand the supply of supportive housing and owned by a service provider or by a housing developer associated with a service provider. That does not mean that the housing cannot or does not follow other housing first principles.

A fairly recent Housing First Checklist published by the U.S. Interagency Council on Homelessness (2016), embraces some of the principles of the Pathways model. However, it focuses more on reducing barriers to housing and stipulating that "compliance" with service plans is not a condition of tenancy than on giving tenants standard leases and the more emphatic "right to choose, modify, or refuse services and supports at any time" (Gilmer et al., 2014).

---

[18] The At Home/Chez Soi study included some project-based housing in Vancouver.

Recall that the central principle at the origin of the Pathways Housing First model is consumer preference.[19]

Making the System Work to End Homelessness

So far we have described the components of the homeless services system. We now turn to how communities—and the federal government—have attempted to combine those components to reduce and end homelessness, and how the service system has evolved in the last quarter century.

The Clinton Administration encouraged local communities to set priorities for the use of federal and local resources—this was the origin of the Continuum of Care planning organizations that continue to submit local applications for HUD funds. Then in the early 2000s, the National Alliance to End Homelessness challenged communities to devise 10-year plans to end homelessness, with a focus on chronic homelessness. HUD Secretary Martinez in the George W. Bush administration, embraced the goal of ending chronic homelessness. The United States Interagency Council on Homelessness brought together leaders of all the relevant state agencies in small groups of states to "academies" where they learned from each other and outside faculty and hammered out plans. (There was not, however, a major infusion of funds.) In New York, Mayor Bloomberg decided that 10 years was too long, so the City's 10-year plan became a 5-year plan in between the time it was written and the time it was published in 2004.[20]

The adoption of the goal of ending chronic homelessness by both the federal government and many communities was spurred by evidence that people with such patterns are costly users of both emergency shelters and hospital emergency rooms, jails, and other expensive "mainstream" services (Culhane, Gross, Parker, Poppe, & Sykes, 2008). Another impulse behind the policy was probably to reduce the most visible and disturbing manifestation of homelessness, people sleeping on the streets of major American cities. The focus on ending chronic homelessness and the federal and local emphasis on permanent supportive housing continued during next two decades. The inventory of permanent supportive housing grew from roughly 189,000 beds in 2007 to 361,000 beds in 2018.

---

[19] A hybrid model of housing assistance, called "sponsor-based" (to distinguish it from "project-based" and "tenant-based") is sometimes permitted by federal funding streams. The service-provider agency has a master lease for a set of housing units and subleases them to its clients. One of us (Jill) took part in a heated discussion convened by HUD a few years ago about whether that model should be expanded (by permitting all housing authorities to follow it) or whether it violates the principles of consumer preference.

[20] One of us (Beth) served as a faculty member for some academies, helped to draft New York City's (NYC) plan, and currently sits on the planning council for Nashville's Continuum of Care. I still have the mug NYC issued as a souvenir, but the City has even more people in emergency shelters today than it did when the plan was issued.

About half of the inventory is explicitly dedicated to people with chronic patterns of homelessness (Henry, Mahathey, et al., 2018).

The Obama Administration in turn created a national strategy to end homelessness, with specific targets for particular population groups experiencing homelessness: veterans, "chronic" individuals, families, and youth (US Interagency Council on Homelessness, 2010). Both federal funders and many cities embraced the new rapid re-housing program model—which sometimes began to be referred to as "housing first" because of its rejection of the "staircase approach" of fixing people's problems before providing them with a lease. As we have seen, this is not the same as the Pathways Housing First model for permanent housing with intensive available service. Rapid re-housing now has about 110,000 beds.

In 2015, the U.S. Interagency Council on Homelessness (and the federal agencies that are represented on the Council, notably HUD and the Department of Health and Human Services) published a joint statement with the National Alliance to End Homelessness recommending that transitional housing facilities be limited to people that have both severe and specific needs and who also prefer support in a congregate residential setting to other options. Among those listed as having severe and specific needs are some people with substance use disorders or in early recovery, some survivors of domestic violence, and some unaccompanied or pregnant and parenting youth (National Alliance to End Homelessness, 2015). HUD and the Veteran's Administration have revised funding accordingly.

The number of transitional housing beds dropped from 211,205 in 2007 to 101,029 in 2018 (Henry, Mahathey, et al., 2018). As Chapter 1 explains, some of this drop may have been renaming transitional housing as rapid re-housing or as emergency shelter rather than a real change in program design. Some of the drop is real. One of us (Jill) knows the director of a family program in Washington, DC who, in response to the negative evidence on transitional housing, has transformed his program into permanent supportive housing for high-needs families with children.

The direction did not much change with the beginning of the Trump Administration, under which the Council produced a new and more low-key federal plan. The new mantra is making homelessness "rare, brief, and one-time," rather than talking about "ending" homelessness (US Interagency Council on Homelessness, 2018b).

For all the talk of ending homelessness and the efforts put into local and federal plans, the numbers of people experiencing homelessness have declined only modestly nationwide and not at all in some cities. HUD's annual reports on numbers of people experiencing homelessness continue to describe some cities and states with year-to-year increases, and some with declining numbers (Henry, Mahathey, et al., 2018). Beds in emergency shelters have increased—from 211,000 in 2007 to 286,000 in 2018 (Henry, Mahathey, et al., 2018), yet people often still are turned away from emergency shelters and put on waiting lists for the other components of the homeless services system. As we will discuss further in Chapter 6, the homelessness crisis response system will never be able to solve homelessness on its own without attention to the social processes that continue to generate it.

Making the System More Efficient and Effective

As cities face insufficient resources within the homeless services system, they have tried to make the system both more effective and more efficient. In some cities, the shift of resources within the system has resulted from deliberate strategic planning by the local Continuum of Care and city agencies to emphasize approaches that limit the time people spend in shelter, that get them back into normal housing as quickly as possible, and that may also be a more cost-effective use of the resources available to the homeless services system.

With encouragement from federal funders, local planners also try to better match people experiencing homelessness to the programs most appropriate to their needs. HUD asks communities to develop a "coordinated entry system," where workers enter everyone who seeks homeless services (or who is contacted by outreach workers) into a database, assess their needs, set priorities among people, and attempt to match people to appropriate resources when they are available (U.S. Department of Housing and Urban Development, n.d.).

There's a lot to like about coordinated entry. People in need have to knock on only one door to have access to whatever services are available, rather than making multiple calls to multiple programs hoping for an opening. When people register with the coordinated entry system, workers know them by name, creating a sense of urgency that programs for "the homeless" lack. Coordinated entry allows a homeless service system to individualize services and to track progress. The system can assign people with the fewest needs to programs that offer the least, reserving more extensive services to people with higher needs, or in a progressive engagement approach, to people who fail when given less. In addition, HUD asks that programs have few barriers (such as sobriety) for entry and that communities focus on especially vulnerable populations, including people whose homelessness is chronic. However, coordinated entry does not, by itself, expand the resources that are critical to ending homelessness, and workers on the ground are reluctant even to ask the necessary questions to enter people into data systems when they have nothing to offer.

Coordinated entry has many challenges. In a well-functioning service system, people who are hardest to house get the most services, so it may seem that services are associated with poor outcomes. (It is also the case that five-alarm fires do more damage than fires to which only one fire company responds, but that is because of the nature of the fires, not ineffectual efforts by the firefighters.) Just as it is fallacious to assume that extensive services given to people with high needs must be failures because many recipients still struggle, it is fallacious to assume that light-touch programs are successes because most graduates do well. The evidence from Family Options and the Georgia effort to construct a statistical comparison group for households offered transitional housing and rapid re-housing suggests that those programs often select the clients most likely to succeed (sometimes called "skimming the cream"). Assessment systems may abet this process. We worry that the resulting sorting of people too often masquerades as successful programming.

We still know too little about how to allocate services to people who experience homelessness. In the Family Options study, we tried and failed to answer the question of whether some types of programs would work better for people with particular characteristics. We could have investigated a myriad of characteristics—perhaps rapid re-housing works better for people with ingrown toenails—so we placed our bets on two composite indicators that seemed most promising. One was the number out of nine psychosocial challenges such as domestic violence or substance use or disability that a family faced. The other was the number out of 15 potential housing barriers they faced including lack of money for a security deposit or to pay rent, past eviction, poor credit history, or lack of transportation to find housing. To our surprise, the impact of each of the interventions—long-term rental subsidies, rapid re-housing, and transitional housing—did not differ depending on the level of challenges or barriers families faced. There is no reason to think the assessment systems in most common use do better. Neither a group of homeless experts assembled by HUD (2015b) nor a recent report from the National Academies of Sciences, Engineering, and Medicine (Kizer et al., 2018) found any evidence supporting the assessment tool in widest use.[21]

A recent examination of this tool, the Vulnerability Index Service Prioritization Decision Assistance Tool (VI-SPDAT) (Community Solutions & OrgCode Consulting Inc., 2014)[22] administered to 1,495 individuals experiencing homelessness in the Midwest found that when the same person received the test more than once (158 cases), the agreement between the scores was not good, even when the two administrations of the test were close in time. Further, total scores were not very good at predicting who in the sample would return to shelter. As in other studies, people who received permanent subsidies, whether permanent supportive housing or subsidies to live in mainstream housing without services, were less likely to return to shelter. (Housing placements did not correspond to the recommended placement in over half of the cases, whether because of lack of resources or for some other reason.) (Brown, Cummings, Lyons, Carrión, & Watson, 2018).

---

[21] Both of us were part of the HUD convening that concluded "The invited experts generally agreed that existing assessment tools do not have a strong evidence base and are limited in their ability to select the best interventions for families and individuals or to predict which families would be the most successful in different interventions." Although some advocated for progressive engagement as an alternative to allocation by assessment, the experts "acknowledged that at this point, the evidence base for progressive engagement is not strong either." Beth was a coauthor of the National Academies report.

[22] A new version of the assessment tool was released in 2015 (OrgCode Consulting Inc. & Community Solutions, 2015).

For all of coordinated entry's advantages, the limited resources of the homeless services system mean that people given priority access to the program for which they appear to be suited often languish on waiting lists: they remain in shelter or on the street until a unit in permanent supportive housing or transitional housing becomes available or until a rapid re-housing program receives a new infusion of funds. Furthermore, cities vary widely in their ability to plan and implement new systems such as coordinated entry, to assess the effectiveness of their implementation, and to respond to their weaknesses. Recently, a small group of cities has been experimenting with variants of coordinated entry called "dynamic prioritization" (referring a high-needs person temporarily to the "best available" program rather than having him remain homeless until the "best" program has an open slot) and with "system-wide problem-solving" (finding second-best solutions such as returning to a doubled-up situation for people with moderate levels of need and insufficient resources to serve them in the homeless services system).[23] The very fact that these efforts are needed show that the homeless services system is underfunded and that ending homelessness will depend in large part on preventing it from occurring, the subject of the next two chapters.

Focused Efforts to End Chronic Homelessness

Outreach to the most vulnerable people experiencing homelessness and coordinated entry were central elements of the 100,000 Homes Campaign, a focused effort launched in 2010 by the nonprofit Common Ground (later Community Solutions), with the audacious goal of housing 100,000 of the nation's most vulnerable people on the streets.[24] As described in a post hoc evaluation (Leopold & Ho, 2015), the campaign built on Common Ground's success in the Street to Home initiative that nearly eliminated homelessness in the Times Square area of New York City and a follow-on effort on Los Angeles Skid Row (Project 50) that uses a housing first approach to permanent supportive housing.

The campaign evolved and developed new tools and also relied on local innovations. It actively recruited cities where 1,000 or more people experienced homelessness (along with some smaller communities), helped communities conduct "registry weeks" where volunteers sought to register every person living in the streets and assess their needs, and offered housing placement Boot Camps, where participants mapped out the barriers to housing and tried to design a more streamlined process for their community. When these efforts did not suffice to put the campaign on track to reach its goals, the Campaign extended its end date to July, 2014, established a common goal for all communities to house 2.5% of

---

[23] One of us (Jill) has been involved in the efforts of a Systems Strengthening Partnership of some of the more sophisticated communities to develop these approaches.

[24] Initially the campaign focused on people who were medically vulnerable, but soon expanded to those whose homelessness was chronic, meaning, per the federal definition, that they had been homeless continuously for a year or more, or had four or more episodes of homelessness in the past 3 years, and had a disability.

their chronically homeless or vulnerable population on the community registry each month, and redesigned the Boot Camps to focus on accessing homeless-specific and mainstream resources. It helped to develop an assessment instrument that built on an earlier effort to identify people at risk of dying on the street to include more information about housing needs.[25] As incentives for communities, it created the 2.5% Club for communities that met the 2.5% placement target and the Fully Committed list for communities that reported their monthly housing placements, even if they did not meet the 2.5% goal.

How did it work? In July, 2014, Community Solutions ended the campaign, reporting that 159 communities had housed 105,580 vulnerable homeless people in permanent housing. The evaluation noted that some of those people would have been housed anyway. Because Community Solutions actively recruited large communities, and those most eager to roll up their sleeves signed on, the researchers were not able to compare reductions in homelessness in the 159 cities to reductions in cities with the same characteristics in a rigorous way. However, several indicators point to the campaign's possible impact: homelessness among veterans, and unsheltered homelessness and chronic homelessness fell more in campaign communities than in noncampaign communities. In a survey of participating communities, roughly three fifths of respondents felt that the campaign increased the community's sense of urgency about ending chronic and veteran homelessness, led the community to feel connected to federal goals, helped to identify and prioritize people in the target groups, and offered the opportunity to learn from other communities. The evaluators pointed out, however, that the campaign could not overcome lack of resources, which it could not offer. Across the communities that took part in the 100,000 Homes Campaign, 38% reported that the campaign helped them to secure more permanent housing resources to a great extent, but (an overlapping) 68% reported that lack of permanent supportive housing was a barrier to meeting housing placement goals (Leopold & Ho, 2015, p. 30).

Nashville and Los Angeles

Nashville and Los Angeles are two very different cities and metropolitan areas, one with moderate numbers of chronically homelessness people and with moderate capacity in its homeless services system, the other a huge region with sophisticated but hard-to-coordinate systems and daunting numbers of people experiencing chronic homelessness. Both cities mounted initiatives focused on ending chronic homelessness, Nashville in direct response to the 100,000 Homes Campaign, while Los Angeles made that campaign part of a larger effort spurred by City and County elected officials and local philanthropy. In Nashville, which has neither a city nor a state income tax, so little money to pay for public services, the City

---

[25] This is the instrument that experts have found lacking in validity, but simply having a way to set priorities, even if that method has little basis in research, is helpful in motivating outreach workers.

sought voluntary contributions to a "How's Nashville" campaign to supplement federal resources (new allocations of HUD-VASH units) and units set aside by the local housing authority for permanent supportive housing. An enterprising Nashville landlord tried to talk his peers into donating 1% of their units to the effort. This landlord was the only one to meet that percentage, but a number of others offered a few units, so in all, about 80 became available, with payments of just $50/month for tenants who could not afford more.

The Los Angeles effort first focused on increasing the capacity of developers to build more permanent supportive housing and persuading owners of affordable housing developments to turn some of their units into supportive housing for people with chronic patterns of homelessness. That effort was somewhat successful but clearly was not going to produce permanent supportive housing on anything like the scale needed to meet the goal of ending chronic homelessness in the Los Angeles region. So the effort to increase permanent supportive housing, led by a funding collaborative called Home for Good, turned to the housing authorities of the City and County of Los Angeles, two of the largest housing authorities in the United States (with overlapping jurisdictions). The housing authorities provided substantial set-asides of regular (not VASH) housing vouchers (Abt Associates, 2018b).[26]

In Nashville, the campaign increased the monthly rate of housing placements by 142%.[27] A housing navigator who worked for a mental health outreach program described how it worked—and continues to work—in that city.[28] The key goals in every case were connecting people to housing and income, not, at least initially, to psychosocial services. The key barriers to overcome often had to do with documents.

LaVerne had a homeless history dating back 15 years or more and a number of barriers, including alcohol dependency and a criminal history, mostly for low-level crimes like public intoxication. From time to time she stayed at the women's Mission until she had some problem with staff and then lived outside for the next 6 months or so, repeating this cycle several times. When she acquired a baby pit bull named Miracle, she was outside for longer, because the Mission did not allow pets. Another navigator helped her get an ID and birth certificate—critical documents to access any sort of subsidy—and a Section 8 (Housing Choice) voucher, but the voucher expired before she found a place. When she resurfaced at the Mission, the new navigator helped her to reapply, and she got another voucher. The navigator found a small landlord (she described him as a slumlord), whose

---

[26] One of us (Jill) works at Abt Associates, a research firm that since 2011 has been the evaluator of the Conrad N. Hilton Foundation's chronic homelessness initiative. The evaluation's primary focus is not the Foundation's grantmaking in support of the initiative but instead the broader public–private partnership established to end chronic homelessness in the Los Angeles region, measuring progress, describing and assessing systems change and its challenges, and making recommendations.

[27] Personal communication, Judith Tackett, Director Metro Homeless Impact Division, September 18, 2018.

[28] Personal communication, Sally B. Lott, September 6, 2018.

units nevertheless passed the HUD inspection required to use vouchers, and who was willing to take vouchers because the money was guaranteed. How's Nashville paid her moving costs and the deposit and got the water and electricity turned on, so LaVerne and Miracle moved in. By the time the landlord later sold the place, LaVerne had made amends with her family and moved in with her son.

In an unusual example, Robbie, who had been homeless for 10 plus years, had been discharged dishonorably from the service, but was erroneously flagged in Social Security Administration records as eligible for VA benefits, so his SSI (Supplemental Security Income for people with disabilities) was cut off. Usually the housing navigators immediately refer any veteran to VA services, because so much more is available to veterans. In this case, the navigator got the VA to correct Robbie's classification and got his SSI benefits restored. With the help of a voucher, Robbie moved into an apartment, where he kept a large tank of tropical fish, and he volunteered at the local food pantry. Robbie's credit was good, so he did not need a lot of help with start-up expenses. His health, on the other hand, was poor. He passed away after 3 years but died in hospice care rather than on the street.

Judy was living in a broken-down car in a Walmart parking lot in West Nashville. After the housing navigator built a relationship with her and helped her to get her documents in order, Judy was happy to move to one of the units provided by private landlords. But what to do about the car with all her belongings? The navigator had Triple A coverage, so called up Triple A and told them her own car had broken down. The tow-truck driver was skeptical—Judy's car had clearly not run in years—but agreed to tow it to Judy's new apartment.

Ralph, an elderly man with dementia had income—social security retirement benefits—but people often stole it. When he had money, he stayed in a cheap hotel until it ran out, and then he would take to the streets. He was also caught in a cycle of payday loans with exorbitant interest rates. The housing navigator got him into senior housing and secured a representative payee who handles his banking. Meals on Wheels helped with food. After several years he moved to a nursing facility, with the help of Adult Protective Services, which would not work with him until he had an address.

Joyce had experienced a lot of violence on the street. To protect herself she "dressed masculine," so that she would be unrecognizable as a woman. Lacking a car, Joyce worked day labor, so her income was unreliable, and she was not always paid what she had earned. The day labor organization, which may have been paying her off the books, refused to provide the pay stubs to prove her income. The navigator secured one of a limited number of year-round bus passes that the local transit authority now provides to the coordinated entry system. With transportation, Joyce could get a better job with stable income and a place in a low-income housing development, subsidized with a housing voucher.

Navigators use a variety of techniques to get people into housing. It can take as long as a year, particularly if there is a delay in getting documents, in securing SSI for someone with disabilities, and securing a housing voucher. People on the street often lose critical documents. Getting a birth certificate issued is relatively easy if the person has an ID but can cost as much as $50 in some states. People who lack IDs have a more difficult time, and every state has different rules. Navigators have sent high school records, medical records, and even jail records to prove someone's identity. But with concerted effort, and resources, much can be done.

In Los Angeles, as well, outreach and placement had to work well for the effort to succeed. That combined City/County effort embraced systems change in the form of a vigorously tested and implemented coordinated entry system. Pulling off coordinated entry was a tall order, given the size of Los Angeles County, which encompasses, but is much larger than, the City of Los Angeles. (In Los Angeles, as in other parts of California, the county government provides public health and social services. The Continuum of Care in the Los Angeles region is a joint City and County entity.) A private nonprofit in each of eight service planning areas (geographic subunits used by Los Angeles County agencies) was selected to run the coordinated entry system and supported by public funding. (In theory, a government agency could run the system, but hiring a nonprofit was deemed quicker and more efficient.)

Although Los Angeles' coordinated entry system was piloted before it was implemented county-wide, implementation across such a large area had some growing pains. Coordinated entry had to make effective use of the organizations contracted by the County Departments of Health and Mental Health to provide service coordination to people with disabilities and chronic health conditions. Challenges included figuring out who provides service when clients move into permanent supportive housing in a completely different part of the county from their preexisting service providers. Despite growing numbers of units, both project-based and tenant-based, there still weren't enough, and housing navigators often were competing for the same housing units (Abt Associates, 2015).

Despite 6 years of effort, the number of people with chronic patterns of homelessness grew instead of shrinking, reaching 17,000 in 2017 (Abt Associates, 2018b). It was clear that more resources would be needed. The widely held belief was that the affordable housing crisis in the Los Angeles region was at the root of the problem. Los Angeles is a poster child for the dynamics we described in Chapter 2—high rents driven by high overall demand for housing along with supply constraints and a housing stock that does not filter down to the substantial percentage of Angelinos with poverty-level incomes.

Home for Good and its allies mounted public campaigns that resulted in two measures, passed by County and City voters and known as Proposition H and Measure HHH. The measures brought substantial additional resources both to the homeless services system and to the affordable housing sector more generally (Abt Associates, 2018a). Accounts of successes for particular individuals are just as inspiring as they are in Nashville. The following is just one example, from a newsletter published by the County Office of the Homeless Initiative.

Kristopher has several mental health diagnoses, including posttraumatic stress disorder and bipolar disorder, and a criminal record for misdemeanors and a felony. After being connected to case management through a mental health agency, he now lives in a two-bedroom apartment with a roommate, supported by rental assistance. His misdemeanors have been expunged, and he is working on getting a certificate of rehabilitation for his felony. He is working as a recovery peer supporter and is about to start college (County of Los Angeles Office of the Homeless Initiative, 2019, p. 10). The number of people in the Los Angeles region with chronic patterns of homelessness was down a bit in the January 2018 point-in-time count but went back in 2019 to essentially the same number as in 2017 (Wright & Kamensky, 2019).

Reducing Homelessness for Veterans

The reduction in homelessness for military veterans, from 73,000 in 2009 to 38,000 in 2018 (Henry, Mahathey, et al., 2018), is a compelling example of what can be done when political will leads to additional resources. Resources provided by the Veteran's Administration include the SSVF program, which provides short-term assistance using a rapid re-housing model, and the VASH supportive housing program, implemented in cooperation with HUD and local housing authorities. HUD-VASH uses a housing first model. An evaluation pointed to considerable technical help in the form of manuals, checklists, and instructional phone calls, and the VA's "hierarchical culture and unified mission" in creating success. "This VA study sheds some light on the political and organizational leverage available when credible leaders seek to transform social policy on a broad scale, particularly when that effort is paired with a substantial bed of resources" (Kertesz et al., 2017, p. 126). The VA also seeks to prevent homelessness, as we will describe in Chapter 5.

Nor is support for ending homelessness among veterans confined to the VA. The United States Interagency Council on Homelessness has created the Mayors' Challenge to End Veteran Homelessness, and HUD asks communities to give priority to veterans. The Interagency Council describes many elements that are needed in community strategies to end veteran homelessness. Some of these are the procedures we have described for all groups: identifying all veterans who experience homelessness; implementing coordinated entry, outreach and engagement; and reducing transitional housing in favor of permanent housing. The Interagency Council also describes reaching beyond the homeless system by engaging private landlords, increasing connections to employment, coordinating with legal services to prevent evictions, navigating outstanding warrants and expunging criminal records, and securing the public benefits to which veterans are entitled (US Interagency Council on Homelessness, 2017b). It is impossible to divvy up credit for the reductions among these various efforts—indeed it is the full court press by all the players that seems critical. As of May, 2019, 3 states and 71 communities including at least one community in 35 states had met the federal "criteria and benchmarks" for ending veteran homelessness (U.S. Department of Veterans Affairs, 2019; U.S. Interagency Council on Homelessness, 2017a, 2018a).[29]

The Finnish Model

The country of Finland has largely succeeded in ending literal homelessness by using an approach that follows the principles of housing first—that is, emphasizing consumer choice and not trying to solve people's problems before connecting them to housing, although not the full Pathways model. Because Finland uses a broad definition of homelessness, including living temporarily with family or friends, they have not yet met their own goals. But even by this broad measure, they have more than halved homelessness as observed in annual point-in-time counts: from more than 18,000 individuals and families in 1987 to about 7,500 in 2016 (Y-Foundation, 2017). Initial efforts to increase social housing and develop a homeless service sector brought the numbers down, but progress stalled around 2004 because of a group of long-term homeless people with considerable support needs—roughly corresponding to the so-called chronic population in the United States (Pleace, 2017; Y-Foundation, 2017). Analysis of the problem led to development of a national homeless strategy based on housing first concepts that brought together all levels of government, quasi-governmental agencies, and the homeless service sector and largely succeeded in housing this group.

A report by the Y-Foundation, which played a central role, credits the housing first approach, which is applied not only to individuals with serious mental illnesses but to everyone, with their success: "In the Housing First model, a dwelling is not a reward that a homeless person receives once their life is back on track. Instead, a dwelling is the foundation on which the rest of life is put back together" (Y-Foundation, 2017, p. 10). However, the report notes "housing naturally cannot be provided unless apartments exist" (p. 10). Thus, constructing and purchasing housing that can be made affordable, along with converting shelters to apartment blocks, was a central part of the Finnish strategy. In a country with a much larger "social housing" sector than the United States, the Y-Foundation is currently the

---

[29] The criteria refer largely to what systems should do, namely identify all veterans experiencing homelessness, regardless of discharge, provide shelter immediately to any who want it, have the capacity to move all veterans into permanent housing swiftly, have plans and resources to address the housing and service needs for veterans entering, returning to, or at risk of homelessness, and use transitional housing only for veterans who have chosen it over permanent housing in order to receive specialized supports. The benchmarks refer more to outcomes: No veteran should experience chronic or long-term homelessness except those in a process (maximum of 90 days) of securing permanent housing, those who have chosen transitional housing over permanent housing, or those who have refused permanent housing. Veterans should move into permanent housing within 90 days of the time they accept it. The numbers exiting homelessness should exceed the numbers entering that state and the numbers placed in transitional programs should be significantly less than the number entering homelessness.

fourth largest landlord in Finland (p. 25). Municipalities provide additional afford-able units. Residents' stories sound very similar to those in the United States:

> An apartment means security—now I have a home to return to. I feel important again now that I am responsible for my own life. I am someone again, I am me. I feel that I have to take care of my own business now. (p. 57)

The report notes that the Finnish version of housing first differs from the Pathways Housing First program in that people pay for affordable housing themselves without special subsidies, using a variety of income sources available to all Finns. These include a housing allowance based on income, along with child allowances, disability, unemployment, student, and pension benefits, and, if still needed as a last resort, social assistance (akin to welfare in the United States). Further, sup-port plans make use of services that are generally available, which is possible because of (as the report understates) "the high standard of social and health services" in Finland. Housing includes scattered-site apartments, some housing in which residents commit to "working towards a life free from substance abuse," (p. 39), some housing reserved for young people (who may share apartments), and some low-threshold supportive[30] housing.

The Finnish supportive housing also differs from the Pathways to Housing model in that most is not scattered site but instead in apartment buildings with common areas and round-the-clock staff. Tenants have leases for their own units but "living is communal," with rules set by the community of residents and staff (p. 27). The Finns acknowledge that "community living does not suit everyone" and that some residents say they live temporarily in supportive housing because they have no choice and hope to move to their own apartments (p. 29). Others are satisfied and plan to stay permanently:

> I haven't had any alcohol for over five years and am a support person for a few friends. I hope that in the future my health will stay stable at the least, if not improve. I want to stay and live in Väinölä, I don't have any urge to leave. Things are good as they are (p. 55).

Service plans are determined with residents with the goal of strengthening their "agency and involvement in their own lives" (p. 80), and providers include "experts by experience" who have been homeless themselves.

The Finns have developed elaborate strategies to combat opposition from neighbors to the development of supportive housing buildings (known in the United States as NIMBYism for Not in My Backyard). Tenants engage in "neigh-borhood work" such as picking up litter, gardening, shoveling snow (this is, after all, Finland), helping older community residents with chores, and maintaining parks. The work provides benefits to the neighborhood and is seen as a "training

---

[30] The Finns use the term "supported" housing.

ground" to help residents "get a handle on life again" (p. 27). Neighbors have access to a 24-hour hotline to report any problems.

The Finns accomplished their success in multiple stages with successive national plans. The latest plan, adopted in 2016, focuses on prevention, on youth and women, and on provisions for migrants and asylum seekers with residence permits (Pleace, 2017; Y-Foundation, 2017).

Whereas the Y-Foundation credits the housing first approach, one of the outside experts brought in to evaluate the efforts argues that two other factors were fundamental: a focus on housing supply and "developing a political consensus, coordination of local, regional and national policy, and bringing together all the key organizations" (Pleace, 2017, p. 101). We highlight a third factor: an impressively self-reflective approach, with ongoing internal and external evaluation and a willingness to adapt based on outside models, evaluator recommendations, and local analyses of shifting needs. Finland is a small and relatively homogenous country that has long had a robust safety net. Nonetheless, it "has gone further and faster in tackling homelessness than equally, or more, prosperous European countries" or indeed than the United States (Pleace, 2017, p. 112).

Summary

Research has shown what works to end homelessness for people who experience it. Supportive housing using a housing first approach works for people who have long histories of homelessness and serious mental illnesses and substance problems. Many people, including most families, become stable and indeed flourish with just an ongoing rental subsidy that makes housing affordable for people who are deeply poor. Long-term housing subsidies are rarely an option for households at the point they experience homelessness unless they are already on a waiting list. Nevertheless, 31% of veterans in the SSVF rapid re-housing program had secured a permanent subsidy at program end, as had over a third of families assigned to usual care 3 years after entering the Family Options study. Getting those subsidies to more people, more quickly would end more homelessness.

To the extent that permanent housing subsidies continue to be inaccessible to people experiencing homelessness, rapid re-housing, at least for families, yields equivalent outcomes to usual care and is cheaper. It is thus preferable to the other options currently available at the start of a homeless episode. Rapid re-housing also allows some people to avoid or shorten stays in emergency shelters, which are often demoralizing and disruptive. We thus support HUD's emphasis on rapid re-housing over transitional housing in its funding of local Continuum of Care programs. However, we should be clear-eyed about the limitations of the evidence. There is no randomized study that shows that rapid re-housing or transitional housing is any better than usual care at ending homelessness or that either has the sort of radiating benefits that long-term subsidies provide for families. Studies show that both transitional housing and rapid re-housing are highly selective in the people they serve, and the relatively good outcomes seen in descriptive studies may be due as much to sorting people as to helping people.[31] The Family Options study suggests that longer-term housing subsidies are often needed.

The progress made in reducing chronic homelessness and the reduction in homelessness among military veterans show not just what specific programs work but what can be accomplished with focus, energy, a willingness to evaluate and adjust, and resources. The most impressive example is Finland, where the infusion of resources has been greatest. There housing first, long-term subsidies, and other means of making housing affordable to everyone has essentially ended literal homelessness. Finland is not the wealthiest country in Europe, nor is it as wealthy as the United States. It has shown that devoting the energy and resources necessary to end homelessness is not a question of wealth but of political will. The Finnish example includes a variety of approaches. Ideally, in the United States individuals and families would be able to choose among a range of housing options, including private apartments with voluntary services fully integrated into communities, more communal arrangements, and sober housing.

The United States can afford the sort of investment Finland has made, if we choose to do so. However currently most people who experience homelessness and indeed most renters with severe cost burdens do not have access to housing subsidies. In many parts of the country, even the waiting lists are closed. The expiration date for the 10-year plans has passed, and although some communities have made progress, particularly in recent years and particularly with respect to veteran homelessness, rates of homelessness remain high. In the final two chapters we turn to an essential part of the effort to end homelessness, preventing homelessness before it occurs for people at high risk and addressing the social conditions that continue to generate homelessness.

---

[31] Rapid re-housing programs are supposed to follow housing first principles; however it is also the case that HUD charges communities to operate coordinated-entry programs using assessment tools to decide on how limited services should be allocated, and these tools often suggest that rapid re-housing is suitable for people with few barriers to housing (U.S. Department of Housing and Urban Development, n.d.).

5

Preventing Homelessness for People at Risk

Chapters 3 and 4 showed that we know how to end homelessness for various groups that experience it. We now turn our discussion to prevention. The human and economic costs of homelessness to the people afflicted and the communities where they live are enormous. We believe that society would be better off if we could prevent people from becoming homeless to begin with. This chapter surveys strategies to prevent homelessness for people at high risk of experiencing it. The following chapter widens the lens to consider what it would take to change the broader societal conditions that generate homelessness and to mend a social safety net that has left many in deep poverty and unstable housing. Both efforts—focused on people at high risk and broader social changes—are likely to be necessary to end homelessness. The scope is different: in one case it is helping people who are at or close to the crisis that plunges them into homelessness; in the other it is keeping a larger number of people from approaching that point.[1]

Turning first to preventing homelessness for people at high risk, we consider mainly strategies that the public health literature would categorize as "primary" prevention—that is, preventing homelessness for a high-risk population before it occurs (although the individuals or families in question may have experienced homelessness in the past). An example might be providing housing or other resources to youth leaving foster care or prisoners who have completed their sentence so that they have some place to go besides the nearest shelter or the street. In the language of public health, "secondary" prevention means early detection and cure of a problem when it has already occurred—nipping it in the bud. Shelter diversion and rapid re-housing might qualify here. "Tertiary" prevention means reducing the undesirable consequences of a condition. In the context of homelessness, tertiary prevention could include soup kitchens, winter shelter

---

[1] Apicello (2010) makes a similar argument.

In the Midst of Plenty: Homelessness and What to Do About It, First Edition.
Marybeth Shinn and Jill Khadduri.
© 2020 Marybeth Shinn and Jill Khadduri. Published 2020 by John Wiley & Sons Ltd.

programs, and efforts to end victimization of people on the streets, as well as combatting city ordinances that criminalize behaviors that people who lack housing are forced to perform in the public square. We do not discuss these programs and efforts. Fighting for the right to lie down in public—or the right of compassionate citizens to distribute food to hungry people in public parks—is a cramped vision of what homeless policy should encompass. Sometimes such fights are necessary, but our goal is to prevent and end homelessness, not to make homelessness a bit less miserable.

Evaluating Prevention for People at High Risk: Efficiency and Effectiveness

To be successful, preventing homelessness before it happens for people at high risk must be both effective—that is, it must stop people from becoming homeless—and also efficient—it must get services to the people most likely to benefit (Burt, Pearson, & Montgomery, 2007). We consider efficiency first, because in a system strapped for resources, getting services to the right people is often the harder problem. In a review of prevention programs funded under the American Recovery and Reinvestment Act of 2009 (the "Stimulus"), Cunningham et al. (2015) note that providers "struggled to determine which households would become homeless without the assistance, yet would do well with [the] short-term financial assistance and light-touch case management" typically on offer (p. xiv).

Further, inefficient targeting too often masquerades as effectiveness. For example, a prevention provider may brag that 90% of people who receive her prevention service avoid homelessness. That could mean that she offers a great program, or it might simply mean she is giving the service to people who were not at high risk to begin with. The provider could raise the percentage to 100%, by offering the service only to millionaires. "Success" should be measured against what would have happened in the absence of the program, often called a "counterfactual." If 90% of program participants would have avoided homelessness without the program, the provider's data would show that her program was singularly ineffective—it made no difference to rates of homelessness.

Even when success is measured appropriately, success rates and failure rates often rise in tandem. To understand why this is so, consider some real data, shown in Figure 5.1, based on 11,105 families who applied for prevention services from the HomeBase prevention program in New York City (described in more detail below). Over the next 3 years, 12.8% of those families entered shelter. Because New York City has a right to shelter, few families with children live in cars or on the street, so shelter entry is a good proxy for literal homelessness.

One of us (Beth) took advantage of the fact that intake workers gathered extensive data on the characteristics of families applying for assistance to develop a model predicting the likelihood of shelter entry for any particular family (Shinn et al., 2013).

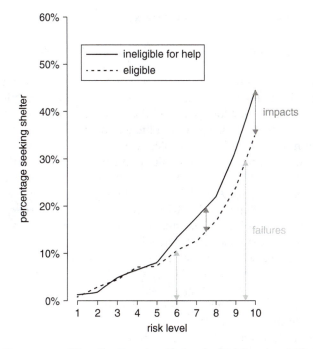

Figure 5.1 Percentage of Families Entering Shelter by Risk Level and Eligibility for Services in New York City. The figure shows that as risk rises, services prevent more homelessness but also have higher failure rates. Shinn, Greer, Bainbridge, Kwon, and Zuiderveen (2013).

In Figure 5.1, the horizontal axis classifies families by risk, according to the model, with families divided into 10 groups of equal size. The vertical axis shows the proportion of each group who entered shelter over the next 3 years. Look first at the upper, solid line, which shows what happened to families in each group whom workers deemed ineligible for services. As risk scores increased, from the bottom 10th of families to the top 10th, the proportion of families who entered shelter also went up. The model worked better than previous approaches to predict homelessness, but it did not work very well: even at the highest level of risk, the majority of families who received no services somehow managed to stay out of shelters. The lower, dotted line shows the proportion of families who were deemed eligible for services and who presumably received them but who nevertheless entered shelters in the next 3 years. It represents the program's failure rate. The vertical distance between the two lines is one estimate of impact—of homelessness prevented. Importantly, as risk scores go up, both failure rates and the impact of the HomeBase intervention increase. At low risk levels there are few failures, but also no evidence the prevention efforts mattered, because there is little risk to avert. At high risk levels, the impact of the program in preventing homelessness is clear, but failure rates are also high. If a program does not have failures, it is probably not delivering services to people at high enough risk to benefit.

Every study of homelessness prevention that has looked has found larger effects for individuals and families who are at higher risk. That would not have to be the case. Medical triage decisions on a battlefield divide patients into three groups—those likely to survive without immediate intervention, those likely to die no matter what is done for them, and those in the middle, for whom medical care might make the difference between life and death. In the case of homelessness prevention, there could, in principle, be a group at such high risk that nothing will prevent them from becoming homelessness. In practice, however, homelessness prevention services have always made the most difference for the people at highest risk (Evans, Sullivan, & Wallskog, 2016; Greer, Shinn, Kwon, & Zuiderveen, 2016; Shinn et al., 2013; Wood, Turnham, & Mills, 2008).

The HomeBase data offer several additional insights. First, they answer the question, why ration services at all? In a world with unlimited resources, there might be no need to ration, but we are very far from that world. As Figure 5.1 shows, about half of the applicants, in risk levels 1–5, had very little risk of entering shelter during the period of the study, whether they got services or not. Overall, during the period under study, workers served more than two thirds of applicants, including about half of the applicants at risk levels 1–5. Those services may have done useful things for people in need, but they did not prevent homelessness because families could avoid shelter without them. In a world with limited resources, it makes sense to concentrate those resources where they will accomplish the most.

Next, the HomeBase data shed light on why workers served low-risk families and neglected some at higher risk. (At the time of the study, each worker decided whom to serve after collecting the intake information.) One reason is that workers' intuitions about risk are not always very good. Workers may operate on lay theories of what causes homelessness—but lay theories are often wrong. The presumed causes may reflect consequences of homelessness or characteristics of the shelter system rather than characteristics that people bring with them to shelters. Lay theories may also miss important predictors. For example, out of home placement as a child is a predictor of homelessness in adulthood (Apicello, 2010; Shinn et al., 2013; Shinn, Knickman, & Weitzman, 1991), probably because people with such histories are less likely to have family to fall back on in hard times, but workers in New York City did not use this factor to decide who should get HomeBase prevention services. In a number of fields from medicine to mental health to education, statistical models are more accurate than professional or clinical judgments, and that turns out to be the case for homelessness as well (Ægisdóttir et al., 2006; Dawes, Faust, & Meehl, 1989; Grove, Zald, Lebow, Snitz, & Nelson, 2000; Meehl, 1954). Workers' intuitions about causes of homelessness can be improved with evidence.

Another reason that workers do not always serve people at the highest risk is more troubling. We call it "the worthy poor trap": Across many programs, people who seem worthy or deserving are more likely to be served than people who are at higher risk. In the case of HomeBase, workers were more likely to give services to high school graduates and people with jobs, but lack of a diploma and unemployment were risk factors. They were more likely to give services to leaseholders threatened with eviction, but people who were doubled up in the same apartment with family or friends or were renting without a lease were at greater risk.

The practice of restricting prevention services to the worthy poor is widespread. Such restrictions echo those of services-first housing programs that require sobriety and participation in treatment before people can come indoors. Service providers must decide whether their goal is to prevent and end homelessness or to reward what they see as good behavior. The latter choice reflects deep-seated values, but the parable of the father who killed the fatted calf for the prodigal son rather than rewarding his dutiful brother provides an alternative value framework. If the goal is to prevent homelessness, worthiness should not be a limiting factor.[2]

A somewhat different argument for giving prevention services to people who are better off is the hope that they will be able to sustain housing after the services end. This practice was widespread among prevention programs funded by the Homelessness Prevention and Rapid Re-Housing Program (HPRP) under the American Recovery and Reinvestment Act of 2009, which struggled with the twin mandates to serve households who would become homeless "but for" the assistance and to provide help to those who could sustain housing afterwards. These instructions suggest triage, as shown in the incorrect but intuitively appealing model for homelessness prevention shown in Figure 5.2.

This intuitive model has several features at odds with actual data. First, the intuitive model suggests many people are too risky to serve—they will not sustain housing and will enter shelter (perhaps not on day one, but soon after services cease) no matter what is done for them. The vertical arrow at risk = 8 suggests a near 100% failure. Actual data suggest that most people manage to avoid shelter, even where risk is high (Greer, 2014; Greer et al., 2016; Shinn et al., 2013). The intuitive model suggests there is a sweet spot for maximum impact somewhere in the middle of the risk continuum, where people would become homeless "but for" assistance. Actual data suggests that the maximum impact is found for people at highest risk. And the intuitive model suggests that services will have an enormous impact (in cost benefit analyses conducted without reference to actual data, the assumption is often that 100% of people will become homeless in the absence of services and 0% when services are offered). The only services that have been found to have that level of impact are long-term subsidies (for families) and subsidies with voluntary services (permanent supportive housing) for people with serious mental illnesses.

---

[2] Requirements could be intended to induce rather than reward good behavior. But as reviewed in Chapter 3, housing itself may provide a platform for people to take control of their lives, leading, at least for families, to reductions in problems such as substance abuse, psychological distress, and domestic violence, whereas psychosocial services without permanent housing had few effects (Gubits et al., 2015, 2016).

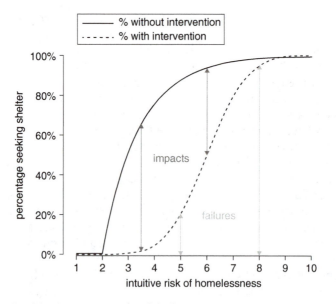

Figure 5.2   Intuitive But Incorrect Model of How Prevention Could Work. In the intuitive model, services have the greatest impact at intermediate levels of risk. Real studies show greatest impact at highest levels of risk.

As a consequence of attempting to avoid failure, prevention programs funded by the Stimulus Act enrolled "a significant share of clients … whose risk of literal homelessness in the short term was low" (Cunningham et al., 2015, p. xvii). The evidence suggests they should have done the opposite—helping households with greater needs, even when the prevention program is modest, is likely to reap larger benefits.

Efficient Allocation of Prevention Services

When providers cannot serve everyone deemed eligible, they can increase the efficiency of prevention efforts by deriving statistical models to select the people to serve. During the period Beth and colleagues studied, HomeBase served two thirds of the poor families who applied but declined to serve 28.4% of families who later entered shelter. By using the screening model derived from the data, they could have reduced those misses to 8.1% (Shinn et al., 2013).[3] New York City adopted the screening model and a parallel model for adult applicants (Greer et al., 2016) to decide who gets full HomeBase services and who is simply given

---

[3] The workers falsely targeted 65.7% of families who avoided shelter (a "false alarm rate" of 65.7%). How many people are missed depends on how many people are targeted. (Targeting everyone would mean missing no one.) For a fair comparison, the reduction in misses (of people who entered shelter despite not being targeted) holds the false alarm rate (of those targeted who did not enter shelter) constant (Shinn et al., 2013).

information about services they can pursue on their own—with one important caveat. The City allowed workers to override the model decisions with supervisor approval. Allowing some worker discretion has two advantages. First, workers are more likely to buy into a screening system if they have some recourse if they think the answer is wrong. Second, the reasons workers want to override the model's decision may give clues to new questions that had not been asked previously, so that they had no chance of becoming part of the model. In this way, models can be updated and improved.

Beth and colleagues have now developed models for three groups—the families and single adults in New York City and a mixed sample of adults and families on the opposite coast in Alameda County, California (Greer, 2014; Greer et al., 2016; Shinn et al., 2013). Although based on different groups and different sets of questions, the resulting models are far more similar than we expected. In every case, the single best predictor of becoming homeless is having been homeless previously. Other prime predictors are being doubled up with another household in the same housing unit or not being a leaseholder, being faced with eviction (including verbal threats as well as legal papers), receiving public assistance (welfare) and having high levels of rent arrears or debt. Note that all these factors reflect housing and economic resources, even though only applicants with low incomes were even considered. Behavioral factors such as reported mental illness, substance abuse, criminal history, and domestic violence did not add to risk anywhere. Some additional factors mattered for the families in New York—being pregnant, having a young child, having a history of involvement with child protective services, adverse experiences in childhood, and discord in the current living situation. Relative youth and reintegrating into the community from an institution also put people at risk in both of the New York samples—reintegration was not asked in California. The similarity of the models provides hope that it may be possible to develop a more general model that could be useful to identify people at risk for homelessness across communities.

These models are limited in several ways. They start with only the client characteristics that workers were already recording—better predictors might lurk in the questions not asked. They are limited to particular locales (two coasts with high housing prices) and particular points in historical time. To be most useful, models should be local and should be updated as conditions change. The models predict only shelter use, not other forms of homelessness or housing instability, although it would be possible to predict any outcome that can be measured accurately. The models are limited to people who applied for prevention services, meaning that an outreach strategy that brought a different set of potential clients to service workers' attention might need a different model. And finally, the models do not predict terribly well. From a moral perspective, rates of homelessness are much too high, but from a statistical perspective, rates are low, making it hard to predict who will succumb. Further, to the extent that homelessness is a matter of bad luck or unpredictable events among people living on the edge, as O'Flaherty suggests (2004, 2010), it may not be possible to improve predictive power very much. Nonetheless, the models can improve workers' decisions substantially.[4] Where resources are scarce, research and statistical models can improve the efficiency of homelessness prevention services.

Predictive models are gaining greater currency. In New York, researchers have used data on later shelter entries to develop a quick three-item screen for emergency-department patients with unhealthy drug or alcohol use (Doran et al., 2019): reporting shelter use in the past year, applying for shelter in the past 3 months, or having ever been incarcerated.

Researchers in Los Angeles used data from a variety of public agencies to develop models to identify people who would become persistently homeless (more than once or for at least a year) among two specific groups: all people who lose jobs and all young people 18–24 receiving public assistance—groups that account for 29% of people who become persistently homeless. (Some members of the group were homeless at the time they entered the sample, and some were not.) The models are more complex than the New York models, integrating data from public agencies on histories of homelessness, employment and unemployment, incarceration, foster care, hospital stays and outpatient services, emergency room visits, medical diagnoses, and receipt of public aid as well as demographic variables, whereas the New York models relied largely on self-reports among people applying for prevention services. In these models, current and past homelessness were again critical predictors, along with disability, employment and incarceration history, and foster care history for youth. Unlike the New York models, which relied on self reports, history of mental health and substance services contributed modestly for the group facing unemployment and more prominently for youth. The Los Angeles models also have high accuracy when identifying people at extremely high risk in the two target groups (Toros, Flaming, & Burns, 2019).[5]

If screening questions identify people at high risk of homelessness, an intake worker can offer or refer them to prevention services on the spot. How one goes from identifying people at high risk by using administrative records for people who have not applied for services to locating those people and getting them primary prevention services (preventing homelessness before it occurs) is less clear. Do you send a letter with an offer of services? Do you alert service providers with

---

[4] Statistical models sometimes can reinforce racial or other biases that have been built into the model. This is particularly true when the outcome to be modeled depends on decisions of people who may hold conscious or unconscious biases. We think the opposite is happening here, where the models direct services to people at greater disadvantage. We looked for and did not find racial bias.

[5] Among 10,000 job losers that the model predicted to be at highest risk of becoming persistently homeless, 73% did so (although this was only 25% of all job losers, including those deemed not at high risk, who became persistently homeless). Among 7,300 18–24-year-olds on public assistance whom the model predicted to be at highest risk, 64% became persistently homeless. Once again, the model missed many people, 76% of those who became persistently homeless. One could reduce misses by targeting more people, but then a lower percentage of those targeted would become persistently homeless.

whom they may have future contacts to make them an offer when they show up? Can you do either in a way that does not label people or create a self-fulfilling prophecy? Secondary prevention (nipping homelessness in the bud) is more plausible here. People who become homeless and have been identified by administrative records to be at high risk for persistent homelessness could be offered the most effective interventions available (such as long-term subsidies or permanent supportive housing) as soon as they enter shelter or are found on the street.[6]

O'Flaherty, Scuttel, and Tseng (2018) suggest that people often possess "private information" not readily captured in statistical models about their risk of homelessness (or other adverse outcomes)—for example, the fact that a cousin who is planning on moving to New Zealand will leave them a place to stay.[7] To take advantage of this information, they argue, it is justifiable to require some inconvenience in accessing preventive services. Only people who know they really need the service will tolerate the inconvenience, allowing services to be focused on those they will help. Requiring people to apply for services or to follow up on a referral might be enough of a hassle to discourage those who do not need the service.

Researchers are making strides in identifying various groups at high risk of homelessness. Most communities, unlike Los Angeles and New York, may not have enough data to develop their own models and could potentially test models developed elsewhere. Additional approaches, besides using statistical models to predict risk, can be used to target prevention services to people with particular life experiences or to communities at high risk. We describe some of them later in this chapter.

Evaluating Effectiveness

After people who are at high risk of becoming homeless are identified, what services work to prevent that event? We know very little. In 1990, the General Accounting Office (now the Government Accountability Office) issued a report entitled *Homelessness: Too early to tell what kinds of prevention assistance work best* (General Accounting Office, 1990). Two decades later a thorough review of the sparse literature on prevention found that "the practice of homelessness prevention is still in its infancy and there is little science base for its implementation" (Apicello, 2010, p. 41). Three decades in, we know a little more, but still not

---

[6] The authors of the Los Angeles study did not calculate model accuracy in predicting persistence among people who became homeless.

[7] O'Flaherty et al. (2018) show that statistical models incorporating less idiosyncratic "private information" do better than models based solely on public information, using questionnaire data from Australia. However, many of their best "private" predictors, including self-assessed current and past homelessness, crowding, and exposure to violence were, in fact, part of the data on which the HomeBase tool was built. O'Flaherty et al. include a thoughtful discussion of the way that answers can be distorted when they are "consequential"—i.e., if people understand that decisions about resources ride on them.

much. As researchers, we may be biased, but we find this lack of research appalling. The federal Emergency Food and Shelter Program (EFSP) began funding short-term rental assistance to prevent homelessness in 1983, although the "program" is little more than a set of cost-allowance guidelines. The year 2012 marked its 30th round of funding,[8] but the program "has never tried to find out whether the assistance it gives prevents households from actually becoming homeless" (Cunningham et al., 2015, p. 4).

The HPRP in 2009 pumped over a billion dollars into homelessness prevention in response to the Great Recession. Communities were required to get money out the door quickly, in order to stimulate the economy, so research took short shrift. The national evaluation (Cunningham et al., 2015) looked at what communities did, not at what worked. The prevention efforts that the program funded may have had some role in mitigating the recession's effects on homelessness. Rates of homelessness barely rose from 2009 to 2010, and they decreased again in 2011 (Henry, Mahathey, et al., 2018). But the program was not designed to show which of the many activities undertaken were more effective than others. The evaluation noted that the "question of whether HPRP was successful in preventing homelessness remains unanswered" (Cunningham et al., 2015, p. 117). Similarly, the screening of all veterans who receive outpatient services for risk of homelessness (described later in this chapter) may be part of the reason that only about half as many veterans experienced homelessness on a single night in January, 2018 (Greer et al., 2016; Henry, Mahathey, et al., 2018) as they did 8 years earlier. Yet in the 35 years since the nation started funding homelessness prevention, few programs have been rigorously evaluated. It is not surprising that communities faced with overwhelming need do not want to divert scarce dollars from services to research, but the Department of Housing and Urban Development (HUD) should commission further studies of prevention. It should not still be "too early to tell what kinds of prevention assistance work best."

Why don't we know more? To estimate the effectiveness of a program we need a counterfactual—a defensible estimate of what would have happened in the absence of services. As in the case of ending homelessness for people who experience it, the most convincing counterfactual for prevention programs is often provided by a randomized experiment, in which people who receive the prevention services are chosen by lottery, and both the "winners" and "losers" of the lottery are followed up to see what happens to them. When there are not enough resources to go around to all who are eligible (or all deemed high risk by a predictive model), allocating them by lottery may be fairer than any other approach. Under such circumstances, we argue, experiments can be done ethically. (Randomization can sometimes be made more politically acceptable by randomizing neighborhoods or social service offices instead of individuals.)

---

[8] The EFSP was made permanent as part of the Stewart B. McKinney Homeless Assistance Act of 1987.

Other research strategies (dubbed quasi-experimental) can also provide strong evidence of effectiveness. For example, researchers have studied the geographic rollout of programs over time (Goodman, Messeri, & O'Flaherty, 2016), what happens to people who apply for help when programs have money or have run out of funds (Evans et al., 2016) and what happens when one state adopts a new program and neighboring states do not (Dworsky, Napolitano, & Courtney, 2013). The national evaluation of the HPRP includes a chapter by Larry Buron and Jacob Klerman recommending several possible studies of prevention programs that use quasi-experimental designs—for example, starting with the application of some version of a targeting model and then comparing outcomes for people just above and below a risk cut-off[9] or implementing a demonstration for people leaving some institutions (e.g., jails, mental hospitals) but not for people leaving other such institutions in the same or similar communities (Cunningham et al., 2015, chapter 10).

On the basis of clever research designs, we have solid evidence that a handful of programs work to prevent homelessness, specifically permanent deep rent subsidies, cash help for households facing evictions, and community-based services provided by New York City's HomeBase prevention program. More suggestive evidence exists for a few additional programs: universal screening of military veterans who apply for any service from the Veteran's Administration, permanent shallow rent subsidies for people with HIV or AIDS, housing with supportive services for people with serious mental illnesses (where effectiveness for *ending* homelessness is quite clear, as shown in Chapter 4), and extension of eligibility for foster care from 18 to 21. Finally, a large number of ideas are worth studying so that we can learn more. In reviewing the programs described below, we classify them by the quality of evidence for effectiveness in preventing homelessness. We also consider efficiency.

Programs with Solid Evidence of Effectiveness

Permanent Deep Housing Subsidies

Chapter 3 showed that housing subsidies that hold housing costs to 30% of household income can end homelessness for families. Subsidies are an important component of Housing First programs that end homelessness and promote stability for people with serious mental illnesses.

Strong experimental evidence shows that housing subsidies also prevent homelessness for poor families. One of us (Jill) was part of a team that evaluated a demonstration program that was not designed to prevent homelessness but happened to provide important evidence. The study originally asked whether housing

---

[9] Greer (2014) employed this design, called regression discontinuity, to evaluate homelessness prevention in Alameda County, but the sample size was insufficient to draw firm conclusions.

vouchers would help families move from welfare to work in the wake of the welfare reform enacted in 1996. The demonstration enrolled families who were eligible for or receiving Temporary Assistance to Needy Families (TANF) and who applied for housing vouchers. These identified families were then randomly assigned to receive a voucher or remain on a waiting list.[10] The evaluation found little evidence that the housing stability created by a housing voucher helped families to work. Instead, to the surprise of the researchers, the headline finding was that vouchers prevent homelessness. Voucher users were much less likely to have experienced homelessness (in a shelter or on the street) during the next 4 years than the control group (3.3% vs. 12.5%).[11] Families using vouchers also were much less likely to be doubled up with friends or relatives, often a precursor to homelessness. As is the case for programs explicitly designed to prevent homelessness, vouchers had the largest impact on homelessness for families that might be considered at higher risk of experiencing homelessness. Here, it was families whose household head was unemployed or who, at the time of random assignment, had only 6 months of eligibility for TANF (Wood et al., 2008).

Housing vouchers used explicitly for preventing homelessness for families and individuals at immediate risk of becoming homeless face the problem of how to identify people at highest risk without creating the perverse incentives we described in Chapter 3: encouraging people to exhibit behaviors that would make them eligible for assistance.[12] For example, if families about to lose TANF income because they had "timed out" or been sanctioned were offered housing vouchers, word would get around that approaching the time limit or failing to comply with TANF rules was a way to get a voucher. One possibility would be to let TANF caseworkers assess whether a family was "gaming" the system or had made real efforts to find work and child care or had extenuating circumstances such as a sick child or a health condition that limited the parent's ability to work. But we have already argued that often caseworkers are not the best judges of who is going to experience homelessness, and discretion invites favoring the worthy poor. Furthermore, the original design of the demonstration of vouchers for welfare families asked TANF caseworkers to refer to the voucher program only those families for whom they thought increased housing stability would provide a platform for employment. It didn't work—in effect, TANF caseworkers sent their

---

[10] The six-site Effects of Housing Vouchers for Welfare Families Study enrolled 8,731 families who were eligible for Welfare to Work vouchers (equivalent to Housing Choice Vouchers described in Chapter 4). Families had to meet the usual eligibility criteria for vouchers: a family income below 50% of the median income for the area, U.S. citizenship or immigration status, and no evictions from publicly funded housing due to recent drug-related criminal activity.

[11] Based on the study's "treatment on treated" or TOT impact estimates. TOT estimates assumed the voucher had no effect on a family who did not use the voucher and also took account of "crossovers"—families in the control group who over the 4-year period rose to the top of the waiting list and also used a voucher.

[12] Economists call this "moral hazard."

entire caseloads to the voucher program.[13] In Chapter 6 we consider a voucher program for all who are poor enough to be eligible, which would eliminate this perverse incentive.

Another approach to using housing vouchers for prevention is to focus on people with "systems involvement" that is patently involuntary (severe mental illness) or sufficiently dire that people are unlikely to use it to improve their position on a waiting list for a housing voucher (prison terms, involvement with the child welfare system). We consider prevention programs linked to the mental health, criminal justice, and foster care systems later in this chapter.

Eviction Prevention: Cash Assistance

Some people enter homelessness from housing that was their own—in the sense that they were renting their own place rather than staying with family or friends.[14] The path from being a renter to being homeless may involve eviction, and some programs to prevent homelessness focus on that pathway. More than 15 million people per year seek assistance from programs to prevent evictions (Evans et al., 2016), but until recently, there was little evidence about whether they were effective in preventing homelessness.

A clever study of the Homeless Prevention Call Center in Chicago, which fields 75,000 call per year and links eligible callers to agencies that provide modest financial assistance, has now provided strong evidence (Evans et al., 2016). The researchers compared outcomes for eligible callers who asked for help on days when agencies had funds and on days when they had run out. Even without help only 2.1% of callers became homeless over the next 6 months; calling when funds were available reduced the likelihood of shelter entry by 76%.[15] The assistance was particularly effective for callers with incomes below 90% of the poverty line (the poorest half of the group). It had little effect for callers with higher incomes, because there was little risk to avert. As in the case of the demonstration of housing vouchers for welfare families and the HomeBase program in New York, prevention efforts had the greatest impact on homelessness for households with the greatest needs. The study could not examine whether additional households avoided eviction, which is enormously disruptive even when it does not lead to literal homelessness (Desmond, 2016), but the fact that the call center calls itself "Homelessness Prevention" suggests that it can reasonably be evaluated on its success in that arena. Authors of the paper argue that financial assistance is cost effective, if one considers both public costs (e.g., shelter and other

---

[13] When this became apparent, HUD dropped the name of the demonstration, Welfare to Work Vouchers, and changed the name of the study to Effects of Housing Vouchers on Welfare Families.

[14] Entering homelessness from housing that the family or individual owned has been extremely rare, even during the foreclosure crisis (Henry, Bishop, de Sousa, Shivji, & Watt, 2018).

[15] Referring back to Figure 5.1, which was based on a different study, these households would be in a low-risk group at the far left of the figure.

services) and private ones (e.g., mortality), although they point out that the evidence here is weaker. It would be more cost effective if limited to poorer households.

Rather than focusing on high-risk households, the Chicago program, like many other eviction prevention programs, cherry-picks people who are at relatively low risk: clients must be able to demonstrate that they will be self-sufficient after they receive the assistance and that financial assistance can resolve the crisis, as well as that the client faces imminent risk of eviction.[16] Households also had to be worthy (our designation, not the program's): their need for help had to stem from an eligible crisis such as job loss or medical emergency rather than enduring poverty. Since households who did not meet these criteria did not receive assistance, the study cannot tell us what would have happened had Chicago expanded eligibility criteria further. It does say that more efficient allocation of all funds to households below 90% of poverty would lead to greater impact, and more cost efficiency.

Even if eviction prevention programs were extended to households facing enduring poverty rather than a single crisis and remained equally effective for this group, they would not prevent the majority of homelessness. People who have a place from which they can be evicted are at lower risk than households that are doubled up in the same unit with another household because they cannot find or afford a place of their own (Greer, 2014; Greer et al., 2016; Shinn et al., 2013). In the Family Options Study of families who experienced homelessness across 12 sites in the United States, only 26% had lived in a place they rented or owned just prior to entering homeless shelters (Gubits et al., 2013, p. 53). Similarly, 26% said that having been evicted was a barrier to securing housing, but 35% cited never having been a leaseholder as a problem (Gubits et al., 2016, p. 2). The national tabulations of data from local communities show that 22% of families and 13% of individuals entered homelessness from their own rental housing in 2017. Many more entered homelessness from someone else's housing (62% of families, 48% of individuals) or in the case of people experiencing homelessness as individuals, from institutional settings (26%) (Henry, Bishop, et al., 2018). However, a prevention program does not need to solve all problems to be a valuable addition to the armamentarium against homelessness.

Community-Based Services: New York City's HomeBase

New York City's HomeBase program provides homelessness prevention services tailored to individual needs via agencies located in community districts throughout the city. (This is the program for which we described targeting efforts earlier in this chapter.) Services include case management

---

[16] The call center also accepts clients at risk of having their utilities shut off, but these clients were not included in the analysis.

and referrals for legal services, day care, domestic violence services, mental health and substance abuse services, education and vocational training, and job placement. Initially HomeBase was located only in community districts from which large numbers of people entered shelters, although it has since been expanded to serve the full city. Local agencies are intended to understand local needs, do appropriate outreach to high risk groups, and provide easy, comfortable access to services. Representatives from the City Department that administers welfare are on-site and can provide short-term assistance (dubbed "one-shots") and help households deal with public assistance, Medicaid, and SNAP (the Supplemental Nutrition Assistance Program also known as food stamps).

After households have exhausted other sources of benefits, HomeBase itself can provide some assistance for rent or rental arrears, furniture such as a crib or bunk bed, or work expenses and training. The program assists clients at risk of losing existing rental subsidies with resolving arrears and completing required recertifications of income and it mediates with landlords and others to help clients maintain their housing. When current living arrangements are no longer viable or when a household is returning to a community after a stay in a shelter or institution, HomeBase can provide relocation assistance and help to maintain stable housing (Fueller, 2016). In essence, HomeBase provides good old-fashioned social work services backed by modest financial resources to households at risk of homelessness.

It works, modestly. One evaluation took advantage of the fact that the program was rolled out across New York City over time, starting with the communities from which the most shelter residents came (Goodman et al., 2016). That is, initially the program targeted high-risk communities as much as high-risk individuals. A second evaluation was a randomized experiment (Rolston, Geyer, Locke, Metraux, & Treglia, 2013). Both studies examined families rather than single adults. The experimental evaluation showed that HomeBase prevented applicants from entering shelter, and the quasi-experiment showed that HomeBase reduced the rates of homelessness in the communities in which it operated. Both analyses suggest that the program is cost effective, based only on the costs of HomeBase and the costs of the shelter stays averted.

The analysis at the community level (community district or census tract) rather than the individual level is particularly important. Studies that show effects only for people who participate in a program could mean that the programs reallocate rather than prevent homelessness. For example, people given priority access to rental subsidies may be less likely to become homeless, but because subsidies are not available to all who are eligible, people pushed further down on the waitlist may be more likely. Thus policymakers should ideally evaluate prevention programs based on their total impact, not just the impact on service applicants or recipients. To our knowledge, the HomeBase quasi-experiment is the only study that does so. It showed the HomeBase reduced total levels of family homelessness by 5–11% in the communities where it operated (Goodman et al., 2016).[17] The study was less clear whether targeting communities at highest risk is critical.

Critical Time Intervention (CTI) for People Discharged from Psychiatric Hospitals

Chapter 3 showed that a structured, 9-month CTI led to reductions in repeat homelessness for currently homeless individuals with serious mental illnesses. That intervention—in which workers follow individuals from institutions to the community, help them to establish ties, and then transfer care—can also prevent homelessness for psychiatric patients who are at risk. Veterans released from psychiatric hospitals in eight sites after the CTI program was implemented also had more time housed over a 1-year follow-up period, less time in institutional placements, and lower levels of addiction severity and psychiatric problems on a standard self-report measure than veterans released from the same hospitals prior to the implementation (Kasprow & Rosenheck, 2007). The reduction in homelessness did not reach statistical significance in this study but did in a subsequent experiment involving 150 formerly hospitalized patients discharged from transitional living facilities on hospital grounds. Reductions in homelessness in the group that received the CTI, compared to a group that received usual care, were most pronounced toward the end of the longer 18-month follow-up period (Herman et al., 2011). The intervention also reduced rehospitalizations (Tomita & Herman, 2012).

Patients being released from psychiatric hospitals are a finite population, so a CTI could plausibly be offered to all who appear to be at risk of homelessness (because of prior homelessness or lack of stable housing plans at discharge). Services may be eligible for Medicaid funding, which would make the intervention scalable—that is, able to be scaled up to cover a large number of people (Byrne & Culhane, 2016). Whether this approach is useful for other populations is less clear. CTI has been recommended for people with mental illnesses being discharged from prisons or jails (Draine & Herman, 2007), but reports from a randomized trial have focused so far on risks for reincarceration rather than housing outcomes (Barrenger, Draine, Angell, & Herman, 2017).

Programs with Suggestive Evidence of Effectiveness

Universal Screening for Veterans

As one element in the full-court press to end homelessness among military veterans, the Veterans Health Administration (VHA) administers a two-item screen for

---

[17] The extent of reduction depended on whether the analysis was conducted at the level of the census tract or at the level of the community district.

current homelessness and imminent risk annually to every veteran who comes in for outpatient services. The Homeless Screening Clinical Reminder asks:

1. In the past 2 months, have you been living in stable housing that you own, rent, or stay in as part of a household?
2. Are you worried or concerned that in the next 2 months you may NOT have stable housing that you own, rent, or stay in as part of a household?

Among 4.3 million veterans who completed the screen in the first year, 0.8% said no to the first questions (screened positive for homelessness), and an additional 1.0% said yes to the second (screened positive for risk); both groups were offered additional services (Byrne et al., 2015, p. 686).

Overall, rates of homelessness on a single night among veterans were cut nearly in half between 2010 and 2018, with the number experiencing unsheltered homelessness cut by more than half (Henry, Mahathey, et al., 2018, p. 54).[18] The screening program presumably contributed to that success, but it is impossible to know how much. Cautions include the fact that only about three fifths of the veterans who screened positive requested services. Of those requesting services, only 71.5% of those who screened positive for homelessness and 65.1% of those who screened positive for risk got the requested services within 30 days. Nonetheless, 83.4% of veterans who initially screened positive for homelessness or risk and who responded to a reassessment 6–12 months later had resolved their housing instability (VA National Center on Homelessness Among Veterans, 2016). In the absence of a counterfactual, we classify the evidence as suggestive. It is not clear how many veterans would have resolved their housing instability without the help of any program.

Further research has identified profiles of veterans who do and do not resolve their housing instability (Byrne et al., 2015) and validated a further second-stage screening tool to assess level of risk in order to guide appropriate services (Montgomery, Fargo, Kane, & Culhane, 2014). This additional research promises to make the screening program more efficient at getting services to people who can benefit most.

Housing Subsidies with Supportive Services for People with Mental Illnesses

In Chapter 3, we examined the strong evidence that supportive housing, particularly housing using the Pathways Housing First approach, is successful in ending homelessness for people with long histories of both homelessness and serious

---

[18] The one-night count of veterans (both sheltered and unsheltered) decreased from 74,087 in 2010 to 37,878 in 2018. The one-night unsheltered count went from 30,650 to 14,566 over the same period (Henry, Mahathey, et al., 2018, p. 54). The decrease among veterans who used shelters at some point during the year was less dramatic, decreasing from 149,635 to 118,380 from 2009 to 2017 (Henry, Bishop, et al., 2018, pp. 5–3, 5–7).

mental illness. More circumstantial evidence suggests that this approach can also prevent homelessness: the rates of homelessness among people admitted to state psychiatric hospitals in Massachusetts declined from 8–10 to 2% during a decade (1993–2003) when the supply of housing with supportive services increased (Burt et al., 2007). It is always a bit dangerous to draw conclusions from two trend lines. Cell phone usage also increased over this period, but probably had little relationship to homelessness. Other changes in Massachusetts at the same time have plausible links to the decline in homelessness for this population—for example, the economic expansion and reduction in unemployment in the 1990s and the expansion, nationally, in the numbers of people receiving disability benefits (Social Security Administration, 2006). Efforts to rule out alternative explanations would make the evidence more convincing that supportive housing was key. Nonetheless, given the strong evidence that supportive housing ends homelessness for people with mental illnesses, it seems plausible that it could also prevent entry into that state. Because the proportion of people who experience serious and persistent mental illness is much smaller than the proportion who are poor, it seems reasonable to target all who desire it for supportive housing assistance.

Shallow, Permanent Subsidies

People in the housing world agree that a "deep" rental subsidy is one that holds housing costs to 30% of the recipient's income and is renewable as long as the recipient meets income and other requirements such as living in a unit that passes inspections and renewing the lease. The contrasting term "shallow" gets used in two ways: for less generous permanent subsidies and for temporary subsidies that may or may not be any less generous during the short time period when they are provided. The double meaning is unfortunate, because evidence from a study of shallow, permanent subsidies has sometimes been taken as support for temporary subsidies such as those provided by rapid re-housing programs.

Evidence for using permanent shallow subsidies for a program targeted to a very specific high-risk group comes from Project Independence, a program that provided a permanent fixed subsidy ($225 per month for a one bedroom in the late 1990s) with limited case management for people living with HIV or AIDS in Alameda County, California, across the Bay from San Francisco. Adults who had a lease and whose incomes were at or below 50% of area median were eligible. After 2 years, 96% of Project Independence program participants but only 10% of a comparison group were still independently housed in a rental unit (Dasinger & Speiglman, 2007). We count the evidence here as suggestive rather than solid for two reasons. First, the outcome was maintenance of an independent rental unit rather than homelessness. Second, the comparison group was made up of clients who, from a retrospective review of agency records, appeared to be eligible for the program. There may have been important differences between those that found their way into Project Independence and others who, although apparently eligible, did not. The Project Independence study raises the question of whether shallow, permanent (or at least long-term) subsidies work for other populations at immediate risk of falling into homelessness such as prisoners reentering society or youth aging out of foster care. We talk about other ways to design rental housing subsidies in Chapter 6.

Eviction Prevention: Legal Representation in Housing Courts

We classified financial assistance to prevent evictions as having solid evidence for preventing homelessness. Two other efforts at eviction prevention—legal representation in housing court and landlord–tenant mediation—have more suggestive evidence. Desmond (2016) describes how tenants who lack representation are overmatched in housing courts by landlords who have legal counsel. And providing legal counsel in housing court to tenants with incomes below poverty led to a reduction in eviction orders from 44% (for tenants without representation) to 10% in a randomized study in New York City—a reduction of 77% (Seron, Frankel, Ryzin, & Kovath, 2001).

Evidence that legal representation of poor tenants will reduce evictions is thus quite solid. The more tentative part of the argument is that reducing orders of eviction will reduce homelessness. It seems quite likely that it will, although less than might be supposed, based on the rigorous study of financial assistance to prevent evictions in Chicago. Recall that only 2.1% of callers to the Chicago eviction hotline at times when no help was available became homeless over the next 6 months (Evans et al., 2016). In the study of predictors of shelter entry among applicants for HomeBase prevention services, 55.3% of families who reported an eviction threat did not enter shelter over the next 3 years. For single adults, a verbal eviction threat was a risk factor for shelter entry, but legal eviction action was surprisingly associated with a lower rather than a higher hazard of entering shelter. This may be because legal evictions were a risk factor that HomeBase could address. The sample of people who were ineligible for HomeBase services (because they lived outside of the eligible community district) were slightly more likely to experience homelessness if they had a legal eviction order.

Eviction Prevention: Landlord–Tenant Mediation

Another approach to preventing eviction in order to prevent homelessness is mediation between landlords and tenants. The evidence here is weaker. (That does not necessarily mean the approach is less effective, simply that we do not know.) We do not credit evidence (frequently offered) that people who received such help were not evicted. Many might have avoided eviction without the help, as did 56% of New Yorkers who arrived at housing court without any legal representation (Seron et al., 2001). One program that targeted individuals with serious mental illnesses who were facing eviction in Western Massachusetts cut the proportion who became homeless by a third, relative to people who were waitlisted but did not receive services (Burt et al., 2007). If those on the waitlist were comparable to those who got services, this suggests that the program was effective, at least for this population. Such programs are relatively inexpensive and should be evaluated more rigorously. Again, it is likely that targeting services to poorer households would yield greater reductions in homelessness.

Programs That Might Be Effective

Many other programs have been proposed for preventing homelessness. Some of these may well have larger effects than those we have just surveyed; others may be useless—in most cases, the lack of research means that we simply do not know. We will focus on ideas that seem the most promising, starting with populations at the highest risk.

Extended Resources for Youth Leaving Foster Care

Youth who age out of foster care are at very high risk of homelessness. Middle-class families do not expect young people to suddenly become independent at age 18 and often, even after a period of housing in college dormitories (subsidized by their parents or college scholarships), many return home to reclaim their bedrooms until they can make it on their own. One in three young adults aged 18–34 lived in their parents' homes in 2015, more than in any other form of housing (Vespa, 2017). So it is hardly remarkable that former foster youth with fewer familial resources to draw on would become homeless at high rates and plausible that offering additional resources to these young people could help.

In the Midwest Evaluation of the Adult Functioning of Former Foster Youth, young people who had entered foster care before they turned 16 for a reason other than delinquency and were still in care at 17 were interviewed repeatedly over time. Between 31 and 46% had experienced an episode of homelessness by age 26, with the uncertainty depending on the assumption one makes about young adults who could not be found. Homelessness here included "not having a regular residence in which to sleep" (Dworsky et al., 2013, p. S319). About two thirds of the 732 youth were from Illinois, which was one of the first states to allow young people to stay in foster care until age 21; the others were from Wisconsin and Iowa, where foster care ended at 18. The Illinois youth were less likely to become homeless before the first follow-up wave of data collection at age 19 but had caught up with their counterparts in other states by age 23, so extended foster care delayed but did not ultimately prevent homelessness. A variety of initiatives might enhance the prevention efforts: longer intervention or extended housing subsidies after youth leave care, second and third chances for youth who leave foster care and then want to return before turning 21, and more assistance to help youth find and maintain stable housing and employment could all help. Additional states have now taken advantage of the Federal partial reimbursement for extending foster care, but more research is needed to understand what additional programs might help young people to avoid homelessness. Although rates of homelessness among former foster youth are so high that targeting the entire population of youth who age out of care makes sense, the Midwest study also showed that youth who had been physically abused, those with mental health problems, those who had run away from foster care, and those with multiple placements were at even higher risk, so further targeting for additional assistance is possible (Dworsky et al., 2013).

Help for People Reentering the Community from Jails and Prisons

Reentering the community was a potent predictor of shelter use for both adults and families in the HomeBase risk models described earlier (Greer et al., 2016; Shinn et al., 2013), and past incarceration was a predictor of persistent homelessness in Los Angeles (Toros et al., 2019). A study that matched shelter records with correctional records found that 11.4% of a cohort of more than 48,000 people released from state prisons to New York City entered a city homeless shelter within 2 years, the majority (6.2%) within the first month after release. (Others may have been homeless on the streets or in other jurisdictions.) A similar proportion (8.5%) of a cohort discharged from state psychiatric hospitals to New York City used city shelters within 2 years (Metraux & Culhane, 2004).

Getting at the same issue from the other side, a quarter of single adults who were not already homeless at the time they entered emergency shelters across the nation in 2017 reported that their previous residence was an institution, most commonly a correctional facility (Henry, Bishop, et al., 2018). An earlier study in New York City with more detail matched data from more than 9,000 single adults who used emergency shelters for the first time in 1997 with data from city and state corrections and city, state, and Veterans Administration hospitals. More than a quarter (28.2%) had been released from one of the institutions in the 90 days prior to entering shelters for the first time, including 18.2% who had used hospitals and 11.3% who had been incarcerated. A few stayed in both types of facility (Metraux, Byrne, & Culhane, 2010). Among all who were sheltered on a specific night (not just first-time shelter users), 23.1% had been incarcerated in the prior 2 years, 17.0% in jail and 7.7% in prison (again with a handful in both). Both institutions, but especially prisons, discharged inmates directly to shelters: among those with a history of incarceration, the gap between incarceration and shelter was a day or less in 37.5% of cases for prison and 22.6% of cases for jails (Metraux & Culhane, 2006). Shelter residents with a history of jail were more likely than other shelter residents to have another subsequent shelter stay; those with a history of prison were less likely. The sequential pattern of shelter and jail use—and possible other unmeasured stops in psychiatric hospitals or detox on what Hopper, Jost, Hay, Welber, and Haugland (1997) dubbed the "institutional circuit"—may point to a need for a more intensive intervention.

A parallel study of 1,426 homeless and marginally housed individuals in San Francisco found that 23.1% had a lifetime history of incarceration in prisons (not including jails). Although all respondents had high health needs, those who had been incarcerated were even more likely than others to have lifetime histories of self-reported poor health, substance abuse, and psychiatric hospitalization, and higher rates of HIV infection by blood test (Kushel, Hahn, Evans, Bangsberg, & Moss, 2005).

Prisoners with serious mental illnesses with or without co-occurring substance use disorders probably need substantial help to reintegrate into the community. Some such individuals would probably benefit from permanent supportive housing.

The CTI, included earlier as a strategy with solid evidence of effectiveness for people leaving psychiatric hospitals, seems likely to be useful for people who travel the institutional circuit but is likely to be overkill for others who may need only brief assistance until they can get on their feet. Curtis, an inmate at Valdosta State Prison in Georgia, was enterprising enough to find one of us (Beth) on the internet and write to say that he lost his home and his money when he entered prison and had no family to turn to. "In three more months I'll be leaving prison with $25 and a bus ticket after serving 4½ years incarcerated." Curtis was confident that his job skills would allow him to secure employment (although as Chapter 2 shows, stigma against former inmates makes finding jobs difficult for many). Nonetheless he sought help finding temporary housing for a few weeks "in a clean environment" until he could get a paycheck or two. Others probably need both bridge housing and help finding employment in order to avoid both homelessness and recidivism. Former prisoners are not the most popular targets for taxpayer largesse. But it is certainly in the public interest for them to become taxpayers themselves rather than returning to jail or prison or becoming homeless. If outright subsidies are unpopular, allowing prisoners to earn and save money while incarcerated or structuring assistance as a loan could reduce homelessness. More research is needed.

Focusing on reentry for prisoners with co-occurring disorders, Osher, Steadman, and Barr (2003) put forward the APIC Model, which stands for Assess needs, Plan, Identify community and correctional programs to meet those needs, and Coordinate. APIC goes far beyond "discharge planning," which can mean little more than giving the released inmate the address of the local homeless shelter. It involves "an ongoing process of communicating, goal setting, assigning accountability, evaluating, and reforming" across correctional and community systems (p. 82). Involvement of the inmate is critical, both in assessing his or her own needs and also in assuring that the inmate does not perceive transition planning as ongoing punishment or restriction on freedom after release. Particularly in jails, where incarceration is often short, planning should begin as soon as a behavioral health issue is identified. According to the model, the plan should address practical issues such as housing, income, food and clothing, transportation, and child care (for inmates who will have responsibility for children), as well as treatment. We are not aware of research showing that this enhanced form of planning for discharge reduces homelessness, but the linkage is plausible.

Two particular challenges for individuals with mental health or other disabilities upon leaving prisons or jails are continuity of medication and disability benefits. Disruptions in medication, whether for psychiatric disabilities, HIV infection, or other pressing medical needs are common on both entry to and exit from prisons and jails (Brinkley-Rubinstein & Turner, 2013). Medication disruptions can lead to health and mental health crises, and in the case of diseases like HIV, development of resistant viral strains that threaten the health of not only the patient, but also the community. Prisoners should be released with an adequate supply of medications and a clear path (often both a prescription and Medicaid benefits) to renew them.

Disability benefits cease when a person is incarcerated, and individuals do not automatically regain eligibility upon release (Social Security Administration, 2015). Some jails and prisons have agreements with the Social Security Administration that facilitate swift reactivation of benefits when a disabled prisoner is released (Osher et al., 2003).

Assembling the required documentation and filing for SSI/SSDI (Supplemental Security Income/Social Security Disability Insurance) benefits can be a difficult process for people who experience homelessness, including people who have been incarcerated. The SSI/SSDI Outreach Access and Recovery (SOAR) project, which is designed to improve initial access to benefits for people who have qualifying disabilities and are at risk of homelessness, dramatically increases the rate at which eligible individuals receive the disability benefits to which they are entitled (Dennis, Lassiter, Connelly, & Lupfer, 2011). A few pioneering communities, including Nashville, have brought SOAR program into jails to help disabled inmates establish income quickly upon release (McCauley & Samples, 2017). Benefits by themselves do not erase barriers to reentry for mentally ill inmates, but they at least provide an income stream that may help to reduce recidivism. We are not aware of evidence that connecting inmates to benefits prevents homelessness, but it seems plausible that it would help.

Programs for youth graduating from foster care, patients leaving psychiatric hospitals, and prisoners leaving carceral institutions are all examples of what Canadian researchers Gaetz, Dej, Richter, and Redman (2016) call "institutional transition support." They see this support as the responsibility of the institutions rather than the receiving communities, as part of a broad-based strategy to end homelessness. Similarly Culhane, Metraux, and Byrne (2011) suggest that substance abuse and criminal justice agencies that discharge clients to communities should take responsibility for temporary housing placements and child welfare agencies should take responsibility for independent living plans and housing supports extending into adulthood for youth leaving their care. And Cunningham et al. (2015) suggest that having "mainstream" agencies provide prevention services for the clients they discharge would be a fruitful area to research. Homelessness researchers and advocates sing a similar tune in wanting this shift in responsibility for homelessness prevention—administrators of the mainstream programs have not yet joined the chorus.

VA-Like Screening for Other Populations at Risk

Another approach to prevention builds on the Veterans Administration's laudable effort to take responsibility for its own population by screening medical patients for risk of homelessness. Researchers in Boston are integrating similar screening into primary care (Sheward et al., 2019). Screening for risk for homelessness could be instituted in other settings, for example, emergency rooms—a possibility under study in New York City (Doran et al., 2019), maternity wards (recall that infants are at high risk of homelessness), or social security offices. In hospitals, perhaps screening should be limited to patients who are uninsured or insured by Medicaid. Of course, there is no point in screening unless preventive services (perhaps akin to those provided by New York City's HomeBase program) are available to those found to be at risk. Research would need both to verify that the screening instrument identified people at reasonably high risk and that the preventive services offered reduced that risk. The difference between these screening efforts and those described earlier in Los Angeles and New York is that the screens (other than the Emergency Room screen under study) are using questions that seem intuitively relevant, without actually examining how well they predict. When relatively low-risk populations are seeking health care or other services, quick screens that are focused on their subjective sense of risk make a lot of sense. The practicality of these intuitive screens would be less clear for applicants for homelessness prevention services, where receipt of desired services might hinge on the answers.

Flexible Cash Grants to Low-Income Households

For many decades, cash grants have been provided to families experiencing a housing crisis, often paid for by the welfare system. With the growth of family homelessness, such programs may be characterized as homelessness prevention. Massachusetts describes its Residential Assistance for Families in Transition (RAFT) program as an alternative to a stay in an emergency shelter, particularly salient because Massachusetts has a "right to shelter" policy and, therefore, a very expensive shelter system (Rog, Henderson, Greer, Kulbicki, & Weinreb, 2017). RAFT provides families with incomes below 50% of area median with up to $4,000 in cash assistance to retain housing, obtain new housing, or otherwise avoid homelessness. The most common use of funds has been to pay rental arrears. A review of the program claims that RAFT saved Massachusetts $31 million in 2017, based on the assumption that all 945 families served who had incomes less than 30% of area median would have gone to shelter and would have stayed in shelter for an average of 351 days (Metro Housing Boston, 2017). Maybe so, but the assumptions that went into this calculation are not plausible. No information is provided about whether any of the families used shelters despite the payments, and the assumption that all would have used shelters in the absence of the payments clearly is wrong.[19] (Recall that only about 13% of applicants for HomeBase prevention services used shelters, and HomeBase did not succeed in averting shelter entry for all.) So our conclusion is that programs such as RAFT may be promising, but we do not yet know how well they are targeted or how effective they are.

Bringing Resources to High-Risk Neighborhoods

In Chapter 2 on the causes of homelessness, we reviewed evidence that the concentrations of poverty found in some city neighborhoods put residents of those neighborhoods at risk of homelessness beyond the risks already associated with their individual vulnerabilities. It may make sense to bring resources into such neighborhoods as an explicit effort to prevent homelessness. New York City's HomeBase is based in neighborhoods (and was originally targeted only to high-risk neighborhoods), but it provides largely individual-level services rather than services to improve neighborhood conditions. In a neighborhood-focused strategy, cities might take legal action against landlords with serious housing code violations (perhaps supported by grants to help them make repairs), bring in banking or credit unions to replace payday lenders and check cashing operations that charge exorbitant fees, and provide preferential access to subsidized child care for neighborhood residents trying to work. Some neighborhoods also need better access to public transit and to health care, especially preventive care. No evidence exists that these broadly focused neighborhood interventions would reduce homelessness, but they deserve a test. Individual and neighborhood-level strategies can be combined, and it would be useful to examine how these efforts might work in tandem.

Integrating Homelessness and Antipoverty Service Systems

A related strategy targeted at local service systems is to integrate the various systems that an individual or family on the verge of homelessness might need. New York's HomeBase program could be thought of as a step in that direction, in that workers seek to connect families with all the services appropriate to their situation. Cities can also integrate the services instead of hiring navigators like HomeBase workers to coordinate them for clients. The evaluation of prevention programs as part of the HPRP concludes that "the case study evidence strongly suggests that more integrated service systems serve clients better when clients

---

[19] The assumptions here seem more in line with the intuitive (but incorrect) model of risk in Figure 5.2 than a model based on data, like Figure 5.1. The review claims that the families served by RAFT who would not have been eligible to enter shelters because they had incomes between 30 and 50% of area median income would have been at risk of experiencing unsheltered homelessness, given the high cost of housing in the Boston metropolitan area, an even less plausible assumption given the rarity of unsheltered homelessness, especially among families.

need help from more than one system" (Cunningham et al., 2015). Services such as housing, employment, budgeting, credit repair, and child care can be offered in coordinated fashion to individuals or families at risk. Recall, however, that the evaluation focused on what communities did, rather than what worked. Service integration makes logical sense, but we have not yet seen rigorous evidence that it reduces homelessness.

Prevention Programs and Cost Benefit Analyses

If the services for people at risk of homelessness are relatively inexpensive, they do not need to be narrowly targeted to be cost effective. Further, programs do not have to be perfectly effective to be worth doing, even if that assessment is based solely on economic considerations. Families who got no special offer of service in the 12 sites of the Family Options study racked up housing and homeless service costs averaging $41,000 over the 3 years after they became homeless. At that rate, a $2,000 prevention program would be cost effective even if it prevented only one family in 20 from becoming homeless, whether because the program was not well-targeted or because it was only modestly effective.

A report on eviction prevention by New York City's Independent Budget Office (2014) highlights an important problem plaguing cost–benefit arguments, sometimes called the "wrong pockets" problem. When costs and benefits accrue to different payers, coordination can be difficult. In the New York eviction prevention case, local government would assume most of the costs, but state and federal governments that contribute to shelter costs would share the benefits. In the case of providing transitional help for people leaving prisons or jails, the costs are incurred by the criminal justice system, and the savings accrue to the homeless services system, although criminal justice might also benefit if interventions reduced recidivism.

Even where the "pockets" can be aligned, total benefits to the public purse might not exceed total costs. Cost–benefit analysis is important, because it can identify more and less efficient ways to attain particular benefits. It is also far from an exact science. Conclusions depend heavily on the assumptions that go into the analyses and to the scope of costs and benefits under consideration. On the other hand, society pays for a variety of things that "promote the general welfare" whether or not they are supported by cost–benefit analyses. We treat medical conditions (through a combination of public and private payments for different groups) not to save money but to alleviate human suffering. We believe homelessness should fall in this category (Kertesz, Baggett, O'Connell, Buck, & Kushel, 2016).

Progressive Engagement

What all the strategies we have surveyed so far have in common is that they identify people who are high risk of homelessness and offer them special services to avoid that state. Alternatives to such targeted interventions can be thought of in two ways. One, the focus of the final chapter, is to address the societal conditions that generate homelessness. The other, called progressive engagement, provides inexpensive services to anyone who appears at risk of becoming homeless. At the outset, providers make no attempt to target the services to those at highest risk. If light-touch services do not resolve the problem, more intensive services follow. For example, households could be offered minimal services such as one-shot rental assistance, legal aid, and help to avoid utility shutoffs, and these inexpensive services could be offered widely. If those prove insufficient, services would move to housing stabilization in an effort to divert people from shelter. Interventions might at that point include mediation with landlords or the household with which the people on the verge of homelessness are living or help with relocation. Those who nonetheless fall through the shelter door (we prefer the image of a trapdoor to a stately horizontal passage), should be offered more help to quickly regain housing—help in accessing housing, move-in costs, or crisis intervention.

Proponents of progressive engagement Culhane et al. (2011) argue that the focus of the homeless services system should shrink, temporally, to the points just before and just after the shelter door. Programs to prevent people from becoming homeless should address households "in the shadow of pending evictions, institutional discharges and strained or untenable co-housing situations" (p. 299). Efforts at housing stabilization would span the period just before and just after households become literally homeless, so that secondary prevention (nipping problems in the bud) essentially merges with primary prevention (preventing problems before they occur). More resource-intensive approaches would be reserved for situations where minimal help did not resolve the problem. Core ideas here include involving "mainstream" services (that is, those offered to all members of a community, not just those who experience homelessness), focusing the homeless services system on housing rather than on serving people who are homeless, offering relatively inexpensive services up front to a large group of people, and reserving expensive services for households for whom more modest interventions prove insufficient.

In the progressive engagement approach, people are identified for greater help not by statistical models, but by failing when offered less. These are essentially the ideas that motivated the rapid re-housing approach described in Chapter 4, where we described concerns about people declining help they thought insufficient and feeling that they were being set up for failure. We have fewer concerns for services provided in front of the shelter door or when people are about to walk out of wherever they are now and go sleep in a bus terminal. Many people on the verge of homelessness are desperate to avoid that state, and a little assistance may help them overcome a crisis or negotiate arrangements that allow them to retain housing. We have not seen rigorous evidence of how this approach works in practice.

Summary

We believe prevention programs have great promise for reducing homelessness, but more research is needed to fulfill that promise. In the case of groups at high risk (people leaving institutions, youth exiting foster care), the central challenge is determining what works. (The CTI for people leaving psychiatric institutions is one proven program.) In the case of programs that have been shown to work such as New York City's HomeBase program of social services with modest financial help or Chicago's financial help to avoid eviction, the challenge is making the programs more efficient and more effective by targeting them to people at high risk. Research on screening models shows that this can be done—not perfectly, but well enough to make programs more cost effective and enable them to extend their reach. (Both the New York and Chicago programs were cost-effective even before additional targeting.)

Programs that have been shown to end homelessness for people who experience it by subsidizing rent (for families) and offering subsidies plus supportive services (for people experiencing mental illness) also work to prevent homelessness. In the case of the relatively small group of people who have serious mental illnesses, the programs could be adopted widely. We discuss wide adoption of housing subsidies for all people who have poverty-level incomes in Chapter 6, on changing social conditions that generate homelessness.

Many other programs might work—but no one has studied them with sufficient rigor so that we know for sure. These include ongoing shallow rental subsidies for various groups in need, legal representation or landlord–tenant or family mediation to prevent eviction, flexible cash grants for low-income households, bringing services to high-risk neighborhoods, and integrating homelessness and antipoverty services. Additional screening programs, both derived from data about risk factors and based on people's self-assessments of risk, should be tested, with services provided.

Modest, low-cost programs are likely to have the most impact when given to people at highest risk, which also means that they will have high failure rates. But programs do not have to work perfectly or to be applicable to all populations to make a serious dent in rates of homelessness. More research here could pay big dividends.

6

Changing Societal Conditions that Generate Homelessness

Throughout this book, we have argued that homelessness is fundamentally the result of broader social policies that put housing costs out of reach for many families and individuals. Many people with incomes below the poverty level are vulnerable, insecure in their housing, and without the resources to cope with a crisis. With so many at risk, trigger events—for example, losing a job, being evicted, or fighting with someone who has provided them with place to live—will send some people into emergency shelters or onto the street. We now turn from policies that prevent homelessness for people at immediate risk of entering a shelter or staying on the street (the topic of Chapter 5) to broader social policies that would keep people from getting to that point.

Homelessness at its core is a problem of deep poverty, coupled with the high costs of housing in late twentieth and early twenty-first century America. Thus any strategy that increases incomes for people on the lowest rungs of the economic ladder or reduces their housing costs will reduce homelessness. Strategies that reduce income volatility will lead to fewer crises that pitch some people into homelessness. Strategies to reduce discrimination in housing, employment, incarceration, and the accumulation of assets will address the disproportionate share of the burden borne by racial minorities and people with mental illness.

Housing

Because the fundamental cause of homelessness is the crisis of housing affordability that emerged in the late 1970s and was the precursor to "modern" homelessness, we turn first to strategies that make housing more affordable for deeply poor families and individuals. We then consider the income side—how to reduce or eliminate deep poverty by increasing wages and strengthening income supports.

In the Midst of Plenty: Homelessness and What to Do About It, First Edition.
Marybeth Shinn and Jill Khadduri.
© 2020 Marybeth Shinn and Jill Khadduri. Published 2020 by John Wiley & Sons Ltd.

Expanding Housing Vouchers

The evidence that deep housing subsidies prevent homelessness is powerful. The main such program is Housing Choice Vouchers. That is the program that produced, through a randomized experiment, the evidence that deep, open-ended housing subsidies prevent poor families from becoming homeless (Wood, Turnham, & Mills, 2008), and it is the program that ended homelessness for families who experienced it in another randomized experiment (Gubits et al., 2018). For the past two decades, the voucher program has grown very little, from about 2 million families and individuals using vouchers to rent private market housing in the early 2000s to about 2.2 million in 2018. Because many more households are eligible for deep housing subsidies, the voucher program uses a waiting list. So do the other types of deep subsidies (agency-owned public housing and assisted housing projects with private owners) that, together with the voucher program, serve about five million households. Lengths of waiting lists vary by community, but typically a family or individual must wait at least 18 months to come to the top of the voucher waitlist. Analysis of a recent survey of 3,210 public housing authorities to determine how they manage their voucher waiting lists found that, for a quarter of those that had not closed their waiting list, it would take at least 7.8 years to serve all households currently on the list; for another quarter, it would take no more than 1.5 years, and half of the public housing authorities were somewhere in between (Dunton, Henry, Kean, & Khadduri, 2014, p. 27). In 2015–2016, the National Low Income Housing Coalition (NLIHC) conducted a survey of 20 public housing authorities[1] and found that the median wait time (for both open and closed waiting lists) was 1.5 years. Wait times are much longer in the large urban areas in which large numbers of people experience homelessness. Larger public housing authorities (those with more than 5,000 voucher and public units combined) had a median wait time of 3 years (National Low Income Housing Coalition, 2016).[2]

As an intervention to prevent large numbers of people from approaching the point where they become vulnerable to falling into homelessness, vouchers are scalable: serving additional households requires only additional resources.

Only about a quarter of renters who qualify for deep housing subsidies under current rules receive them (Collinson, Ellen, & Ludwig, 2015). However, that does not mean that we need to provide deep housing subsidies to 20 million new households. First, some of those who technically qualify for housing assistance would receive either no assistance or a very small amount, because paying 30% of

---

[1] Sometimes called public housing agencies. These local entities manage the Housing Choice Voucher program and often also own public housing developments.

[2] Waiting times are somewhat shorter for public housing.

their income (under the voucher subsidy formula) would pay the entire private market rent the program is permitted to subsidize.[3]

Second, vouchers and the other deep housing subsidies can be reserved for people with extremely low incomes (less than 30% of the area median or the federal poverty level).[4] To the extent that housing authorities continue to transform public housing projects so that they have a broader mix of incomes, this can (and should) be accompanied by replacing public housing units no longer occupied by the poorest households with vouchers.

Finally, some portion of people who are poor have not yet started their first job as an adult or have suffered a temporary reverse (job loss, family break-up, a medical crisis) and do not expect to be poor for a long enough period of time to apply for housing assistance. An analysis of data from the Census Bureau's Survey of Income and Program Participation showed that severe rent burdens, a metric the U.S. Department of Housing and Urban Development (HUD) uses to track housing needs, do not necessarily last year after year for particular households. Of households who had no housing assistance and paid more than half their income for rent in 2001, 45% no longer had severe rent burdens in 2002, in about half the cases because their incomes had increased (U.S. Department of Housing and Urban Development, 2007).[5]

Finally, not all people who apply for housing assistance end up using it. In some cases this is because their current units do not pass inspections, and a move does not seem worth the trouble. Families recruited in homeless shelters as part of the Family Options Study used Housing Choice Vouchers at much higher rates than is typical for families on voucher waiting lists (Solari & Khadduri, 2017), presumably because their needs were more acute. Nevertheless, the process of locating a unit can be daunting, as shown in the study of discrimination against voucher holders described in Chapter 3. Authors of that study suggested several policies that would help: outlawing landlord discrimination on the basis of source of income,[6] extending the time permitted for a search from 60 days to 120 days, and offering assistance in the housing search (Cunningham et al., 2018). Some public housing authorities have made efforts to help families through the process, but generally through recruiting additional landlords to be part of the Housing

---

[3] The same logic applies to public housing and privately owned Section 8 projects: 30% of a household's income would be more than the housing is worth, and the household could do better elsewhere.

[4] In many parts of the U.S., 30% of area median income is roughly the equivalent of the federal poverty level. In areas where it is lower, the HUD definition of extremely low income is the same as the federal poverty level, which in 2018 was $12,140 for a single person and $20,780 for a family of three (U.S. Department of Health and Human Services, 2019).

[5] The next most common reasons were that their rent went down or that they now were living in assisted housing.

[6] Such laws have been shown to improve the rate at which households succeed in using vouchers (Bell, Sard, & Koepnick, 2018; Finkel & Buron, 2001). Bell et al. (2018) suggest education and enforcement mechanisms to make laws more effective.

Choice Voucher program rather than providing direct help to locate housing to particular families and individuals.[7] In some communities, improvements in management to assure that public housing authorities pay rent on time and conduct housing inspections promptly might induce more landlords to participate (Cunningham et al., 2018).

How many vouchers would be needed to make them available to all households with incomes below 30% of the area median? One of us (Jill) produced, with colleagues,[8] estimates for the Housing Commission of the Bipartisan Policy Center that started with the 11.1 million renters shown by the American Housing Survey (AHS) to have incomes below 30% of the area median[9] and used participation rates in the Supplemental Nutrition Assistance Program (SNAP) (food stamps) to estimate that 8.9 million of these households would apply for rental housing assistance. We then applied an estimate of the rate at which those found eligible for housing assistance would actually use the assistance, which unlike SNAP requires considerably more action on the part of the household (people found eligible for SNAP receive an electronic debit card they take to a grocery store). Not all households issued a housing voucher try to rent a unit and not all who do find an eligible unit and a willing landlord. Some households offered a unit in a public or assisted housing project turn it down. The result was an estimate of 6.7 million households with extremely low incomes who need and would use housing assistance.[10] But 3.6 million households with incomes below 30% of the area median already receive assistance, leaving a gap of only 3.1 million households. Part of that gap would be filled over time, as households with incomes above 30% of area media moved out of their assisted housing projects or gave up their vouchers through natural turnover, part of the Bipartisan Policy Center's proposal. That would leave a gap of only 2.9 million new subsidies that would be needed by 2023, a policy goal the Bipartisan Policy Center deemed plausible (Bipartisan Policy Center, 2013, 2015a, 2015b). The cost estimate of this expansion of housing assistance was $30.8 billion a year when fully phased in, less than 1% of the $3.7 trillion that the U.S. federal government spent directly[11] in the year the Bipartisan Policy Center made the recommendation (Bipartisan Policy Center, 2015a; U.S. Office of Management and Budget, 2019).

---

[7] When individualized help in finding housing has been provided, it generally has been by "mobility" programs that, in response to fair housing settlements, help families find housing in neighborhoods without concentrations of poor people and minorities. A court-ordered settlement often provides the funding for these programs (Solari & Khadduri, 2017). In the 2019 appropriations bill, the U.S. Congress enacted a new housing mobility demonstration, with some incremental vouchers and funding for mobility support services and regional agreements to facilitate using vouchers across jurisdictional lines.

[8] Larry Buron, Bulbul Kaul, and Jeff Lubell.

[9] This is a lower income limit than currently used.

[10] We used a "success rate" of 70% for vouchers and 95% for public housing and assisted housing projects and the regionally varying subsidy standard used for the voucher program.

[11] This does not include revenue foregone from "tax expenditures."

Vouchers are more scalable than the other forms of deep housing subsidy, because they use housing that already exists in the private market and because it costs less to subsidize a household with a voucher than to build new housing for poor people (Olsen, 2010; U.S. General Accounting Office, 2001; Weicher, 2012). Scalability does not mean it is feasible to move immediately from 2.2 million vouchers to 5 million vouchers, since the program is actively administered by public housing authorities that would have to hire, train, and deploy additional staff to take additional households through the process of using a voucher and finding housing that meets, or can be brought up to, HUD's quality standards.[12]

Nor is it necessary for significant strides toward ending homelessness to reach the Bipartisan Policy Center's goal of making the program available to everyone who would apply and use the program if it were available to all households with incomes below 30% of the area median. What is needed is a return to the time when 300,000 "incremental" units with deep housing subsidies were funded each year and then added to the permanent size of the programs (Weicher, 2012) along with an allocation formula for the new vouchers that tilts heavily toward the places with the greatest shortages of affordable housing. With an increment of 300,000 vouchers per year, the program might never reach an "open enrollment" status without waiting lists, but wait times would get much shorter, and housing authorities would be willing to put people at risk of homelessness high on the list. Strengthening the income side of the safety net (recommended later in this chapter) would slow the growth in the number of renters with extremely low incomes and make wait lists for vouchers even shorter. What it takes is the political will to strengthen the income side of safety net and return to the growth in deep rent subsidies last seen in the late 1970s.

Less Expensive Housing Subsidies for Poor Renters

Since the beginning of the program in the 1970s, a voucher has always added more to a family's resources than food stamps or welfare … when the family was fortunate enough to have a voucher. The per unit costs of a voucher might be reduced somewhat while still keeping the housing subsidy large enough to protect against homelessness.

---

[12] Most housing occupied by poor renters either meets the quality standard or has deficiencies HUD deems "moderate" and could be brought up to standard fairly easily. HUD classifies poor households as having worst case housing needs if they pay more than 50% of their income for rent and utilities or have housing deemed severely inadequate. Of households so classified, 95.6% have only severe rent burdens rather than severely inadequate housing (Watson, Steffan, Martin, & Vandenbroucke, 2017).

The subsidy provided by the Housing Choice Voucher program is based on a payment standard keyed to local rents minus 30% of the household's income.[13] The level of the payment standard is essentially arbitrary and set by a political negotiation. When first established, it was somewhat above the middle of market rents across each metropolitan area or group of nonmetropolitan counties. The standard was reduced in the 1980s to yield rents at about the middle of the market.[14] The modest reductions of the 1980s had little discernable effect on the program's outcomes—for example, on what percentage of families trying to use vouchers were able to use them. This observation is not based on rigorous evidence; because the reductions in the subsidy standard were made everywhere at once, it was not possible to compare places where the standard was reduced with places where it was not. However, a recent study by Collinson and Ganong (2018) suggests that, when it comes to voucher subsidy standards, higher is not necessarily better. They estimate that, when HUD adjusted the subsidy standard upward in 2005 to correct for some technical errors, voucher users did not, on average, rent better units. Instead, much of the increase in the maximum allowable subsidy was captured by landlords in the form of higher rents. They use a second "natural experiment," an increase in the subsidy standard permitted in some metropolitan areas in 2001, and come to the same conclusion.

Adjusting the subsidy standard is a better way to control program costs than increasing the percentage of income households are expected to pay, because that percentage can be thought of as a "rent tax" on income. Currently, for every additional dollar of income, voucher users pays 30 cents more as their share of the rent, already a very high marginal tax rate that can deter efforts to increase earnings. Reducing the subsidy standard makes the voucher less valuable, dollar-for-dollar, for households at all income levels.[15]

Edgar Olsen has proposed repeatedly that the voucher subsidy be reduced substantially in order to make a program without a waiting list feasible. He argues that smaller but more widespread rent subsidies would lead to substantial reductions in homelessness and free the homeless services system to focus on very short-term emergency assistance and on helping people experiencing homelessness to use the vouchers to which they would have access (Olsen, 2010). Olsen acknowledges that the size of the reduction matters—that there is some level of reduction below which households with poverty-level incomes would not be able to participate in the voucher program. In theory, housing markets would adjust

---

[13] Technically the payment standard is pegged to Fair Market Rents published by HUD, with some discretion by the public housing authority to set the standard a bit higher or lower. Program rules require some adjustments to the income on which 30% is based.

[14] Rents originally were set at the 50th percentile of local private market rents, but only units with recent movers and in standard condition were included. Jill participated in internal analysis at HUD that concluded that rents at the 40th percentile (with similar exclusions) would be at about the middle of the market.

[15] Another way to reduce the value of a voucher is to increase tenant payments—for example, to 35% of income, a bad idea because it would increase the "rent tax."

to a lower subsidy level by creating housing units at rents that could be reached by the smaller subsidy. We think that unlikely, since there is a floor on the cost of operating rental housing. We discuss approaches to lowering that floor via regulatory changes that permit very small houses or more multiple occupant housing (including subdivision of existing structures) later in the chapter. However, we don't really know the extent to which regulatory changes would reduce the costs of rental housing or what the optimal level of the voucher subsidy is. A few public housing authorities that are permitted to operate outside many statutory and regulatory constraints are experimenting with "thinning the soup."[16]

Reducing the subsidy level for the current voucher program also faces a timing challenge—unless done in connection with an expansion of the program that has sufficient political support, it is likely simply to result in thinner subsidies for the current 2.2 million households.

A change to the design of the voucher program currently under way might have the effect of reducing program costs. For a small but expanding number of metropolitan areas, the HUD estimates to which the subsidy standard is pegged are now set at the level of zip codes rather than for the metropolitan area as a whole. The purpose is to permit more use of vouchers in the relatively higher cost portions of metropolitan areas, given research evidence that neighborhood quality has an effect on the life trajectories of children (Chetty & Hendren, 2018). However, since many voucher users are likely to continue to live in lower-cost neighborhoods, the new policy could create lower per unit program costs overall. Early evaluation findings suggest that may be the case, but it is too early to tell (Dastrup, Finkel, Burnett, & de Sousa, 2018).[17]

Deeper Targeting of Rent Subsidies

Targeting existing vouchers exclusively to households with poverty-level incomes (30% of area median income)[18] or even to households in deep poverty such as those below 15% of area median income[19] could yield a substantial reduction in

---

[16] "Thinning the soup" is how the Tacoma, WA housing authority describes its approach. For any particular household, a lower payment standard might mean renting a less expensive unit or might mean renting the same unit and paying more than 30% of income, which is permitted by voucher program rules, up to a point.

[17] The study by Collinson and Ganong (2018) that estimated the effect of across-the-board changes in the voucher subsidy standard also examined the effect of zip code-level Fair Market Rents in Dallas, the first metropolitan area in which this policy change was implemented, and concluded that it encouraged voucher users to rent housing in better neighborhoods and was cost-neutral.

[18] Or the federal poverty level, when 30% of the income level in the area is lower than the poverty level.

[19] As noted in earlier chapters, households in deep poverty have incomes below half the federal poverty level. For areas where 15% of area median income is lower than half the poverty level, the definition could be the higher of 15% of area median income or deep poverty, in parallel to the current definition of extremely low income.

homelessness. Offering vouchers to all families in deep poverty rather than to those already in shelter would avoid the problem of perverse incentives discussed in Chapter 3: entering a shelter in order to get a housing voucher (Khadduri, 2008).

Current rules require 75% of vouchers and 40% of public housing units and units in privately owned deep subsidy projects to be reserved for households with incomes below 30% of area median or the federal poverty level. In reality, there is no difference among the programs—in all three types of assistance, about three quarters of households have incomes that are at least that low (U.S. Department of Housing and Urban Development, 2018b). Income mixing in public and assisted housing has always been more aspirational than real—found in only a few projects and not very effective in creating social interaction among poor and non-poor households (Chaskin & Joseph, 2015; Khadduri & Martin, 1997). As part of its strategy for extending housing assistance to all renters with incomes below 30% of median, the Bipartisan Policy Center proposed limiting all new occupants of public housing and assisted housing projects to households with incomes this low (Bipartisan Policy Center, 2013).

Temporary Rent Subsidies

Another approach to strengthening the housing aspect of the safety net would be to offer subsidies at the current subsidy standard but available to a particular household for a limited time, so that other households could take their place when the subsidy ends. Subsidies could be phased out rather than ended abruptly. In effect, this is the rapid re-housing model discussed in the Chapter 4 as an approach to resolving an immediate episode of homelessness, only in this case the time-limited subsidies would be used as a part of the safety net to keep a large number of households from approaching homelessness. Subsidies would likely need to last substantially longer than the average of 6–9 months that proved ineffective for keeping families housed in the Family Options Study (Gubits et al., 2018).

Phased out subsidies have been proposed as a way of encouraging work by putting people on notice that they will have to have enough income to pay the rent at a specified future time. Here we consider them as a way of reducing the cost of making housing subsidies available to a larger fraction of those who need them, by offering them to households in deep poverty who might be expected to gain income over time—for example, as child care responsibilities diminish over time or as an adult acquires skills through education or training. A 5-year subsidy or one keyed to the age of the youngest child in a household would allow a family with young children to raise them to school age, when many expenses and risk for homelessness go down. It is not clear that this would actually save much money. Many working age household heads without a disability already use housing assistance for only a few years, even though they are able to continue to use it as long as their low incomes make them eligible (Lubell, Shroder, & Steffen, 2003).

About half of working age households without a disability who left assisted housing in 2015 had a length of stay of less than 3 years (McClure, 2017).

While actual patterns in the use of housing assistance imply that time-limited subsidies might be adequate for many, there are issues with moving in that direction. Allowing subsidies to expire could be perilous politically for government officials, making limits to be enforced at some future time less than totally credible to recipients. Using authority provided under a demonstration program, a few public housing authorities have experimented with time-limited voucher subsidies, and in 2019 HUD began a study of the impact of having the assistance phase down over time. The pattern as of 2014 was that public housing authorities had not enforced the time period rigorously but instead permitted many families to continue to try to increase their incomes to the point where they could afford housing on their own (Khadduri et al., 2014). Subsidies with an end point associated with the age of the youngest child (at the time the subsidy is awarded) might be more politically palatable and would address a genuine need for young families.

Rent Subsidies Through the Tax System

Expanding rent subsidies for households with poverty-level incomes is a matter of political will rather than technical feasibility. In the United States, there appears to be more political will for using the tax system to address social problems than for spending money through direct appropriations. The history of deep, project-based subsidies illustrates the point. The Section 8 New Construction program, enacted in 1974, lasted only a few years and then was repealed. It was replaced fairly quickly by the Low Income Housing Tax Credit (LIHTC), which has lasted more than 30 years.

A current proposal by the Center on Budget and Policy Priorities tries to mimic the success of LIHTC. Structured much like the voucher program, it would reduce rents for poor renters.[20] Instead of a voucher payment from a public housing authority, the owner of rental housing would receive a federal tax credit for the difference between the rent and the tenant payment. States would be given an allocation of tax credits from a national pool—the example given is $6 billion per year—and hold competitions to award the credits to owners of particular developments that would be permitted to use the allocation of credits for 15 years (Fischer, Sard, & Mazzara, 2017). So this is not really a proposal for an expansion of deep housing subsidies with the aim of making them available to all poor renters. Instead, it is a "project-based" approach with a limited budget—modeled on the LIHTC and likely to be used, initially, mainly to add deep subsidies to units produced under that program.[21] However, it would be possible to enact a more

---

[20] Households with income below the higher of the federal poverty level or extremely low income (30% of area median income).

[21] A weakness of the proposal is that, like LIHTC, it would be allocated to states on a per capita basis and would not provide more resources to states with greater shortages of affordable housing.

open-ended housing subsidy through the tax system, a demand-side subsidy that would go directly to poor renters as a refundable tax credit. Housing advocate Cushing Dolbeare proposed such an approach in the early 2000s, making the point that the tax system subsidizes middle income and, especially, wealthier homeowners through the deductibility of mortgage interest, property taxes, and capital gains (Dolbeare, 2001). Such proposals have continued and may have gained currency lately.

Housing Subsidies for Particularly Vulnerable Groups

Since the early 2000s, "incremental" units of deep housing subsidies—incremental in the sense that they add units to the overall stock of assisted housing—have been added only for special population groups.[22] As it happens, these special programs generally have been for types of households relevant to preventing homelessness. That may have helped generate the political will behind the appropriations of funds—for example, the federal budget enacted in the spring of 2018 for the fiscal year already under way as of that date included funds for 48,000 vouchers to help people with disabilities live in housing of their choice in the community[23] and 2,600 vouchers for families at risk of losing their children to foster care because they lacked adequate housing. The only other new vouchers were for a 5,000-unit expansion of the Veteran's Administration Supportive Housing (VASH) program for homeless veterans (Rice, 2018).

Special allocations of vouchers are among the ways that HUD provides deep rent subsidies for people with disabilities. There is no requirement that they be linked with services but, at the public housing authority's discretion, they can be, creating supportive housing. Even if not linked to services, vouchers strengthen the safety net for people with disabilities, adding to the Supplemental Security Income (SSI) income that we know helps protect against repeated homelessness (Glendening & Shinn, 2018). SSI income alone is not sufficient to protect people with disabilities from severe rent burdens (Souza et al., 2011).

The vouchers for families at risk of losing their children to foster care[24] are linked to the child welfare system, based on the premise that lack of stable housing may be one of the factors that keeps families from providing a safe environment for their children. Families experiencing homelessness have high rates of separation from their children, both in the years preceding their entry into shelter

---

[22] The Housing Choice Voucher grew substantially in the 1990s, but that was mainly because vouchers were allocated to public housing agencies to replace units that left the public housing and project-based portions of the assisted housing stock, with no resulting net growth—and even possibly some shrinkage—of the overall stock of assisted housing.

[23] Called "mainstream" vouchers, because they permit people with disabilities to live in mainstream housing rather than in specialized programs or institutions. An earlier name for the program was nonelderly disabled or NED vouchers.

[24] Called family reunification program (FUP) vouchers.

and during and after a shelter stay (Cowal, Shinn, Weitzman, Stojanovic, & Labay, 2002; Culhane, Webb, Grim, Metraux, & Culhane, 2003; Park, Metraux, & Culhane, 2004; Shinn, Brown, & Gubits, 2017; Shinn, Gibbons-Benton, & Brown, 2015; Walton, Wood, & Dunton, 2018), and there is evidence that vouchers can improve housing stability and some child welfare outcomes (Fowler & Chavira, 2014; Gubits et al., 2018; Pergamit, Cunningham, & Hanson, 2017; Pergamit, Cunningham, Hanson, & Stanczyk, 2019). Continuing to expand special allocations of vouchers to keep high-risk families intact would help strengthen the safety net in a way highly relevant to preventing homelessness.

The U.S. Partnership on Mobility from Poverty, a group of researchers supported by the Gates Foundation, has proposed an alternative to linking vouchers to the child welfare system that is more ambitious and would reach a larger group of people. A substantial infusion of vouchers, 100,000 each year for 5 years, would be reserved for families with at least one child under 6 years of age and either a history of homelessness or housing instability or current residence in an area of concentrated poverty. The authors point out that long waiting lists can make families wait for a voucher until past the time when having the voucher would be of greatest benefit to a child. Vouchers would be paired with services to help families move to high-opportunity neighborhoods and home visiting services that support new parents caring for their children in the earliest years (Sard, Cunningham, & Greenstein, 2018). We applaud this proposal for its strengthening of the safety net as well as for its focus on homelessness but note that 100,000 incremental vouchers a year would not go far enough toward meeting the level of need among renters with extremely low incomes. The targeting to families with young children means that families would be served at the period of greatest risk.

A final special voucher program that has received frequent allocations of incremental units is VASH, HUD vouchers administered through housing agencies, with the Veterans Administration identifying veterans who need supportive housing and providing the associated services. The program is targeted to veterans with disabling conditions who have already experienced homelessness or are on the brink of doing so (as described in Chapters 3 and 4). We mention it here in connection with the willingness of legislators to add to the overall stock of housing vouchers through funding for special populations deemed to be at high risk of homelessness.

Building Housing for Poor Renters

So far in this chapter we have focused on ways of scaling up the Housing Choice Voucher program, with possible modifications that make the existing stock of privately owned rental housing more affordable. Vouchers are much easier to scale up than programs that build new housing (or redevelop existing housing to make it like new). In addition, the literature is clear that demand-side subsidies are more cost-effective than strategies that rely on construction (Ellen, Schill, Schwartz, & Voicu, 2003; Olsen, 2010; U.S. General Accounting Office, 2001;

Wallace, Struening, & Susser, 1993; Weicher, 2012). Economic analysis also has shown that, under many market circumstances, supply-side housing programs substitute for new housing that would have been built in the absence of the sub-sidy—although not necessarily in the same locations or at the same rent levels (Malpezzi & Vandell, 2002; Murray, 1999). In addition, it has proven difficult to target supply-side subsidies to people with the lowest incomes.

However, there are some circumstances in which a demand-side subsidy may be less effective and, therefore, programs that subsidize the construction of new affordable housing are called for. A perennial concern about exclusive reliance on the voucher approach is that adding to the demand for housing may result in higher rents overall and be harmful to households that do not benefit from a rent subsidy. That issue was addressed through a demonstration program in the 1970s, in the experiments that led up to the enactment of a demand-side subsidy in 1974 (the current voucher program under a different name). The Housing Allowance Supply Experiment saturated two housing markets—Green Bay, WI and South Bend, IN—with vouchers and found that they had essentially no effect on rents (Lowry, 1983).

A more recent analysis of rent data by Scott Susin suggested that housing vouchers may have an inflationary effect. Susin (2002) found that housing mar-kets with a larger allocation of incremental vouchers (at the time that was still happening) had greater rent increases, with those increases concentrated in the bottom third of rents and concluded that vouchers may have been hurting unsubsidized low-income renters more than they were helping subsidized rent-ers. Susin's analysis has two weaknesses. First, it depends on the assumption that voucher units are concentrated in the bottom third of the housing market, which is not the case. The whole point of a voucher with the subsidy standards that have existed since the start of the program is that they permit a household to rent at the middle of the housing market, not the bottom. Vouchers are dispersed across metropolitan neighborhoods that have rental housing, although not to the extent that fair housing advocates can and should want (Devine, Gray, Rubin, & Taghavi, 2003; Mazzara & Knudsen, 2019). In lower-rent neighborhoods, they tend to subsidize the better, relatively higher-rent units (Desmond, 2016). The other weakness of Susin's analysis is that he could not control for other factors that may have influenced rents during the period he studied.

Yet more recent analysis, by Eriksen and Ross (2015), controls for potential unobservable factors that affect rents at the same time as an influx of housing vouchers by constructing a panel series of rents for the same units from American Housing Survey data and using it to estimate the effect of an increase in the num-ber of vouchers that occurred between 2000 and 2002. The authors conclude that metropolitan areas with larger increases in vouchers did not experience "statistically significant or economically meaningful" increases in rents across all rental units in 134 Metropolitan Statistical Areas (MSAs). Looking separately at units with rents at various levels compared to the subsidy standard, they find that rents increased by a small amount ($2.93 per month) for units with rents between 80 and 100% of the Fair Market Rent. In contrast, for units with rents below 80% of Fair Market Rent, the infusion of vouchers actually decreased rents. The largest effects on rents were an increase in rents close to the Fair Market Rent in metropolitan areas with supply constraints, and a decrease in rents below 80% of the Fair Market Rent in metropolitan areas without such constraints. In our view the upshot is that an expansion of the voucher program is not likely to cause rent inflation except in particular metropolitan areas.[25]

Eriksen and Ross (2015) are not the only economists to point out that some cities and metropolitan areas are constrained in their ability to increase the supply of housing in response to an increase in demand. Sometimes this has to do with physical limits on the amount of buildable land found in some densely populated coastal areas. Furthermore, as economists argue and have demonstrated empirically, in some places the regulatory environment in which housing developers operate increases the price of land and the cost of construction, limiting the extent to which building can respond to demand for housing. Raphael (2010) links tight regulatory environments to rates of homelessness—this is certainly not the only factor but, along with the large number of renters with high incomes in places like New York City and urban California, it helps to explain why both high rent burdens and homelessness are most common in those locations.

Supply-side subsidies for rental housing have a role to play in strengthening the housing safety net. Doing this effectively faces two challenges, but we think it can be done. The first challenge that needs to be addressed is that, given the cost of building a new unit *and* making it affordable for a renter with a poverty-level income, supply-side programs tend to be lightly targeted. That is, they do not go to the households with greatest needs. The second challenge is that the politics of allocating subsidies makes it difficult for a federal program to direct supply-side subsidies only to places they are most needed. The LIHTC illustrates these challenges. First, it is allocated per capita rather than in a way that directs more resources to places with housing shortages. While it is unlikely that Congress will be willing to change the basic, per capita, allocation of the LIHTC, a possible improvement would be an add-on to the tax credit with a better formula.

Second, without being coupled with a deep subsidy, the LIHTC does not provide rents low enough to be affordable to households in poverty. A study conducted relatively early in the history of the program found that only 23% of program residents who did not also have tenant-based vouchers or project-based Section 8 assistance had incomes below 30% of area median (Buron, Nolden, Heintz, & Stewart, 2000). A more recent study based on data provided by 18

---

[25] This is a different issue from whether public housing authorities sometimes agree to pay above-market rents for particular voucher units. Desmond and Perkins (2016) use a survey of tenants in Milwaukee to compare voucher rents to rents of unassisted units and find a $58 "rent premium" for units with a voucher holding tenant. In a study of communities in which the use of vouchers was controversial, Khadduri and colleagues observed some significant overpayment for voucher units in certain neighborhoods in several cities (Churchill, Holin, Khadduri, & Turnham, 2001).

states found that just 45% of tenants have extremely low income, and the overwhelming majority of such tenants are using housing vouchers or another deep rent subsidy (O'Regan & Horn, 2013). Such doubling up of the subsidy—using vouchers in LIHTC units—has become common. Although this does not add to the number of poor families and individuals for whom housing has been made affordable, the LIHTC can relieve constraints on supply in places where vouchers are relatively difficult to use. With a sufficient number of vouchers, this tax credit and other capital subsidies could be spread over a larger number of units.

A new program, the National Housing Trust Fund (2015), tries to overcome the challenges of targeting supply subsidies to the people who most need housing subsidies and of allocating funds to the places where market constraints make the use of vouchers difficult. At least 75% of subsidized units must serve the poor, and the allocation formula is heavily targeted to the places that need deep subsidies and an expanded supply.[26] Like proposals to use the tax system for rent subsidies, the National Housing Trust Fund represents an attempt to overcome the reluctance of the U.S. Congress to appropriate adequate amounts of on-budget funding for the Housing Choice Voucher program by finding another source of revenue for deep rent subsidies—in this case by using a percentage of the large volume of business of the government secondary market institutions that securitize mortgage loans, Fannie Mae and Freddie Mac. The National Housing Trust Fund was originally enacted in 2007, but funding was suspended when the federal government took control of the secondary market enterprises. That suspension was lifted at the end of 2014 by the federal agency responsible for overseeing Fannie Mae and Freddie Mac (National Housing Trust Fund, 2015).

The National Housing Trust Fund distributed nearly $174 million in 2016 and $267 million in 2017, much less than is needed but a start. In the early going, most states were not using funds to build additional affordable housing but instead to deepen the targeting of units already produced or under development using the LIHTC or state-funded programs (Gramlich, 2017). A possible improvement to the Trust Fund would be to require that monies be used to support housing that would not have been built otherwise.

Because supply constraints are located predominately in certain parts of the country—the wealthier parts and (perhaps a related fact) places that have constraining housing regulations, supply-side programs on the scale needed to support a stronger housing safety net will need to be funded in part by states and cities from their own tax revenue (or related resources such as trust funds fed by fees). An add-on to the LIHTC might encourage such funding by requiring a match of state or local own-source funding. States with an adequate supply of housing available to potential voucher users would be unlikely to provide the match needed to access the additional quota of tax credit authority.

---

[26] The allocation formula gives substantial weight to the mismatch between affordable units and households with extremely low incomes and to the percentage of such households with high rent burdens.

In the Los Angeles region, city Proposition HHH and county Measure H have enacted substantial local funding for affordable housing, explicitly motivated by the upsurge in the numbers of people experiencing homelessness in the region but with eligible uses of funds that go beyond permanent supportive housing for people experiencing homelessness. Proposition HHH is a $1.2 billion bond issue by the City of Los Angeles. Measure H is a quarter cent sales tax expected to raise $3.55 billion over 10 years (Abt Associates, 2018a).

States and localities can take other actions to increase the affordability of housing. For example, inclusionary zoning is an effort to produce affordable housing without direct public subsidies. Inclusionary zoning ordinances can be mandatory, requiring that a fraction of new units be affordable. Or they can provide voluntary incentives, for example, allowing greater building height or density in exchange for providing affordable units. They also vary in how deeply targeted those units are. An analysis of programs in the San Francisco metropolitan area and suburban Boston suggests that the amount of housing produced under inclusionary zoning has been modest, and that during times when housing is appreciating, inclusionary zoning may depress production or increase costs (Schuetz, Meltzer, & Been, 2011).

Overturning exclusionary zoning would have a larger effect, permitting higher density housing and rental as well as homeownership housing in urban neighborhoods. For example, Minneapolis has eliminated single-family zoning to allow duplexes and triplexes in every neighborhood, city-wide (Mervosh, 2018). Oregon has passed legislation to require cities with more than 10,000 people to allow duplexes everywhere (Wamsley, 2019). Advocates hope that these moves will make housing more affordable and allow greater racial and socioeconomic integration. One reason the housing crisis in Los Angeles is so severe is that it has moved in the opposite direction over the last half century. In 1960, zoning permitted a capacity for 10 million people, but by 1990 it had downzoned, so that it had capacity for only 3.9 million (Morrow, 2013). According to one calculation, that means that the city's population is now 93% of the maximum that current zoning would allow (Morrow as quoted in Badger & Bui, 2019).

Communities with supply constraints should experiment with regulatory reforms that have the effect of reducing the cost of housing—for example, streamlining the process for acquiring permissions and permits (time definitely is money in the world of housing development). Regulatory changes can also permit nontraditional housing types such as co-housing, micro-apartments, or tiny houses. California recently updated laws allowing for "accessory dwelling units" also called granny flats, backyard cottages and secondary units (California Department of Housing & Community Development, 2018). Some cities have older single-family houses that could be subdivided if regulations permitted, and permitting placement of mobile homes could be a reasonable option for expanding rental housing in some places. Fannie Mae is exploring ways to support more affordable housing including modular construction of multifamily homes (Hayward, 2019) and financing for nonprofit or resident owned-manufactured housing developments (trailer parks) (Villarreal, 2019).

Single Room Occupancy rentals (now dubbed "co-living"), with small private spaces and additional common space, are making a comeback in expensive cities (Bowles, 2018). The waiting list for co-living in San Francisco and the tiny house movement (Mears, 2015) in many parts of the country suggests that even middle class renters and aspiring professionals often are willing to live in small spaces with shared amenities. Zoning changes and modest tax incentives might encourage development of small units affordable to people, especially single adults, who are living on the margins and who might otherwise become homeless. Officials in Philadelphia have called for legalizing rooming houses, bringing existing arrangements out of the shadows and permitting better regulation of quality (Lind, 2018).[27]

Although many people need little more than an affordable place to live in order to avoid homelessness, some will need more support. Supportive housing with services provided by Assertive Community Treatment (ACT) teams keeps people with long histories of homelessness and serious mental illnesses housed, as in the initial Pathways to Housing model described in Chapter 3. But such supportive housing is expensive. Even the model of supportive housing with services provided by case managers that the At Home/Chez Soi program found effective for people with lesser needs is not cheap. Relatively few people need this level of ongoing support, although an individual's needs and wishes may vary over time. (One advantage of the scattered-site model of supportive housing in comparison to facilities is that it is easy to adjust the level of supports up or down without requiring tenants to move.)

An alternative model harnesses informal social supports to provide housing in the community at low cost for people with modest needs who might otherwise require more expensive programming or extensive family support to stay housed. For example, the Friendship House model in Nashville and several other university towns offers inexpensive housing to some people, often graduate students, in exchange for providing informal supports to more vulnerable tenants with intellectual disabilities (the "friends"). Both students and friends have small private units in houses or small-scale apartment buildings, along with some common space. Students organize weekly common meals and take responsibility for reaching out to specific friends. The students are not service providers but provide community and the sort of help one might expect from a friendly neighbor. A professional provides back-up and some programming, but with a much larger caseload than would be possible without the student supporters (personal communication, Jaco Hamman, April 8, 2019).

None of these alternatives can be brought to scale as quickly as housing vouchers, they will not appeal to everyone, and they are not a substitute for additional public investment in housing. But zoning changes, tax breaks, and modest public

---

[27] Should these trends become more widespread, HUD might consider changes to the questions asked in the AHS that measure housing quality or define a housing "unit," so as not to add artificially to the number of units in the U.S. housing stock considered "inadequate" or "moderately inadequate."

investment in alternative forms of housing can augment the supply of decent units affordable to people at the bottom of the income distribution. Creative approaches to provision of services in affordable housing can keep even vulnerable people housed.

Incomes

Incomes form the other half of the housing affordability equation. With more income, people can avoid the severe rent burdens that are the hallmark of the affordability crisis for poor and deeply poor families and individuals. Just as the United States in the late twentieth and early twenty-first century has failed to address the housing side of the safety net, so too it has failed to provide the minimum levels of income that would lift people out of deep poverty.

Multiple strategies can raise incomes. Some would help people gain the skills needed for work, remove barriers to working, and provide earnings sufficient to lift working families and individuals out of poverty. Others, acknowledging that many people cannot work and that earnings may not be sufficient to provide for basic needs, would provide transfer income at more adequate levels and with fewer people ineligible. Still others would make necessities other than housing more affordable. The expansion of Medicaid under the Affordable Care Act (Obamacare) has already allowed some households to escape financial catastrophe, and take-up by the remaining states would provide a cushion to their poor residents.

Supporting Work and Earnings

Turning first to strategies to support work, raising the minimum wage, which has remained at $7.25/hour since 2009, has intuitive appeal. Until the early 1990s, most economists believed that raising the minimum wage would depress employment, particularly at the bottom of the wage scale. An influential paper by Card and Krueger (1993) suggested this was an empirical question—one that could be put to test—when New Jersey raised its minimum wage, from $4.25 to $5.05 per hour. They found no adverse effects of the raise in comparison to nearby Pennsylvania, where the minimum remained unchanged. More recent studies that compare states and contiguous counties across state lines have reached similar conclusions, supporting the view that a modest increase in the minimum wage would have little effect on employment (Cengiz, Dube, Lindner, & Zipperer, 2019; Dube, Lester, & Reich, 2010).

Some analysts question whether the minimum wage benefits mainly households that would otherwise live in poverty or instead additional earners in more affluent households (Holzer, 2015b; Sawhill & Karpilow, 2014). However, a recent study finds that minimum wages have led to net increases in incomes at the bottom of the income distribution (Dube, 2018).

A modest increase in the minimum wage would benefit a large portion of the workforce. For example, almost one of every six employees works at less than 125% of the current minimum wage (taking state and local minimum wages into account) (Belman & Wolfson, 2014). Some states and cities are experimenting with large increases in the minimum, and existing research findings that modest increases do not reduce employment or hours may not extend to large rises. We do not pretend to be experts on the subject and do not suggest the optimal level of a federal minimum wage or of levels chosen by states.

A measure that would complement increases in federal or state minimum wages is boosting the Earned Income Tax Credit (EITC), which was created in 1975 and had major expansions the 1990s. Under the EITC, people who are employed in low-income households with children receive a supplement to their wages in the form of a refundable tax credit, incentivizing work (the credit increases with additional earnings up to a phase out point) and increasing cash income. An extensive body of evidence has shown positive effects of the EITC on employment and on lifting families out of poverty. Expanding the much less generous benefits available for households without children is an idea that garners bipartisan support (Marr, Huang, Murray, & Sherman, 2016). Another attractive proposal for changing the EITC is to make it more generous for families with very young children (Sawhill & Karpilow, 2014). Some analysts are concerned that the EITC also subsidizes low-wage employers, but evidence for this is not strong.[28]

Noting the durability of the EITC and its expansion over time, Stegman and coauthors (2004) proposed adding a supplement to the EITC as a complement to the Housing Choice Voucher program, which then could be targeted more heavily to those who cannot work. Their proposal was not a housing program, but instead an expansion of the EITC benefit sufficient to alleviate severe rent burdens for a large number of working families and individuals by scaling a supplement that would vary over time to current rent levels—not the rents actually paid by the credit's recipients but instead typical rents paid by households across the United Sates. The supplement would follow the structure of the EITC, phasing up with additional earnings up to a certain point, and thus would counteract one of the arguments against the voucher subsidy model—that it discourages work. With an expanded EITC reducing rent burdens for working families, the voucher program could increasingly serve the elderly and people with disabilities. Commenters on the proposal noted its targeting inefficiency (not getting to the

---

[28] Most antipoverty programs are more generous when household earnings are lower rather than higher, so they make work less rewarding. Therefore, they require employers to pay more to induce people to work (and take on related expenses such as transportation or clothing). In contrast, the EITC increases the returns for low-wage employment, so it may also serve indirectly to hold down wage costs for low-wage employers, who can induce people to work for less. Analysts have concluded that the empirical evidence for this is not strong (Burtless, 2015; National Academies of Sciences Engineering and Medicine, 2019, pp. D5–2).

right people) compared to on-budget spending on housing subsidies and compared to an approach that linked a tax credit explicitly to a family's actual rent burden (Carr, Rengert, & Huh, 2004; Dolbeare, 2004). Another weakness of the proposal from the standpoint of preventing homelessness is that it leaves out major groups of households most vulnerable to becoming homeless: nonworking families and younger individuals without disabilities, many of whom have limited ability to work because of child care responsibilities or health problems that are not severe enough to support an SSI disability determination but nonetheless limit work (Walton, Dastrup, & Khadduri, 2018).

Yet another approach is to enact policies that enhance workers' bargaining power to negotiate for a larger proportion of the economic benefits that have flowed largely to wealthy Americans in the past decades. These include strengthening unions and requiring representation of workers on corporate boards. Rather than legislating a higher minimum wage or providing direct subsidies via the EITC, such policies might enable workers to secure higher wages from the private sector.

Policies that depend on working such as raising the minimum wage, strengthening the EITC, or increasing workers' bargaining power would not end poverty (or deep poverty) for the many people with poverty-level incomes who cannot work.

Broad-Based Transfer Programs

Next we consider transfer or benefit programs that do not depend on work, at least for families. The most widely used such program is the food stamps program, now called the Supplemental Nutrition Assistance Program or SNAP. Although restricted to purchases of food, SNAP is very close to cash because benefit levels are lower than food expenditures. With benefits loaded onto a debit card, SNAP is easy to use. Most states have online applications, and participation rates are high (Oliveira, Prell, Tiehan, & Smallwood, 2018). An easy way to move more people out of deep poverty[29] by providing more income to meet all basic needs (income not spent on food is available for other things) would be to increase SNAP benefits, something that was done temporarily during the Great Recession. As of 2017, the maximum monthly benefit (for a household with no income) was $194 for a single person and $511 for a family of four. Arguably this is not sufficient to cover food costs (Ziliak, 2016), so raising the benefit level would not change the "near cash" character of the program.

Starting in the 1990s, "able-bodied adults without children" have been required to work or else are limited to receiving benefits for only 3 of 36 months, with some ability of states to waive this requirement. Few states waive it entirely (Bolen & Dean, 2018; Oliveira et al., 2018). We think imposing work requirements

---

[29] See Chapter 2 on causes for measures of poverty that take transfer payments such as food stamps into account.

on SNAP (food stamps) beneficiaries is a bad idea. Work requirements add substantially to the program's administrative costs. They discourage participation by forcing people to prove they are actively seeking work and removing benefits from those who appear to be able to work but in reality are not. Ending the work requirement for childless adults could have a significant impact on homelessness.

A broader transfer program proposed by some on both the right and the left is a universal basic income. A National Academies panel charged by Congress with examining policies to reduce child poverty by half used simulations to suggest that a Universal Basic Income of $250 per month to all citizens, children, and adults, would be effective in reducing deep poverty, but at a very high cost, $322–$624 billion annually, depending on policy and tax choices (2019, D-5-12). We report on less expensive proposals after considering current income supports directed at families.

Income Support for Families

Income support for families with children was turned into the Temporary Assistance to Needy Families (TANF) block grant in 1996, and since then benefits and participation levels have eroded substantially, as states have chosen to use their combined federal and state funds for things other than cash (Floyd, 2017; Floyd, Pavetti, & Schott, 2017).

In the last 5 years, 16 states have increased their TANF grants by at least $40 per month for a family of three. New Hampshire's benefit was calibrated to 60% of the poverty line, ensuring that it will no longer lose value due to inflation. New Jersey and Tennessee implemented their first grant increases since the late 1980s (Burnside & Floyd, 2019). Despite these recent increases by some states, the generally smaller benefit levels and the reduction in participation have weakened this part of the safety net. (The time-limited nature of the assistance probably has been less important).

The experience with TANF shows that, once a program has become a block grant, it can be difficult to turn back. The Obama Administration suggested legislative changes that would have required states to spend an increasing amount of their TANF funds on "core benefits and services," defined as "basic assistance, work related assistance for needy families, and child care," but when phased in that would still have covered only 60% of the combination of federal and state TANF funding.[30] The proposals, which were put forth in the final year of the Administration, would also have added "reducing child poverty" to the legislative purposes of the TANF program (U.S. Department of Health and Human Services, 2016b, p. 346).

---

[30] To draw down federal TANF funds, states are required to demonstrate that their own spending on TANF represents a Maintenance of Effort (MOE). The proposals would also have tightened the rules on what can be counted as MOE.

An idea that may have more traction than stronger federal mandates for state use of TANF funds is increasing the Child Tax Credit and making it fully refundable so that families with no or little earnings could receive the full credit. A refundable tax credit for young children (for example, for children under three or under six) would be similar to the family cash allowance common in most industrialized nations. Those allowances often have the objective of encouraging births in societies with an aging population, so they are available to families at all income levels. In the U.S., where immigration, at least until now, has forestalled aging of the population, the objective would be to lift children out of poverty, so either an income limit or making the benefit taxable would make sense. An income-tested tax credit for children would complement the EITC by providing support during the period when a parent is least likely to work, especially in the absence of widespread, affordable child care. And because families with young children are especially likely to become homeless, as Chapter 2 showed, it would put cash in the hands of families particularly vulnerable to homelessness.

Child Care

The relationship between the high cost of child care and family homelessness was illustrated by Michelle, who lost her job and her housing when she could not pay for child care for her newborn. (We introduced Michelle in Chapter 1.) The United States spends less, as a proportion of GDP, than any other country in the Organization for Economic Co-Operation and Development (OECD) on early childhood education and care. OECD is a membership organization of wealthier countries, 36 as of this writing. As a consequence of the low U.S. level of investment in child care, low-income families pay three times as large a proportion of their income for child care as the OECD average. Low-income couples pay an average of 39% of disposable income (after taking all benefits into consideration), compared to the OECD average of 13%. Low-income single mothers pay 42%, compared to the OECD average of 14% (Browne & Neumann, 2017).[31]

Many studies show the positive impact of care on children's outcomes, if the child care is of high quality.[32] A study of a particular high-quality program in the U.S. used an experimental design and followed children long-term. The authors estimated annual "social rates of return" of 7–10%, largely reflecting increases in adult earnings and reductions in crime and welfare use (Heckman, Moon, Pinto, Savelyev, & Yavitz, 2010).[33] Child care also supports parents, enabling them to participate in paid labor. The Child and Dependent Care Tax Credit, a federal

---

[31] Low income is defined as the 20th percentile of single mothers and of families, by income—that is, 80% of that type of household has more disposable income and 20% has less.

[32] For an international review of this evidence, see van Huizen and Plantenga (2015).

[33] This estimate corrects some methodological shortcomings of previous, higher estimates of rates of return for the HighScope Perry Preschool program. We cite it largely to show that one should not stint on quality to save money.

benefit administered through the tax code, allows families to subtract a portion of their child care costs from their income tax. However, that tax credit is not refundable, meaning that the poorest families who pay only social security taxes but not income taxes receive no help. Making it refundable or supporting child care costs in other ways would help families with young children. As we have shown earlier, poor families with young children are at particularly high risk of homelessness.

The National Academies panel (2019) that was charged with assessing policies that would cut child poverty in half did not have ending homelessness as part of their charge, but their recommendations dovetail with many of our own. They found that no single policy (other than an exorbitantly costly universal income) would do the trick, nor would a package of policy changes focused solely on work. They came up with two packages, with different price tags. The less expensive package, dubbed the "means tested support and work package," included an expanded EITC, an expanded and fully refundable Child Care Tax Credit, an expanded Housing Choice Voucher program (so that 70% of eligible families received vouchers), and expanded SNAP benefits. The panel calculated that this array of policies would cost $90.7 billion per year and reduce both child poverty and deep poverty by half. A slightly costlier package included the same expanded ETIC and Child Care Tax Credit and also increased the minimum wage, initiated a child allowance and a child support assurance program, and eliminated eligibility restrictions related to immigration. Because it did not include housing supports, it would do less to prevent homelessness.

Income Support for People with Disabilities

The U.S. safety net for people with disabilities could also be strengthened. The Social Security Disability Insurance (SSDI) program provides benefits for workers (or their dependents) who have paid social security taxes long enough that they are eligible for payments from the Social Security Disability Trust Fund. Supplemental Security Income (SSI) provides benefits for people with disabilities and very low income and assets. Recipients of both programs need to demonstrate that they have a disability that makes them unable to engage in any "substantial gainful activity" because of a "medically-determinable physical or mental impairment" that is expected to last for at least 12 months or result in death.

Both forms of disability benefits help protect people from becoming homeless. Recall from Chapter 1 that rates of disability among people experiencing homelessness are high: half of individual adults (49%) and a fifth (22%) of adults in families who used homeless shelters in 2017 (Henry, Bishop, de Sousa, Shivji, & Watt, 2018).[34] In the Family Options Study, where 38% of families found in

---

[34] Not all of these self-reported disabilities would qualify for disability benefits.

emergency shelters reported a member with a disability, families who received disability benefits were less likely to return to homelessness in the 20 months after they entered shelters (Glendening & Shinn, 2018).

Benefit levels for federal disability benefits are modest and increases are justified. As of 2019, the maximum federal benefit level for SSI, the less generous of the two programs, was $771 per month for an individual and $1,157 per month for a couple, with supplements provided by most states. People with disability benefits as their only source of income often struggle to pay for housing (illustrated by William, whom we introduced in Chapter 1).

Counteracting Income Volatility—Overcoming Bad Luck

The basic idea of a social safety net is to help people navigate tough times. When eviction prevention programs give support only to people who can show that their financial problems stem from a one-time event not under their control and that they will be able to shoulder the rent again after a one-time infusion of cash, they are trying to overcome volatility and bad luck. We have argued that those programs might do more good if they did not restrict themselves to demonstrably worthy recipients with short-term needs but extended to people faced with more enduring poverty. However, we believe that programs designed to reduce volatility in incomes have a role to play in preventing homelessness.

The unemployment insurance program is the most important such strategy that helps to stabilize both households (when a wage-earner is laid off) and communities (because recipients still have money to spend in an economic downturn), but not everyone is covered. The share of unemployed workers receiving unemployment insurance fell from nearly half (49%) in the 1950s to a little over a quarter (27%) in the 2010s. To some extent this reflects the growth in the proportion of nontraditional workers (independent contractors and freelancers), who are excluded, and part-time, contingent, and on-call workers, who often have difficulty meeting the work history requirements (McKay, Pollack, & Fitzpayne, 2018). According to one study, nontraditional workers, who experience more income volatility than traditional workers, accounted for 94% of the net job growth between 2005 and 2015 (Katz & Krueger, 2016). However, recent Bureau of Labor Statistics data show that "contingent workers," those who do not expect their jobs to last, are only 3.8% of the U.S. labor force, with another 10.1% in alternative employment arrangements such as independent contractors, on-call workers, and temporary help agency workers (Bureau of Labor Statistics, 2018).

Even more important than changing employment patterns may be changing state requirements that make many low-wage workers ineligible for unemployment insurance. A 2016 report sponsored by the Center for American Progress, the National Employment Law Project, and Georgetown Law School recommends stronger federal standards for eligibility that would keep people from falling through the cracks because they cannot easily demonstrate they left employment through no fault of their own, that they have sufficient work histories to qualify, and that they are actively seeking work. The report also recommends strengthening the unemployment insurance system's reemployment services (West et al., 2016) The Obama Administration made some proposals in 2016 that would have extended unemployment insurance coverage to "part-time workers, newer labor market entrants, certain low-income and intermittent workers, and workers who leave work for compelling family reasons such as to move with a spouse, escape domestic violence, or care for an ill family member" (The White House, 2016). In the absence of federal legislation, states should consider making such reforms, which would help individuals and families with the volatile work and family situations typical of those who fall into homelessness.

An Aspen Institute report (McKay et al., 2018) considers multiple strategies to extend and update unemployment insurance. One example would create mandatory short-term individual "security accounts" for workers in all types of employment, funded by the government for low-income workers.[35] Workers could access the account for short-term benefits after a variety of qualifying events (for example, a major reduction in earnings, whether or not due to a layoff), with excess accumulations funneled into a retirement account (Gruber, 2016).

Countering Social Exclusion

The social exclusion that has led to the overrepresentation of African Americans and people with disabilities among those experiencing homelessness will not be overcome easily, but many of the proposals already mentioned will chip away. The National Academies (2019) panel on child poverty calculated that the package of policies that included increases in housing vouchers, the EITC, SNAP (food stamps), and the child care tax credit would not only halve child poverty and enhance employment but also differentially benefit African Americans. Outlawing "source of income" discrimination in housing will prevent landlords from taking use of housing vouchers as a proxy for race as a way of discriminating against black renters. Calculating the payment standard for vouchers based on the zip code or Small Area Fair Market Rent (SAFMR), rather than the average Fair Market Rent for an entire metro area, will enable African American users of housing vouchers to afford homes in more affluent areas.[36] Increases in disability benefits will allow people who cannot work to have more housing opportunities, and some of the alternative housing models we have discussed explicitly benefit people with disabilities who need extra support to live independently. The 1999

---

[35] For disabled people, ABLE accounts, created by the Achieving a Better Life Experience Act of 2014, serve a similar purpose. They provide tax-advantaged savings accounts that allow disabled people to build assets without losing SSA eligibility.

[36] As of this writing, HUD suspended the rollout of SAFMRs to all metropolitan areas. We think the policy should be made universal.

Olmstead Supreme Court decision and subsequent guidance require government-supported housing providers to place residents with disabilities in the most community-integrated setting possible (*Olmstead v. L.C.*, 1999).

Recognition of the role of governments—federal, state, and local—in creating and maintaining not merely *de facto* but *de jure* segregation suggests that government should do more to dismantle it. Currently government does a much better job of documenting illegal discrimination in housing (via paired testing studies) than of enforcing the law. HUD sued Facebook for practicing discrimination by targeting housing ads on the basis of race, religion, and national origin but did so only after the company settled a suit brought by various activist groups (Associated Press, 2019), and 2 years after HUD had scaled back an inquiry into Facebook's policies on advertising housing (Benner, Thrush, & Isaac, 2019). As long as paired testers uncover high levels of illegal discrimination against prospective minority renters and home buyers and against disabled renters, as has been shown in every study conducted to date, federal enforcement efforts need to be more aggressive. In addition to fines or other penalties against landlords found to discriminate, settlement agreements should include set-asides of units for groups that have been discriminated against.

One primary way that local governments have actively promoted segregation is exclusionary zoning, so governments have a responsibility to dismantle it. Doing away with zoning policies that prohibit multifamily housing or require large lots for single family homes will make construction of affordable housing less costly and permit more racial integration.

The Fair Housing Act, part of the Civil Rights Act of 1968, not only prohibited discrimination but also required all federal housing programs to be administered by federal agencies and their grantees in a manner that affirmatively furthers fair housing. Over the years, the federal government has failed to take the lead, leaving the responsibility to members of class action suits and their lawyers. A 2010 report by the Government Accountability Office (GAO) noted that "Grantee's compliance with [Affirmatively Furthering Fair Housing] requirements and the effectiveness of HUD's oversight and enforcement have been called into question through litigation and reports and testimonies for some years" (Government Accountability Office, 2010, p. 2).

Starting in the 1990s, HUD in principle required communities to prepare "analyses of impediments" to fair housing, but not all communities prepared them, and many analyses were cursory or out of date. The "vast majority" lacked time frames or signatures of elected officials, so accountability was unclear. The GAO report blamed HUD's "limited approach to establishing [Analysis of Impediments] regulatory requirements, and its limited oversight and enforcement…" (Government Accountability Office, 2010, p. 31).

Finally, during the Obama Administration, HUD published the Affirmatively Furthering Fair Housing rule that had been promised for decades. This was in July 2015, nearly half a century after the passage of the Fair Housing Act. Under the rule, all jurisdictions that receive federal money for housing and urban development are required to analyze and create a plan to identify and dismantle barriers to fair housing on the basis of race, disability, and other categories. Further, communities must affirmatively work to undo the harm caused by segregation, setting goals and timelines. HUD's review and acceptance of the community's plan is a prerequisite for its receiving HUD funds. Because the requirement for a plan applied to communities on a rolling basis, depending on local planning cycles for HUD funds, only a few communities completed their plans before HUD, under a new Administration, suspended implementation of the rule. A coalition of civil rights groups is challenging the suspension in court (*National Fair Housing Alliance et al. v. Carson*). Housing advocates have identified some of the plans prepared before the rule was suspended, including those from New Orleans and Seattle, as models for other communities (Capps, 2018; City of New Orleans & Housing Authority of New Orleans, 2016; City of Seattle & Seattle Housing Authority, 2017).

Robust oversight and enforcement by HUD and other federal agencies[37] of the mandate for affirmatively furthering fair housing could begin to provide some redress for historical *de jure* segregation and current *de facto* segregation. Rothstein (2017) suggests going further than withholding HUD grants by also denying homeowners part of the mortgage tax deduction in communities that fail to implement affirmative fair housing plans or to suburbs with less than a "fair share" of African Americans, as determined by coming close to the proportion in the metropolitan area. "Close" might mean within 10% points, so that in a metropolitan area that is 15% African American, a suburb with fewer than 5% African Americans would be required to integrate. Such economic penalties would give white homeowners a stake in fair housing in their communities.

Tradeoffs and Combinations for Making Housing Affordable

Reaching the goal of making housing affordable to low-income renters depends on many strategies. Some can be used together, and some can be traded off. For example, we have suggested that an increase of 300,000 Housing Choice Vouchers per year might be sufficient to prevent homelessness, if combined with strategies that raise incomes at the bottom of the income distribution.

Strategies for enhancing incomes also can be combined or traded off. For example, a higher minimum wage might be compatible with keeping the EITC at its current level.

A major expansion of the Housing Choice Voucher program comes closest to a silver bullet for ending homelessness, but we expect that some mix of most of the strategies we survey—an all-of-the-above approach—will be necessary. We are

---

[37] The mandate extends beyond HUD programs—for example, to the Low Income Housing Tax Credit program, which is administered by the U.S. Treasury.

agnostic as to the particular mix, recognizing that policies have numerous effects and policymakers will want to choose ones that serve additional goals besides ending homelessness. Similarly, the National Academies (2019) panel came up with two quite different packages of policies that would work to halve child poverty. Between the two of them, we prefer the approach that would also reduce homelessness.

Strategies for expanding affordable housing may vary from place to place, depending on such things as how much of the population is living in unsafe housing, vacancy rates in housing that could be made affordable with subsidies, and current zoning and other regulatory restrictions. States and cities will need to take some responsibility for making housing more affordable.

Summary

In this chapter, we argue that to stop generating homelessness society must make more housing affordable. Some people with serious mental illnesses or other disabilities will need additional supports, but everyone needs housing. The proposals we make in this chapter combine with the approaches to ending homelessness for people who experience it surveyed in Chapters 3 and 4 and the strategies for targeted prevention efforts for high risk groups from Chapter 5 to form a comprehensive strategy to prevent and end homelessness.

The fastest and most effective way to increase the supply of affordable housing is via an expansion of the Housing Choice Voucher program that holds a household's rental costs to 30% of their adjusted income. We propose a return to the time when 300,000 additional housing subsidies were added each year. This would not be an "open enrollment" program, but this amount of expansion would shorten substantially the waiting time for a housing voucher and protect large numbers of families and individuals from falling into homelessness.

More broadly, because housing affordability depends on the relationship between incomes and housing costs, anything that raises incomes for people at the bottom of the distribution or that lowers their housing costs will contribute. We consider a variety of approaches to both sides of the equation.

On the housing side, in addition to proposing a substantial expansion of the Housing Choice Voucher program, we suggest ways to make rental subsidies such as vouchers less expensive and to target them to the poorest households and particularly vulnerable groups.

An expansion of the housing voucher subsidies used in the current stock of private market housing is not the complete answer. New construction of dedicated affordable housing developments takes longer than expansion of the voucher program, but may be needed in some parts of the country—in particular, in areas that, through regulation, have limited the ability of the private market to expand the supply of housing. In such areas, zoning, and other regulatory changes should be implemented to permit the construction of less costly forms of housing and the creation of additional low-cost housing through subdividing existing housing units. Current proposals to expand the National Housing Trust Fund should continue to focus on serving the poorest households and continue to have an allocation formula linked to housing affordability. An expansion might also be linked to reform of local housing regulations and require matching funds from states.

On the income side, we suggest ways to support work and earnings such as increases in the minimum wage and in the EITC—with particular expansions for childless adults who currently get very little help and for families with young children. More generous disability benefits and payments in the TANF program would help extremely disadvantaged groups. Expansion of SNAP (food stamps) and Medicaid and making the Child Care Tax Credit more generous and fully refundable would help households pay for necessities that compete with rent. And strengthening unemployment insurance would help workers weather disruptions in income.

Finally, policy must tackle social exclusion that puts minorities and people with disabilities at special risk of homelessness. If expansion of the Housing Choice Voucher program is the primary lever to reduce homelessness, legislation that prohibits landlords from discriminating on the basis of the source of the rent payment is needed everywhere. HUD must do a better job of enforcing existing laws against housing discrimination, which remains rampant, and restore implementation of the rule that requires communities to affirmatively further fair housing as a condition for the receipt of federal funds.

The United States can learn from Finnish example, described in Chapter 4. The Finns' success in this task built on developing a political consensus and coordination of local, regional, and national policy (Pleace, 2017). It also required continual evaluation and a willingness to adapt strategies on the basis of data and changing needs. The most important ingredient was political will.

Finding the Political Will to End Homelessness

The central message of this book is that homelessness is a choice, not a choice by people sleeping on the streets but a choice by the rest of us to look the other way. The United States is a wealthy country, with both the resources and, as we have tried to show, the knowledge to end homelessness. We know that making housing affordable with Housing Choice Vouchers both prevents and ends homelessness for families. We know that supportive housing—affordable housing with low barriers to entry and services that people choose—ends homelessness for individuals with serious mental illnesses. We know that strategies targeted to high-risk groups can reduce entry into homelessness, and we argue that expanding the social safety net, tackling social exclusion, and undertaking any of a variety of strategies to make housing affordable will prevent homelessness for many more. What we need is political will.

We view homelessness as the most extreme manifestation of inequality in incomes and wealth. In the years after World War II, the United States was less wealthy than it is today, but that wealth was more widely shared. Research by Piketty (2014) shows that the top income decile (the top 10% of households by income) received about a third of the total income from the end of World War II to 1980. Then began a "spectacular" rise in inequality, so that by 2000–2010, the United States had "regained the record levels observed in 1910-1920" (pp. 275, 276). The top 1% of Americans enjoyed almost a fifth of the total income in the early 2010s, a share higher than in other Anglophone countries and over twice the share of the top 1% in Continental Europe and Japan (Piketty, 2014, chapter 9). Wealth is even more skewed than income. The share of wealth owned by just the top 1% of families "has regularly grown since the late 1970s and reached 42% in 2012" (Saez & Zucman, 2016). The rise of incomes at the top was mirrored by the decline at the bottom. From 2000 to 2016, the number of households earning less than $15,000 and the number earning more than $150,000 (in constant dollars) each increased by 37%, but the number in that vast middle increased by only 16%, a pattern sometimes described as the hollowing out of the middle class (Joint Center for Housing Studies of Harvard University, 2018, p. 16). It is not surprising that most Americans do not feel that they are "in the midst of plenty."

These changes have been abetted by social policy. From 1932 to 1980, the average top federal income tax rate (not including state taxes) averaged 81%, and in 1980, the top tax rate on estates, inherited wealth, stood at 80% (Piketty, 2014). The top federal tax rate is 37% today, with the top rate on capital gains only 20% and no estate tax at all for estates less than $11.4 million (Internal Revenue Service, 2018a, 2018b, p. 1, n.d.). Wealthy homeowners receive more benefits (exclusion of mortgage interest on mortgages up to $750,000 and favorable treatment of capital gains on homes) than low income renters get in the form of housing subsidies (Internal Revenue Service, 2019; Schuetz, 2018). The 2017 Tax Cut and Jobs Act, provided most of its benefits to the wealthiest tax payers (Huang, Herrera, & Duke, 2017; Joint Committee On Taxation, 2017).

Homelessness, we argue, is a consequence of these changes over the past decades. The postwar period of relative equality was also the period in which homelessness declined and many social scientists thought it was at an end. Instead, homelessness increased as incomes at the bottom failed to keep up with the costs of housing. The inequality that leads some to live in mansions and others in the streets is not an inexorable consequence of market forces. It is a consequence of social policies. We could choose differently.

References

ABLE National Resource Center. (n.d.). *What are ABLE accounts?* Retrieved from https://www.ablenrc.org/what-is-able/what-are-able-acounts

Abt Associates. (2015). *A coordinated entry system for Los Angeles: Lessons from early implementation.* Retrieved from https://www.abtassociates.com/sites/default/files/migrated_files/cff627d2-7b04-40d4-9578-7fab3a364657.pdf

Abt Associates. (2018a). *Developing and passing Proposition HHH and Measure H: How it happened and lessons learned.* Retrieved from Hilton Foundation website: https://www.hiltonfoundation.org/learning/developing-and-passing-proposition-hhh-and-measure-h

Abt Associates. (2018b). *Evaluation of the Conrad N. Hilton Foundation Chronic Homelessness Initiative: 2018 Annual Report.* Retrieved from Hilton Foundation website: https://hilton-production.s3.amazonaws.com/documents/354/attachments/Abt_Associates_Homelessness_2018_Report.pdf?1539278965

Adams, G., Snyder, K., & Sandfort, J. R. (2002). *Navigating the child care subsidy system: Policies and practices that affect access and retention.* New Federalism Series A, No. A-50. Washington, DC: The Urban Institute.

Adams, J., Rosenheck, R., Gee, L., Seibyl, C. L., & Kushel, M. (2007). Hospitalized younger: A comparison of a national sample of homeless and housed inpatient veterans. *Journal of Health Care for the Poor and Underserved, 18*(1), 173–184. doi:10.1353/hpu.2007.0000

Ægisdóttir, S., White, M. J., Spengler, P. M., Maugherman, A. S., Anderson, L. A., Cook, R. S., … Rush, J. D. (2006). The meta-analysis of clinical judgment project: Fifty-six years of accumulated research on clinical versus statistical prediction. *The Counseling Psychologist, 34*(3), 341–382. doi:10.1177/0011000005285875

Alesina, A., & Glaeser, E. L. (2004). *Fighting poverty in the U.S. and Europe: A world of difference.* Oxford, UK: Oxford University Press.

Alexander, M. (2011). *The new Jim Crow.* New York, NY: The New Press.

Anderson, M. (1964). *The federal bulldozer: A critical analysis of urban renewal, 1949–1962.* Cambridge, MA: MIT Press.

In the Midst of Plenty: Homelessness and What to Do About It, First Edition.
Marybeth Shinn and Jill Khadduri.
© 2020 Marybeth Shinn and Jill Khadduri. Published 2020 by John Wiley & Sons Ltd.

Apicello, J. (2010). A paradigm shift in housing and homeless services: Applying the population and high-risk framework to preventing homelessness. *The Open Health Services and Policy Journal, 3*, 41–52. doi:1874-9240/10

Associated Press. (2019). US charges Facebook with high-tech housing discrimination. *New York Times.* Retrieved from https://www.apnews.com/e48ed9941ff 14766979e0fef232f4729

Aubry, T., Goering, P., Veldhuizen, S., Adair, C. E., Bourque, J., Distasio, J., ... Tsemberis, S. (2016). A multiple-city RCT of housing first with assertive community treatment for homeless Canadians with serious mental illness. *Psychiatric Services, 67*, 275–281. doi:10.1176/appi.ps.201400587

Aubry, T., Tsemberis, S., Adair, C. E., Veldhuizen, S., Streiner, D., Latimer, E., ... Goering, P. (2015). One-year outcomes of a randomized controlled trial of housing first with ACT in five Canadian cities. *Psychiatric Services, 66*, 463–469. doi:10.1176/appi. ps.201400167

Aurand, A., Cooper, A., Emmanuel, D., Rafi, I., & Yentel, D. (2019). *Out of reach 2019.* Retrieved from National Low Income Housing Coalition website: https://reports. nlihc.org/sites/default/files/oor/OOR_2019.pdf

Badger, E., & Bui, Q. (2019). Cities start to question an American ideal: A house with a yard on every lot. *New York Times.* Retrieved from https://www.nytimes.com/ interactive/2019/06/18/upshot/cities-across-america-question-single-family-zoning.html

Baggett, T. P., Hwang, S. W., O'Connell, J. J., Porneala, B. C., Stringfellow, E. J., Orav, J. E., ... Rigotti, N. A. (2013). Mortality among homeless adults in Boston: Shifts in causes of death over a 15-year period. *JAMA Internal Medicine, 173*(3), 189–195. doi:10.1001/jamainternmed.2013.1604

Bahr, H. M. (1968). *Homelessness and disaffiliation.* New York, NY: Columbia University Bureau of Applied Social Research.

Bahr, H. M. (1970). *Disaffiliated men.* Toronto, Canada: University of Toronto.

Bahr, H. M. (1973). *Skid row: An introduction to disaffiliation.* New York, NY: Oxford University Press.

Bahr, H. M., & Caplow, T. (1973). *Old men drunk and sober.* New York, NY: New York University Press.

Barr, A. (2004). Evaluation research. In D. K. Padgett (Ed.), *The qualitative research experience* (pp. 152–161). Wadsworth/Thomson Learning: Belmont, CA.

Barrenger, S. L., Draine, J., Angell, B., & Herman, D. (2017). Reincarceration risk among men with mental illnesses leaving prison: A risk environment analysis. *Community Mental Health Journal, 53*, 883–892. doi:10.1007/s10597-017-0113-z

Barron, J. (2009, September 8). *State discriminated against mentally ill, judge rules.* The New York Times, p. A24.

Basler, B. (1985, December 17). Koch limits using welfare hotels. *The New York Times.* Retrieved from https://www.nytimes.com/1985/12/17/nyregion/koch-limits-using-welfare-hotels.html

Bassuk, E. L., DeCandia, C. J., Tsertsvadze, A., & Richard, M. K. (2014). The effectiveness of housing interventions and housing and service interventions on ending family homelessness: A systematic review. *American Journal of Orthopsychiatry, 84*(5), 457–474. doi:10.1037/ort0000020

Bassuk, E. L., & Rosenberg, L. (1988). Why does family homelessness occur? A case-control study. *American Journal of Public Health, 78*(7), 783–788. doi:10.2105/ AJPH.78.7.783

Bassuk, E. L., Weinreb, L. F., Buckner, J. C., Browne, A., Salomon, A., & Bassuk, S. S. (1996). The characteristics and needs of sheltered homeless and low-income housed mothers. *Journal of the American Medical Association, 276*(8), 640–646. doi:10.1001/jama.1996.03540080062031

Batty, M., Bricker, J., Briggs, J., Holmquist, E., McIntosh, S., Moore, K., ... Henriques Volz, A. (2019). *Introducing the distributional financial accounts of the United States* (Finance and Economics Discussion Series 2019-017). Retrieved from Federal Reserve System website: https://www.federalreserve.gov/econres/feds/files/2019017pap.pdf

Bell, A., Sard, B., & Koepnick, B. (2018). *Prohibiting discrimination against renters using housing vouchers improves results: Lessons from cities and states that have enacted source of income laws.* Retrieved from Center on Budget and Policy Priorities website: https://www.cbpp.org/sites/default/files/atoms/files/10-10-18hous.pdf

Belman, D., & Wolfson, P. J. (2014). Introduction. In D. Belman & P. J. Wolfson (Eds.), *What does the minimum wage do?* (pp. 1–18). Kalamazoo, MI: W.E. Upjohn Institute for Employment Research.

Benner, K., Thrush, G., & Isaac, M. (2019). Facebook engages in housing discrimination with its ad practices, U.S. says. *New York Times.* Retrieved from https://www.nytimes.com/2019/03/28/us/politics/facebook-housing-discrimination.html

Bernard, K. E. (2019). *Nashville's point-in-time count: An analysis of shelter utilization and homeless encampments.* (Unpublished thesis). Human and Organizational Development, Vanderbilt University, Nashville, TN.

Bernstein, N. (2001, February 7). Homeless shelters in New York fill to highest levels since 80's. *The New York Times.* Retrieved from https://www.nytimes.com/2001/02/08/nyregion/homeless-shelters-in-new-york-fill-to-highest-level-since-80-s.html

Bertrand, M., & Mullainathan, S. (2004). Are Emily and Greg more employable than Lakisha and Jamal? A field experiment on labor market discrimination. *The American Economic Review, 94*(4), 991–1013. doi:10.3386/w9873

Bipartisan Policy Center. (2013). *Housing America's future: New directions for national policy.* Retrieved from https://bipartisanpolicy.org/report/housing-americas-future-new-directions-national-policy

Bipartisan Policy Center. (2015a). *Background memorandum: Measuring likely participation in an open-enrollment housing voucher program for extremely low-income households.* Retrieved from https://bipartisanpolicy.org/wp-content/uploads/2019/03/Housing-Voucher-Recommendation-Memo-January-2015.pdf

Bipartisan Policy Center. (2015b). Housing the families who need it most is within our reach. Retrieved from https://bipartisanpolicy.org/library/housing-the-families-who-need-it-most-is-within-our-reach

Bogue, D. J. (1963). *Skid row in American cities.* Chicago, IL: University of Chicago Press.

Bolen, E., & Dean, S. (2018). *Waivers add key state flexibility to SNAP's three-month time limit.* Retrieved from Center on Budget & Policy Priorities website: https://www.cbpp.org/sites/default/files/atoms/files/3-24-17fa.pdf

Bourquin, R. (2015). *Emergency Assistance (EA) shelter: The top ten things for advocates to know.* Retrieved from https://www.masslegalservices.org/content/emergency-assistance-ea-shelter-top-ten-things-advocates-know

Bowles, N. (2018). Dorm living for professionals comes to San Francisco. *New York Times.* Retrieved from https://www.nytimes.com/2018/03/04/technology/dorm-living-grown-ups-san-francisco.html?module=inline

Brehm, J. W. (1956). Postdecision changes in the desirability of alternatives. *Journal of Abnormal and Social Psychology, 52*(3), 384–389. doi:10.1037/h0041006

Brinkley-Rubinstein, L., & Turner, W. L. (2013). Health impact of incarceration on HIV-positive African American males: A qualitative exploration. *AIDS Patient Care and STDs, 27*(8), 450–458. doi:10.1089/apc.2012.0457

Bronson, J., & Berzofsky, M. (2017). *Indicators of mental health problems reported by prisoners and jail inmates, 2011–12* (NCJ250612). Retrieved from Bureau of Justice Statistics website: https://www.bjs.gov/content/pub/pdf/imhprpji1112.pdf

Broton, K., & Goldrick-Rab, S. (2018). Going without: An exploration of food and housing insecurity among undergraduates. *Educational Researcher, 47*(2), 121–133. doi:10.3102/0013189X17741303

Brown, M., Cummings, C., Lyons, J., Carrión, A., & Watson, D. P. (2018). Reliability and validity of the Vulnerability Index-Service Prioritization Decision Assistance Tool (VI-SPDAT) in real-world implementation. *Journal of Social Distress & the Homeless, 27*(2), 110–117. doi:10.1080/10530789.2018.1482991

Brown, S. R., Shinn, M., & Khadduri, J. (2017). *Well-being of young children after experiencing homelessness*. Retrieved from Administration for Children & Families website: https://www.acf.hhs.gov/opre/resource/well-being-of-young-children-after-experiencing-homelessness

Browne, A., & Bassuk, S. S. (1997). Intimate violence in the lives of homeless and poor housed women: Prevalence and patterns in an ethnically diverse sample. *American Journal of Orthopsychiatry, 67*(2), 261–278. doi:10.1037/h0080230

Browne, J., & Neumann, D. (2017). *OECD tax wedge and effective tax rates on labour: Childcare costs in 2015* (No. VS/2015/0427 (DI150030)). Retrieved from Organisation for Economic Co-operation and Development website: https://taxben.oecd.org/tax-ben-resources/Childcare-costs-in-2015.pdf

Bureau of Labor Statistics. (2018). Contingent and alternative employment arrangements—May 2017 [Press release]. Retrieved from https://www.bls.gov/news.release/pdf/conemp.pdf

Burnside, A., & Floyd, I. (2019). *TANF benefits remain low despite recent increases in some states*. Retrieved from Center on Budget & Policy Priorities website: https://www.cbpp.org/sites/default/files/atoms/files/10-30-14tanf.pdf

Buron, L., Nolden, S., Heintz, K., & Stewart, J. (2000). *Assessment of the economic and social characteristics of LIHTC residents and neighborhoods: Final report*. Washington, DC: Government Printing Office.

Burrows, R. (1997). The social distribution of the experience of homelessness. In R. Burrows, N. Pleace, & D. Quilgars (Eds.), *Homelessness and social policy* (pp. 50–68). London, UK: Routledge.

Burt, M. R. (2010). *Life after transitional housing for homeless families*. Retrieved from U.S Department of Housing and Urban Development website: https://www.huduser.gov/portal/publications/povsoc/trans_hsg.html

Burt, M. R., Aron, L. Y., Douglas, T., Valente, J., Lee, E., & Iwen, B. (1999). *Homelessness: Programs and the people they serve. Findings of the National Survey of Homeless Assistance Providers and Clients*. Retrieved from Urban Institute website: https://www.urban.org/research/publication/homelessness-programs-and-people-they-serve-findings-national-survey-homeless-assistance-providers-and-clients

Burt, M. R., Pearson, C. L., & Montgomery, A. E. (2007). *Homelessness: Prevention, strategies and effectiveness*. New York, NY: Nova Science Publishers, Inc.

Burtless, G. (2015). Does the government subsidize low-wage employers? Retrieved from Brookings website: https://www.brookings.edu/opinions/does-the-government-subsidize-low-wage-employers

Bush, H., & Shinn, M. (2017). Families' experiences of doubling up after homelessness. *Cityscape, 19*(3), 331–356.

Byrne, T., & Culhane, D. P. (2016). *Medicaid funding for critical time intervention: A scalable solution to crisis homelessness?* Paper presented at the Reckoning with Homelessness Conference, New York University.

Byrne, T., Fargo, J. D., Montgomery, A. E., Roberts, C. B., Culhane, D. P., & Kane, V. (2015). Screening for homelessness in the Veterans Health Administration: Monitoring housing stability through repeat screening. *Public Health Reports, 130*(6), 684–692. doi:10.1177/003335491513000618

Byrne, T., Treglia, D., Culhane, D. P., Kuhn, J., & Kane, V. (2015). Predictors of homelessness among families and single adults after exit from homelessness prevention and rapid re-housing programs: Evidence from the Department of Veterans Affairs Supportive Services for veteran families program. *Housing Policy Debate, 26*(1), 252–272. doi:10.1080/10511482.2015.1060249

California Department of Housing & Community Development. (2018). Accessory Dwelling Units (ADUs). Retrieved from www.hcd.ca.gov/policy-research/AccessoryDwellingUnits.shtml

Capps, K. (2018). The Trump Administration just derailed a key Obama rule on housing segregation. *CityLab*. Retrieved from https://www.citylab.com/equity/2018/01/the-trump-administration-derailed-a-key-obama-rule-on-housing-segregation/549746

Card, D., & Krueger, A. B. (1993). *Minimun wages and employment: A case study of the fast food industry in New Jersey and Pennsylvania* (Working Paper No. 4509). Retrieved from National Bureau of Economic Research website: https://www.nber.org/papers/w4509.pdf

Carliner, M., & Marya, E. (2016). *Rental housing: An international comparison.* Retrieved from The Harvard Joint Center for Housing Studies website: http://www.jchs.harvard.edu/sites/default/files/international_rental_housing_carliner_marya.pdf

Carr, J. H., Rengert, K. M., & Huh, K. (2004). Comment on Michael A. Stegman, Walter R. Davis, and Roberto Quercia's "the earned income tax credit as an instrument of housing policy". *Housing Policy Debate, 15*(2), 289–300. doi:10.1080/10511482.2004.9521503

Castellanos, H. D. (2016). The role of institutional placement, family conflict, and homosexuality in homelessness pathways among Latino LGBT youth in New York City. *Journal of Homosexuality, 63*(5), 601–632. doi:10.1080/00918369.2015.1111108

Cengiz, D., Dube, A., Lindner, A., & Zipperer, B. (2019). The effect of minimum wages on low-wage jobs. *The Quarterly Journal of Economics.* doi:10.1093/qje/qjz014

Chaskin, R. J., & Joseph, M. L. (2015). *Integrating the inner city: The promise and perils of mixed-income public housing transformation.* Chicago, IL: University of Chicago Press.

Chaudry, A. (2004). *Putting children first: How low-wage mothers manage child care.* New York, NY: Russell Sage.

Chetty, R., & Hendren, N. (2018). The impacts of neighborhoods on intergenerational mobility I: Childhood exposure effects. *The Quarterly Journal of Economics, 133*(3), 1107–1162. doi:10.1093/qje/qjy007

Churchill, S., Holin, M. J., Khadduri, J., & Turnham, J. (2001). *Strategies that enhance community relations in the tenant-based Housing Choice Voucher Programs.* Retrieved from U.S. Department of Housing and Urban Development website: https://www. huduser.gov/portal/Publications/pdf/hcvp_finalrpt.pdf

City of New Orleans, & Housing Authority of New Orleans. (2016). *Office of Community Development 2016 Assessment of Fair Housing.* Retrieved from https://www.nola.gov/ community-development/documents/2016-updated-afh-plan-090516/ afh-plan-090516-final

City of Seattle, & Seattle Housing Authority. (2017). *2017 City of Seattle and Seattle Housing Authority Joint Assessment of Fair Housing.* Retrieved from Seattle gov website: https:// www.seattle.gov/Documents/Departments/HumanServices/CDBG/2017% 20AFH%20Final.4.25.17V2.pdf

Clatts, M. C., Goldsamt, L., Huso, Y., & Gwadz, M. V. (2005). Homelessness and drug abuse among young men who have sex with men in New York city: A preliminary epidemiological trajectory. *Journal of Adolescence, 28*, 201–214. doi:10.1016/ j.adolescence.2005.02.003

Cohen, R., Yetvin, W., & Khadduri, J. (2019). *Understanding encampments of people experiencing homelessness and community responses: Emerging evidence as of late 2018.* Retrieved from U.S. Department of Housing and Urban Development: https:// www.huduser.gov/portal/publications/Understanding-Encampments.html

Collinson, R., Ellen, I. G., & Ludwig, J. (2015). *Low-income housing policy* (Working Paper 21071). Retrieved from National Bureau of Economic Research website: https://www.nber.org/papers/w21071.pdf

Collinson, R., & Ganong, P. (2018). How do changes in housing voucher design affect rent and neighborhood quality? *American Economic Journal: Economic Policy, 10*(2), 62–89. doi:10.1257/pol.20150176

Community Solutions & OrgCode Consulting Inc. (2014). *The Vulnerability Index-Service Prioritization Decision Assistance Tool (VI-SPDAT)* (Manual for single person households). Author.

Conley, D. (1999). *Being black, living in the red: Race, wealth, and social policy in America.* Berkeley, CA: University of California Press.

Couloute, L., & Kopf, D. (2018). *Out of prison & out of work: Unemployment among formerly incarcerated people.* Retrieved from Prison Policy Initiative website: https:// www.prisonpolicy.org/reports/outofwork.html

County of Los Angeles Office of the Homeless Initiative. (2019). *Quarterly Report 12.* Retrieved from http://homeless.lacounty.gov/wp-content/uploads/2019/02/ Homeless-Initiative-Quarterly-Rpt-No.12-.pdf

Cowal, K., Shinn, M., Weitzman, B. C., Stojanovic, D., & Labay, L. (2002). Mother-child separations among homeless and housed families receiving public assistance in New York City. *American Journal of Community Psychology, 30*(5), 711–730. doi:10.1023/A:1016325332527

Cragg, M., & O'Flaherty, B. (1999). Do homeless shelter conditions determine shelter population? The case of Dinkins deluge. *Journal of Urban Economics, 46*(3), 377–415. doi:10.1006/juec.1998.2128

Crenshaw, K. (1989). Demarginalizing the intersection of race and sex: A black feminist critique of antidiscrimination doctrine, feminist theory, and antiracist politics. *University of Chicago Legal Forum, 1989*, 139–167.

Culhane, D. P. (1992). The quandaries of shelter reform: An appraisal of efforts to "manage" homelessness. *Social Service Review, 63*, 429–440. doi: 10.1086/603931

Culhane, D. P., Dejowski, E. F., Ibanez, J., Needham, E., & Macchia, I. (1994). Public shelter admission rates in Philadelphia and New York City: The implications of turnover for sheltered population counts. *Housing Policy Debate, 5*(2), 107–140. doi:10.1080/10511482.1994.9521155

Culhane, D. P., Gross, K. S., Parker, W. D., Poppe, B., & Sykes, E. (2008). *Accountability, cost-effectiveness, and program performance: Progress since 1998.* Retrieved from http://repository.upenn.edu/spp_papers/114

Culhane, D. P., Lee, C.-M., & Wachter, S. M. (1996). Where the homeless come from: A study of the prior address distribution of families admitted to public shelters in New York City and Philadelphia. *Housing Policy Debate, 7*(2), 327–365. doi:10.1080/10511482.1996.9521224

Culhane, D. P., Metraux, S., & Byrne, T. (2011). A prevention-centered approach to homelessness assistance: A paradigm shift. *Housing Policy Debate, 21*(2), 295–315. doi:10.1080/10511482.2010.536246

Culhane, D. P., Metraux, S., Byrne, T., Stino, M., & Bainbridge, J. (2013). The age structure of contemporary homlessness: Evidence and implications for public policy. *Analyses of Social Issues and Public Policy, 13*(1), 228–244. doi:10.1111/asap.12004

Culhane, D. P., Metraux, S., Park, J. M., Schretzman, M., & Valente, J. (2007). Testing a typology of family homelessness based on patterns of public shelter utilization in four U.S. jurisdictions: Implications for policy and program planning. *Housing Policy Debate, 18*(1), 1–28.

Culhane, J. F., Webb, D., Grim, S., Metraux, S., & Culhane, D. (2003). Prevalence of child welfare services involvement among homeless and low-income mothers: A five-year birth cohort study. *Journal of Sociology & Social Welfare, 30*(3), 79–95.

Cunningham, M., Burt, M. R., Scott, M., Locke, G., Buron, L., Klerman, J., … Stillman, L. (2015). *Prevention programs funded by the homelessness prevention and rapid rehousing program.* Retrieved from U.S. Department of Housing and Urban Development website: https://www.huduser.gov/portal/sites/default/files/pdf/HPRP-report.pdf

Cunningham, M., Galvez, M., Aranda, C. L., Santos, R., Wissoker, D., Oneto, A., … Crawford, J. (2018). *A pilot study of landlord acceptance of housing choice vouchers: Executive summary.* Retrieved from U.S. Department of Housing and Urban Development website: https://www.huduser.gov/portal/publications/pilot-study-landlord-acceptance-hcv-exec-summ.html

Cutuli, J. J., Montgomery, A. E., Evans-Chase, M., & Culhane, D. P. (2017). Childhood adversity, adult homelessness and the intergenerational transmission of risk: A population-representative study of individuals in households with children. *Child and Family Social Work, 22*(1), 116–125. doi:10.1111/cfs.12207

Darity, W., Hamilton, D., Paul, M., Aja, A., Price, A., Moore, A., & Chiopris, C. (2018). *What we get wrong about closing the racial wealth gap.* Retrieved from Duke University Center on Social Equity website: https://socialequity.duke.edu/sites/socialequity.duke.edu/files/site-images/FINAL%20COMPLETE%20REPORT_.pdf

Dasinger, L. K., & Speiglman, R. (2007). Homelessness prevention: The effect of a shallow rent subsidy program on housing outcomes among people with HIV or AIDS. *AIDS and Behavior, 11*, S128–S139. doi:10.1007/s10461-007-9250-7

Dastrup, S., Finkel, M., Burnett, K., & de Sousa, T. (2018). *Small area fair market rent demonstration evaluation: Final report.* Retrieved from U.S. Department of Housing and Urban Development website: https://www.huduser.gov/portal/publications/Small-Area-FMR-Evaluation-Final-Report.html

Davidson, C., Neighbors, C., Hall, G., Hogue, A., Cho, R., Kutner, B., & Morgenstern, J. (2014). Association of Housing First implementation and key outcomes among homeless persons with problematic substance abuse. *Psychiatric Services, 65*(11), 1318–1324. doi:10.1176/appi.ps.201300195

Dawes, R. M., Faust, D., & Meehl, P. E. (1989). Clinical versus actuarial judgment. *Science, 243*(4899), 1668–1674. Retrieved from http://www.jstor.org/stable/1703476

de Vet, R., Beijersbergen, M. D., Jonker, I. E., Lako, D. A. M., van Hermert, A. M., Herman, D. B., & Wolf, J. R. L. M. (2017). Critical time intervention for homeless people making the transition to community living: A randomized control trial. *American Journal of Community Psychology, 60*(175–186). doi:10.1002/ajcp.12150

Dennis, D., Lassiter, M., Connelly, W. H., & Lupfer, K. S. (2011). Helping adults who are homeless gain disability benefits: The SSI/SSDI Outreach, Access, and Recovery (SOAR) program. *Psychiatric Services, 62*(11), 1373–1376. doi:10.1176/ps.62.11.pss6211_1373

Desmond, M. (2016). *Evicted: Poverty and profit in the American city.* New York, NY: Crown Publishers.

Desmond, M., & Perkins, K. L. (2016). Are landlords overcharging housing voucher holders? *City and Community, 15*(2), 137–162. doi:10.1111/cico.12180

Devine, D. J., Gray, R. W., Rubin, L., & Taghavi, L. B. (2003). *Housing Choice Voucher location patterns: Implications for participants and neighborhood welfare.* Retrieved from U.S. Department of Housing and Urban Development website: https://www.huduser.gov/publications/pdf/location_paper.pdf

Dolbeare, C. N. (1991). *Out of reach: Why everyday people can't find affordable housing* (2nd ed.). Washington, DC: Low Income Housing Information Service.

Dolbeare, C. N. (1992). *The widening gap: Housing needs of low income families: Findings from the American Housing Survey 1989.* Washington, DC: Low Income Housing Information Service.

Dolbeare, C. N. (2001). Housing affordability: Challenge and context. *Cityscape, 5*(2), 111–130. Retrieved from https://www.jstor.org/stable/20868520

Dolbeare, C. N. (2004). Comment on Michael A. Stegman, Walter R. Davis, and Roberto Quercia's "the earned income tax credit as an instrument of housing policy". *Housing Policy Debate, 15*(2), 261–277. doi:10.1080/10511482.2004.9521501

Doran, K. M., Johns, E., Shinn, M., Schretzman, M., Shelley, D., McCormack, R. P., ... Mijanovich, T. (2019, September). *Predicting imminent homelessness among Emergency Department Patients with unhealthy alcohol or drug use.* INEBRIA, Lubeck, Germany.

Dordick, G., O'Flaherty, B., Brounstein, J., Sinha, S., & Yoo, J. (2018). What happens when you give money to panhandlers? The case of downtown Manhattan. *Journal of Urban Economics, 108*, 107–123. doi:10.1016/j.jue.2018.09.005

Draine, J., & Herman, D. B. (2007). Critical time intervention for reentry from prison for persons with mental illness. *Psychiatric Services, 58*(12), 1577–1581. doi:10.1176/ps.2007.58.12.1577

Draine, J., Salzer, M. S., Culhane, D. P., & Hadley, T. R. (2002). Role of social disadvantage in crime, joblessness, and homelessness among persons with serious mental illness. *Psychiatric Services, 53*(5), 565–573. doi:10.1176/appi.ps.53.5.565

Dube, A. (2018). *Minimum wages and the distribution of family incomes* (Working Paper 25240). Retrieved from National Bureau of Economic Research website: https://www.nber.org/papers/w25240

Dube, A., Lester, T. W., & Reich, M. (2010). Minimum wage effects across state borders: Estimates using contiguous counties. *Review of Economics and Statistics, 92*(4), 945–964. doi:10.1162/REST_a_00039

Dunton, L., & Brown, S. R. (2019). *Rapid re-housing in 2018: Program features and assistance models.* Rockville, MD: Abt Associates.

Dunton, L., Henry, M., Kean, E., & Khadduri, J. (2014). *Study of PHAs' efforts to serve people experiencing homelessness.* Retrieved from U.S. Department of Housing & Urban Development website: https://www.huduser.gov/portal/publications/pha_homelessness.pdf

Durso, L. E., & Gates, G. J. (2012). *Serving our youth. Findings from a national survey of service providers working with lesbian, gay, bisexual, and transgender youth who are homeless or at risk of becoming homeless.* Retrieved from The Williams Institute website: https://williamsinstitute.law.ucla.edu/wp-content/uploads/Durso-Gates-LGBT-Homeless-Youth-Survey-July-2012.pdf

Dworsky, A., Napolitano, L., & Courtney, M. (2013). Homelessness during the transition from foster care to adulthood. *American Journal of Public Health, 103*(S2), S318–S323. doi:10.2105/AJPH.2013.301455

Ecker, J., Aubry, T., & Sylvestre, J. (2019). A review of the literature on LGBTQ adults who experience homelessness. *Journal of Homosexuality, 66*(3), 297–323. doi:10.1080/00918369.2017.1413277

Edin, K., DeLuca, S., & Owens, A. (2012). Constrained compliance: Solving the puzzle of MTO's lease-up rates and why mobility matters. *Cityscape: A Journal of Policy Development and Research, 14*(2), 181–194.

Edin, K., & Shaefer, H. L. (2015). *$2.00 a day.* New York, NY: Houghlin Mifflin Harcourt Publishing.

Eggers, F. J., & Moumen, F. (2013a). *American Housing Survey: Housing adequacy and quality as measured by the AHS.* Retrieved from U.S. Census Bureau website: https://www.census.gov/content/dam/Census/programs-surveys/ahs/publications/HousingAdequacy.pdf

Eggers, F. J., & Moumen, F. (2013b). *Analysis of trends in household composition using American Housing Survey data.* Bethesda, MD: US Depatment of Housing and Urban Development, Office of Policy Development and Research.

Ellen, I. G., Schill, M. H., Schwartz, A. E., & Voicu, I. (2003). *Housing production subsidies and neighborhood revitalization: New York City's ten-year capital plan for housing.* Retrieved from Federal Reserve Bank of New York website: https://www.newyorkfed.org/medialibrary/media/research/epr/03v09n2/0306elle.pdf

Eriksen, M. D., & Ross, A. (2015). Housing vouchers and the price of rental housing. *American Economic Journal: Economic Policy, 7*(3), 154–176. doi:10.1257/pol.20130064

European Federation of National Associations Working with the Homeless AISBL. (2017). ETHOS – Eurpoean Typology of Homelessness and Housing Exclusion. Retrieved from https://www.feantsa.org/download/ethos2484215748748239888.pdf

Evans, W. N., Sullivan, J. X., & Wallskog, M. (2016). The impact of homelessness prevention programs on homelessness. *Science, 353*(6300), 694–699. doi:10.1126/science.aag0833

Falk, G. (2014). *Temporary Assistance for Needy Families (TANF): Eligibility and benefit amounts in state TANF cash assistance programs* (R43634). Retrieved from Federation of American Scientists website: https://fas.org/sgp/crs/misc/R43634.pdf

Family and Youth Services Bureau. (n.d.). *Runaway and homeless youth.* Retrieved from https://www.acf.hhs.gov/fysb/rhy-interoperability

Fazel, S., Geddes, J. R., & Kushel, M. (2014). The health of homeless people in high-income countries: Descriptive epidemiology, health consequences, and clinical and policy reccomendations. *Lancet, 384,* 1529–1540. doi:10.1016/S0140-6736(14)61132-6

Fazel, S., Khosla, V., Doll, H., & Geddes, J. (2008). The prevalence of mental disorders among the homeless in Western countries: Systematic review and meta-regression analysis. *PLoS Medicine, 5*(12), 1670–1681. doi:10.1371/journal.pmed.0050225

Feins, J. D., Fosburg, L. B., & Locke, G. (1994). *Evaluation of the Emergency Shelter Grants Program volume 1: Findings.* Washington, DC: U.S. Department of Housing and Urban Development.

Felton, B. J., & Shinn, M. (1981). Ideology and practice of deinstitutionalization. *Journal of Social Issues, 37*(3), 158–172. doi:10.1111/j.1540-4560.1981.tb00835.x

Fertig, A. R., & Reingold, D. A. (2008). Homelessness among at risk families with children in twenty American cities. *Social Service Review, 82*(3), 485–510. doi:10.1086/592335

Festinger, L., & Carlsmith, J. M. (1959). Cognitive consequences of forced compliance. *Journal of Abnormal and Social Psychology, 58*(2), 203–210. doi:10.1037/h0041593

Finkel, M., & Buron, L. (2001). *Study on Section 8 voucher success rates: Volume 1 Quantative study of success rates in metropolitan areas.* Retrieved from U.S. Department of Housing and Urban Development website: https://www.huduser.gov/publications/pdf/sec8success.pdf

Finkel, M., Henry, M., Matthews, N., & Spellman, B. (2016). *Rapid Re-housing Demonstration program: Part II: Demonstration findings-Outcomes evaluation.* Retrieved from U.S. Department of Housing and Urban Development website: https://www.huduser.gov/portal/sites/default/files/pdf/RRHD-PartII-Outcomes.pdf

Firdion, J.-M., & Marpsat, M. (2003). Homeless research in France: Definition of homelessness, research, and legislation in its last developments. *Constructing Understanding of the Homeless Population.* Retrieved from https://www.academia.edu/17203384/Homeless_research_in_France_definition_of_homelessness_research_and_legislation_and_its_last_developments

Firdion, J.-M., & Marpsat, M. (2007). A research program on homelessness in France. *Journal of Social Issues, 63*(3), 567–588. doi:10.1111/j.1540-4560.2007.00524.x

Fischer, S. N., Shinn, M., Shrout, P., & Tsemberis, S. (2008). Homelessness, mental illness, and criminal activity: Examining patterns over time. *American Journal of Community Psychology, 42,* 251–265. doi:10.1007/s10464-008-9210-z

Fischer, W., Sard, B., & Mazzara, A. (2017). *Renters' credit would help low-wage workers, seniors, and people with disabilities afford housing.* Retrieved from Center on Budget Policy Priorities website: https://www.cbpp.org/research/housing/renters-credit-would-help-low-wage-workers-seniors-and-people-with-disabilities

Fisher, B. W., Mayberry, L. S., Shinn, M., & Khadduri, J. (2014). Leaving homelessness behind: Housing decisions among families exiting shelter. *Housing Policy Debate, 24*(2), 364–386. doi:10.1080/10511482.2013.852603

Fisher, J., & Smeeding, T. (2016). *Income inequality. State of the Union: The Poverty and Inequality Report,* 32–38. Retrieved from Standford Center on Poverty & Inequality website: http://inequality.stanford.edu/sites/default/files/Pathways-SOTU-2016-2.pdf

Floyd, I. (2017). *As TANF ages, its performance as a safety net and work program worsens.* Retrieved from Center on Budget and Policy Priorities website: https://www.cbpp.org/blog/as-tanf-ages-its-performance-as-a-safety-net-and-work-program-worsens

Floyd, I., Pavetti, L., & Schott, L. (2017). Lessons from TANF: Initial unequal state block-grant funding formula grew more unequal over time. Retrieved from Center on Budget and Policy Priorities website: https://www.cbpp.org/research/family-income-support/lessons-from-tanf-initial-unequal-state-block-grant-funding-formula

Fontenot, K., Semega, J., & Kollar, M. (2018). *Income and poverty in the United States. (PGO-263).* Washington, DC: United States Census Bureau.

Forry, N. D., Daneri, P., & Howarth, G. (2013). *Child care subsidy literature review* (OPRE Brief 2013-60). Retrieved from Administration for Children and Families website: https://www.acf.hhs.gov/sites/default/files/opre/subsidy_literature_review.pdf

Fowler, P. J., & Chavira, D. (2014). Family unification program: Housing services for homeless child welfare-involved families. *Housing Policy Debate, 24*(4), 802–814. doi: 10.1080/10511482.2014.881902

Fox, L. (2018). *The supplemental poverty measure.* Retrieved from U.S. Census Bureau website: https://www.census.gov/content/dam/Census/library/publications/2018/demo/p60-265.pdf.

Friedman, S., Reynolds, A., Scovill, S., Brassier, F. R., Campbell, R., & Ballou, M. (2013). *An estimate of housing discrimination against same-sex couples.* Retrieved from U.S. Department of Housing and Urban Development website: https://www.huduser.gov/portal/publications/fairhsg/discrim_samesex.html.

Fueller, R. (2016, May 11). *HomeBase homelessness prevention presentation.* Paper presented at the Reckoning with Homelessness Conference, New York, NY.

Furman Center for Real Estate and Urban Policy. (2006). *Housing policy in New York City: A brief history* (Working paper 06-01). Retrieved from http://furmancenter.org/files/publications/AHistoryofHousingPolicycombined0601_000.pdf

Gaetz, S. (2014). Can housing first work for youth? *European Journal of Homelessness, 8*(2), 159–175.

Gaetz, S., Dej, E., Richter, T., & Redman, M. (2016). *The state of homelessness in Canada.* Toronto, Canada: Canadian Observatory on Homlessness Press.

Gaetz, S., & Scott, F. (2012). *Live, learn, grow: Supporting transitions to adulthood for homeless youth – A framework for the foyer in Canada.* Retrieved from The Homeless Hub website: https://homelesshub.ca/sites/default/files/foyer_report23112012.pdf

Galster, G., & Godfrey, E. (2005). By words and deeds: Racial steering by real estate agents in the U.S. in 2000. *Journal of the American Planning Association, 71*(3), 251–268. doi:10.1080/01944360508976697

Garriga, C., Ricketts, L. R., & Schlagenhauf, D. E. (2017). The homeownership experience of minorities during the great recession. *Federal Reserve Bank of St. Louis Review, 99*(1), 139–167. doi:10.20955/r.2017.139-67

General Accounting Office. (1977). *Returning the mentally disabled to the community: Government needs to do more.* (HRD-76-152). Retrieved from https://www.gao.gov/assets/120/117385.pdf.

General Accounting Office. (1990). *Too early to tell what kind of prevention assistance work best.* Retrieved from https://www.gao.gov/assets/150/148923.pdf

Gilmer, T. P., Stefancic, A., Katz, M. L., Sklar, M., Tsemberis, S., & Palinkas, L. A. (2014). Fidelity to the housing first model and effectiveness of permanent supported housing programs in California. *Psychiatric Services, 65*(11). doi:10.1176/appi.ps.201300447

Glendening, Z., & Shinn, M. (2018). *Predicting repeated and persistent family homelessness: Do families' characteristics and experiences matter?* (OPRE Report No.2018–104). Retrieved from Office of Planning, Research & Evaluation website: https://www.acf.hhs.gov/sites/default/files/opre/opre_persistent_homelesss_brief_10_9_18_508_compliant.pdf

Goering, P., Veldhuizen, S., Nelson, G. B., Stefancic, A., Tsemberis, S., Adair, C. E., ... Streiner, D. L. (2016). Further validation of the pathways housing first fidelity scale. *Psychiatric Services, 67*, 111–114. doi:10.1176/appi.ps.201400359

Goering, P., Veldhuizen, S., Watson, A., Adair, C. E., Kopp, B., Latimer, E., ... Aubry, T. (2014). *National At Home/Chez Soi final report.* Retrieved from Mental Health Commission of Canada website: https://www.mentalhealthcommission.ca/sites/default/files/mhcc_at_home_report_national_cross-site_eng_2_0.pdf

Goodman, L. A. (1991). The prevalence of abuse among homeless and housed poor mothers: A comparison study. *American Journal of Orthopsychiatry, 61*(4), 489–500. doi:10.1037/h0079287

Goodman, S., Messeri, P., & O'Flaherty, B. (2016). Homelessness prevention in New York City: On average, it works. *Journal of Housing Economics, 31*, 14–34. doi:10.1016/j.jhe.2015.12.001

Gordon, L. A. (1989, January 9). Letter to the editor. *The New York Times.*

Gornick, J. C., & Jäntti, M. (2016). Poverty. In *State of the Union: The Poverty and Inequality Report* [Special issue], 15–24. Retrieved from Stanford Center of Poverty and Inequality website: http://inequality.stanford.edu/sites/default/files/Pathways-SOTU-2016-2.pdf.

Gosselin, P., & Zimmerman, S. (2008). *Trends in income volatility and Risk, 1970–2004.* Paper presented at the Association for Public Policy Analysis and Management Fall Research Conference, Los Angeles, CA.

Government Accountability Office. (2010). *Housing and community grants: HUD needs to enhance its requirements and oversight of jurisdictions' fair housing plans* (GAO-10-905). Retrieved from https://www.gao.gov/assets/320/311065.pdf

Gramlich, E. (2017). *Housing the lowest income people: An analysis of national housing trust fund draft allocation plans.* Retrieved from National Low Income Housing Coalition website: https://nlihc.org/sites/default/files/NHTF_Allocation-Report_2017.pdf

Greer, A. L. (2014). *Preventing homelessness in Alameda County, CA and New York City, NY: Investigating effectiveness and efficiency* (Dissertation). Human and Organizational Development, Vanderbilt University, Nashville, TN.

Greer, A. L., Shinn, M., Kwon, J., & Zuiderveen, S. (2016). Targeting services to individuals most likely to enter shelter: Evaluating the efficiency of homelessness prevention. *Social Service Review, 90*(1), 130–155. doi:10.1086/686466

Grigsby, C., Baumann, D., Gregorich, S. E., & Roberts-Gray, C. (1990). Disaffiliation to entrenchment: A model for understanding homelessness. *Journal of Social Issues, 46*(4), 141–156. doi:10.1111/j.1540-4560.1990.tb01803.x

Grove, W. M., Zald, D. H., Lebow, B. S., Snitz, B. E., & Nelson, C. (2000). Clinical versus mechanical prediction: A meta-analysis. *Psychological Assessment, 12*(1), 19–30. doi:10.1037/1040-3590.12.1.19

Gruber, J. (2016). *Security accounts as short term social insurance and long term savings: Expanding financial security for workers in the new economy.* Fresh Perspective Series. Retrieved from The Aspen Institute website: https://www.aspeninstitute.org/publications/gruber

Gubits, D., Bishop, K., Dunton, L., Wood, M., Albanese, T., Spellman, B. E., & Khadduri, J. (2017). *Understanding rapid re-housing. Systematic review of rapid re-housing outcomes literature.* Washington, DC: U.S. Department of Housing and Urban Development.

Gubits, D., McCall, T., Brown, S. R., & Wood, M. (2017). *Family options study summary report.* Retrieved from U.S. Department of Housing and Urban Development website: https://www.huduser.gov/portal/sites/default/files/pdf/FamilyOptionsStudySummaryReport.pdf

Gubits, D., Shinn, M., Bell, S. H., Wood, M., Dastrup, S. R., Solari, C. D., ... Spellman, B. E. (2015). *Family options study: Short-term impacts of housing and services interventions for homeless families.* Retrieved from U.S. Department of Housing and Urban Development website: http://www.huduser.org/portal//portal/sites/default/files/pdf/FamilyOptionsStudy_final.pdf

Gubits, D., Shinn, M., Wood, M., Bell, S. H., Dastrup, S. R., Solari, C. D., ... Kattel, U. (2016). *Family options study: 3-year impacts of housing and services interventions for homeless families.* Retrieved from U.S. Department of Housing and Urban Development website: https://www.huduser.gov/portal/sites/default/files/pdf/Family-Options-Study-Full-Report.pdf

Gubits, D., Shinn, M., Wood, M., Brown, S. R., Dastrup, S. R., & Bell, S. H. (2018). What interventions work best for families who experience homelessness? Impact estimates from the family options study. *Journal of Policy Analysis & Management, 37*(4), 835–866. doi:10.1002/pam.22071

Gubits, D., Wood, M., McInnis, D., Brown, S. R., Spellman, B., Bell, S. H., & in partnership with Shinn, M. (2013). *Data collection and analysis plan: Family Options Study.* Retrieved from U.S. Department of Housing and Urban Development website: https://www.huduser.gov/portal/publications/pdf/HUD_501_family_options_Data_Collection_Analysis_Plan_v2.pdf

Gulcur, L., Stefancic, A., Shinn, M., Tsemberis, S., & Fischer, S. N. (2003). Housing, hospitalization and cost outcomes for homeless individuals with psychiatric disabilities participating in continuum of care and housing first programmes [special issue]. *Journal of Community & Applied Social Psychology, 13*(2), 171–186. doi:10.1002/casp.723

Hahn, J. A., Kushel, M. B., Bangsberg, D. R., Riley, E., & Moss, A. R. (2006). The aging of the homeless population: Fourteen-year trends in San Francisco. *General Journal of Internal Medicine, 21*, 775–778. doi:10.1111/j.1525-1497.2006.00493.x

Hammel, J., Smith, J., Scovill, S., Campbell, R., & Duan, R. (2017). *Study of rental housing discrimination on the basis of mental disabilities: Final report.* Retrieved from U.S. Department of Housing and Urban Development website: https://www.huduser.gov/portal/sites/default/files/pdf/MentalDisabilities-FinalPaper.pdf.

Hanratty, M. (2017). Do local economic conditions affect homelessness? Impact of area housing market factors, unemployment, and poverty on community homelessness rates. *Housing Policy Debate, 27*(4), 640–655. doi:10.1080/10511482.2017.1282885

Hardiman, D. L., Lynch, C., Martin, M., Vandenbroucke, D. A., & Yao, Y. G. D. (2010). *Worst case housing needs 2007: A report to Congress.* Retrieved from U. S. Department of Housing and Urban Development website: https://www.huduser.gov/portal/publications/affhsg/wc_HsgNeeds07.html.

Haveman, R., Blank, R., Moffitt, R., Smeeding, T., & Wallace, G. (2015). The war on poverty: 50 years later. *Journal of Policy Analysis and Management, 34*(3), 593–638. doi:10.1002/pam.21846

Hayes, M.A, Zonneville, M., & Bassuk, E. (2013). *The SHIFT Study: Final report.* Retrieved from American Institutes for Research website: https://www.air.org/sites/default/files/SHIFT_Service_and_Housing_Interventions_for_Families_in_Transition_final_report.pdf

Hayward, J. (2019). Affordable housing crisis demands renewed focus on housing supply. *Perspectives.* Retrieved from Fannie Mae website: http://www.fanniemae.com/portal/research-insights/perspectives/affordable-housing-supply-hayward-031219.html

Heckman, J. J., Moon, S. H., Pinto, R., Savelyev, P. A., & Yavitz, A. (2010). The rate of return to the HighScope Perry Preschool Program. *Journal of Public Economics, 94*, 114–128. doi:10.1016/j.jpubeco.2009.11.001

Heflin, C. M., & Pattillo, M. (2006). Poverty in the family: Race, siblings, and socioeconomic heterogeneity. *Social Science Research, 35*(4), 804–822. doi:10.1016/j.ssresearch.2004.09.002

Henry, M., Bishop, K., de Sousa, T., Shivji, A., & Watt, R. (2018). *The 2017 Annual Homeless Assessment Report (AHAR) to Congress Part 2: Estimates of Homelessness in the United States.* Retrieved from U.S. Department of Housing and Urban Development website: https://www.hudexchange.info/resource/5769/2017-ahar-part-2-estimates-of-homelessness-in-the-us

Henry, M., Mahathey, A., Morrill, T., Robinson, A., Shivji, A., and Watt, R. (2018). *The 2018 Annual Homeless Assessment Report (AHAR) to Congress Part 1: Point-in-time Estimates of Homelessness.* Retrieved from The U.S Department of Housing and Urban Development: https://www.hudexchange.info/resources/documents/2018-AHAR-Part-1.pdf

Herbert, C. E., & Belsky, E. S. (2008). The homeownership experience of low-income and minority households: A review and synthesis of the literature. *Cityscape: A Journal of Policy Development and Research, 10*(2), 5–59. Retrieved from https://www.huduser.gov/portal/Publications/PDF/hisp_homeown9.pdf

Herman, D. B., Conover, S., Gorroochurn, P., Hinterland, K., Hoepner, L., & Susser, E. S. (2011). Randomized trial of critical time intervention to prevent homelessness after hospital discharge. *Psychiatric Services, 62*(7), 713–719. doi:10.1176/ps.62.7.pss6207_0713

Holzer, H. J. (2015a). Should the earned income tax credit rise for childless adults? *IZA World of Labor, 184.* doi:10.15185/izawol.184

Holzer, H. J. (2015b). A $15-hour minimum wage could harm America's poorest workers. Retrieved from Brookings website: https://www.brookings.edu/opinions/a-15-hour-minimum-wage-could-harm-americas-poorest-workers

Homelessness Task Force. (2008). *The road home: A national approach to reducing homelessness.* Retrieved from www.abc.net.au/cm/lb/4895838/data/the-road-home---a-national-approach-to-reducing-homelessness-data.pdf

Hopper, E. K., Bassuk, E. L., & Olivet, J. (2010). Shelter from the storm: Trauma-informed care in homelessness services settings. *The Open Health Services and Policy Journal, 3*, 80–100. doi:10.2174/1874924001003020080

Hopper, K. (1990). Public shelter as "a hybrid institution": Homeless men in historical perspective. *Journal of Social Issues, 46*(4), 13–29. doi:10.1111/j.1540-4560.1990.tb01796.x

Hopper, K. (2003). *Reckoning with homelessness.* Ithaca, NY: Cornell University Press.

Hopper, K., Jost, J., Hay, T., Welber, S., & Haugland, G. (1997). Homelessness, severe mental illness, and the institutional circut. *Psychiatric Services, 48*(5), 659–665. doi:10.1176/ps.48.5.659

Hopper, K., & Milburn, N. G. (1996). Homelessness among African Americans: A historical and contemporary perspective. In Jim Baumohl for the National Coalition for the Homeless (Ed.), *Homelessness in America* (pp. 123–131). Phoenix, AZ: Oryx Press.

Hopper, K., Shinn, M., Laska, E., Meisner, M., & Wanderling, J. (2008). Estimating numbers of unsheltered homeless people through plant-caputre and postcount survey methods. *American Journal of Public Health, 98*, 1438–1442. doi:10.2105/AJPH.2005.083600

Howie the Harp (1990). Independent living with support services: The goal and future for mental health consumers [Special issue]. *Psychosocial Rehabilitation Journal, 13*(4), 85–89. doi:10.1037/h0099471

Hoynes, H. W, & Schanzenbach, D. W. (2018). Safety net investments in children. *Brookings Papers on Economic Activity*, 89–150. doi:10.1353/eca.2018.0001

Huang, C.-C., Herrera, G., & Duke, B. (2017). *JCT estimates: Final GOP tax bill skewed to top, hurts many low- and middle-income Americans.* Retrieved from Center on Budget and Policy Priorities website: https://www.cbpp.org/sites/default/files/atoms/files/12-19-17tax.pdf

Hurlburt, M. S., Hough, R. L., & Wood, P. A. (1996). Effects of substance abuse on housing stability of homeless mentally ill persons in supported housing. *Psychiatric Services, 47*(7), 731–736. doi:10.1176/ps.47.7.731

Immergluck, D. (2009). *Foreclosed: High-risk lending, deregulation, and the undermining of America's mortgage market.* Ithaca, NY: Cornell University Press.

Ingram, K. M., Corning, A. F., & Schmidt, L. D. (1996). The relationship of victimization experiences to psychological well-being among homeless women and low-income housed women. *Journal of Counseling Psychology, 43*(2), 218–227. doi:10.1037/0022-0167.43.2.218

Internal Revenue Service. (2018a). Helpful facts to know about capital gains and losses. Retrieved from https://www.irs.gov/newsroom/helpful-facts-to-know-about-capital-gains-and-losses

Internal Revenue Service. (2018b). *Publication 5307, Tax Reform: Basics for Individuals and Families.* (Catalog Number 71626U). Retrieved from https://www.irs.gov/pub/irs-pdf/p5307.pdf.

Internal Revenue Service. (2019). *Publication 936, Home mortgage interest deduction.* Retrieved from https://www.irs.gov/pub/irs-pdf/p936.pdf.

Internal Revenue Service. (n.d.). Estate tax. Retrieved from https://www.irs.gov/businesses/small-businesses-self-employed/estate-tax

Jasinski, J. L., Wesely, J. K., Wright, J. D., & Mustaine, E. E. (2010). *Hard lives, mean streets: Violence in the lives of homeless women*. Boston, MA: Northeastern University Press.

Jefferson, A., Thomas, H., Khadduri, J., & Mahathey, A. (2019). *Understanding rapid re-housing: Findings from initial interviews with rapid re-housing participants*. Rockville, MD: Abt Associates.

Jencks, C. (1994). *The homeless*. Cambridge, MA: Harvard University Press.

Joint Center for Housing Studies of Harvard University. (2008). America's rental housing: The key to a balanced national policy. Retrieved from http://www.jchs.harvard.edu/publications/rental/rh08_americas_rental_housing/rh08_americas_rental_housing.pdf

Joint Center for Housing Studies of Harvard University. (2016). *The state of the nation's housing*. Retrieved from https://www.jchs.harvard.edu/sites/default/files/jchs_2016_state_of_the_nations_housing_lowres_1.pdf

Joint Center for Housing Studies of Harvard University. (2017a). *America's rental housing 2017*. Retrieved from https://www.jchs.harvard.edu/sites/default/files/harvard_jchs_americas_rental_housing_2017_0.pdf

Joint Center for Housing Studies of Harvard University. (2017b). *The state of the nation's housing*. Retrieved from http://www.jchs.harvard.edu/sites/jchs.harvard.edu/files/harvard_jchs_state_of_the_nations_housing_2017.pdf

Joint Center for Housing Studies of Harvard University. (2018). *The state of the nation's housing*. Retrieved from https://www.jchs.harvard.edu/sites/default/files/Harvard_JCHS_State_of_the_Nations_Housing_2018.pdf

Joint Committee On Taxation. (2017). *Distributional effects of the conference agreement for H.R.1, the "tax cuts and jobs act"* (JCX-68-17). Retrieved from https://www.jct.gov/publications.html?func=startdown&id=5054

Kaeble, D., & Cowhig, M. (2018). *Correctional populations in the United States, 2016*. Retrieved from Bureau of Justice Statistics website: https://www.bjs.gov/content/pub/pdf/cpus16.pdf

Kain, J. F. (1968). Housing segregation, Negro employment, and metropolitan decentralization. *Quarterly Journal of Economics, 82*, 175–197. doi:10.2307/1885893

Kalleberg, A. L. (2011). *Good jobs, bad jobs: The rise of polarized and precarious employment systems in the United States, 1970s to 2000s*. New York, NY: Russell Sage Foundation.

Kasprow, W. J., & Rosenheck, R. A. (2007). Outcomes of critical time intervention case management of homeless veterans after psychiatric hospitalization. *Psychiatric Services, 58*(7), 929–935. doi:10.1176/appi.ps.58.7.929

Katz, L. F., & Krueger, A. B. (2016). *The rise and nature of alternative work arrangements in the United States, 1995–2015*. Retrieved from https://krueger.princeton.edu/sites/default/files/akrueger/files/katz_krueger_cws_-_march_29_20165.pdf

Kertesz, S. G., Austin, E. L., Holmes, S. K., DeRussy, A. J., Van Deusen Lukas, C., & Pollio, D. E. (2017). Housing first on a large scale: Fidelity strengths and challenges in the VA's HUD-VASH program. *Psychological Services, 14*(2), 118–128. doi:10.1037/ser0000123

Kertesz, S. G., Austin, E. L., Holmes, S. K., Pollio, D. E., Schumacher, J. E., White, B. & Lukas, C. V. (2014). Making housing first happen: Organizational leadership in VA's expansion of permenant supportive housing. *Journal of General Internal Medicine, 29*(Supplement 4), 835–844.

Kertesz, S. G., Baggett, T. P., O'Connell, J. J., Buck, D. S., & Kushel, M. B. (2016). Permanent supportive housing for homeless people: Reframing the debate. *New England Journal of Medicine, 375*(22), 2115–2117. doi:10.1056/NEJMp1608326

Kertesz, S. G., Crouch, K., Milby, J. B., Cusimano, R. E., & Schumacher, J. E. (2009). Housing First for homeless persons with active addiction: Are we overreaching? *The Milbank Quarterly, 87*(2), 495–534. doi:10.1111/j.1468-0009.2009.00565.x

Kertesz, S. G., & Johnson, G. (2017). Housing First: Lessons from the United States and challenges for Australia. *The Australian Economic Review, 50*(2), 220–228. doi:10.1111/1467-8462.12217

Khadduri, J. (2008). *Housing vouchers are critical for ending family homelessness.* Retrieved from Researchgate website: https://www.researchgate.net/publication/238710714_Housing_Vouchers_Are_Critical_for_Ending_Family_Homelessness

Khadduri, J. (2015). The founding and evolution of HUD: Fifty years, 1965–2015. In U.S. Department of Housing and Urban Development (Ed.), *HUD at 50: Creating Pathways to Opportunity* (pp. 5–102). Washington, DC: U.S. Department of Housing and Urban Development.

Khadduri, J., Burnett, K., & Rodda, D. (2003). *Targeting housing production subsidies: Literature review.* Retrieved from U.S. Department of Housing and Urban Development website: https://www.huduser.gov/publications/pdf/targetinglitreview.pdf

Khadduri, J., & Martin, M. (1997). Mixed-income housing in the HUD multifamily stock. *Cityscape, 3*(2), 33–69. Retrieved from https://www.jstor.org/stable/41486510

Khadduri, J., Vandawalker, M., Cohen, R., Lubell, J., Buron, L., Freiman, L., & Kean, E. (2014). Innovations in the moving to work demonstration. Retrieved from: http://utahnahro.org/assets/moving-to-work-demonstration.pdf

Kizer, K. W., Brush, B., Hayashi, S., Hwang, S., Katz, M., Mujahid, M., ... Wenzel, S. (2018). *Permanent supportive housing: Evaluating the evidence for improving health outcomes among people experiencing chronic homelessness.* Washington, DC: The National Academies of Sciences, Engineering, Medicine.

Kochhar, R., & Fry, R. (2014). *Wealth inequality has widened along racial, ethnic lines since end of Great Recession.* Retrieved from Pew Research Center website: https://www.pewresearch.org/fact-tank/2014/12/12/racial-wealth-gaps-great-recession

Koebel, C. T., & Murray, M. S. (1999). Extended families and their housing in the US. *Housing Studies, 14*(2), 124–143. doi:10.1080/02673039982885

Kozol, J. (1988). *Rachel and her children.* New York, NY: Crown Publishers.

Kuhn, R., & Culhane, D. P. (1998). Applying cluster analysis to test a typology of homelessness by pattern of shelter utilization: Results from the analysis of administrative data. *American Journal of Community Psychology, 26*(2), 207–232. doi:10.1023/A:1022176402357

Kushel, M. B., Hahn, J. A., Evans, J. L., Bangsberg, D. R., & Moss, A. R. (2005). Revolving doors: Imprisonment among the homeless and marginally housed population. *American Journal of Public Health, 95*(10), 1747–1752. doi:10.2105/AJPH.2005.065094

Lee, B. A., & Farrell, C. R. (2003). Buddy, can you spare a dime? Homelessness, panhandling, and the public. *Urban Affairs Review, 38*(3), 299–324. doi:10.1177/1078087402238804

Lee, C. M., Mangurian, C., Tieu, L., Ponath, C., Guzman, D., & Kushel, M. (2017). Childhood adversities associated with poor adult mental health outcomes in older homeless adults: Results from the HOPE HOME study. *American Journal of Geriatric Psychiatry*, *25*(2), 107–117. doi:10.1016/j.jagp.2016.07.019

Leopold, J., Culhane, D. P., & Khadduri, J. (2017). *Where do homeless people come from? Movement of households from their prior residences into homeless residential facilities in Michigan and Iowa.* Rockville, MD: Abt Associates.

Leopold, J., & Ho, H. (2015). *Evaluation of the 100,000 homes campaign.* Retrieved from Urban Institute website: https://www.urban.org/sites/default/files/publication/44391/2000148-Evaluation-of-the-100000-Homes-Campaign.pdf

Levin, I., Borlagdan, J., Mallett, S., & Ben, J. (2015). A critical examination of the youth foyer model for alleviating homelessness: Strengthening a promising evidence base. *Acoustics, Speech, and Signal Processing Newsletter, IEEE*, (4. [Online]). doi:10.21307/eb-2015-004

Levy, D. K., Turner, M. A., Santos, R., Wissoker, D., Aranda, C. L., Pitingolo, R., & Ho, H. (2015). *Discrimination in the rental housing market against people who are deaf and people who use wheelchairs: National study findings.* Retrieved from U.S. Department of Housing and Urban Development website: https://www.huduser.gov/portal/sites/default/files/pdf/housing_discrimination_disability.pdf

Lind, D. (2018). Affordable housing is your spare bedroom. *New York Times.* Retrieved from https://www.nytimes.com/2018/06/12/opinion/affordable-housing-co-living-single-room-occupancy.html

Link, B. G., Susser, E., Stueve, A., Phelan, J., Moore, R., & Struening, E. (1994). Lifetime and five-year prevalence of homelessness in the United States. *American Journal of Public Health*, *84*(12), 1907–1912. doi:10.2105/AJPH.84.12.1907

Logan, J. R. (2013). The persistence of segregation in the 21st century metropolis. *City and Community*, *12*(2), 160–168. doi:10.1111/cico.12021

Lowry, I. S. (1983). *Experimenting with housing allowances: The final report of the housing assistance supply experiment.* Cambridge, MA: Oelgeschlager, Gunn & Hain.

Lubell, J. M., Shroder, M. D., & Steffen, B. L. (2003). Work participation and length of stay in HUD-assisted housing. *Cityscape*, *6*(2), 207–223. Retrieved from https://www.jstor.org/stable/20868552

Macnaughton, E., Nelson, G., Worton, S. K., Tsemberis, S., Stergiopoulos, V., Aubry, T., ... Goering, P. (2018). Navigating complex implementation contexts: Overcoming barriers and achieving outcomes in a national initiative to scale out Housing First in Canada. *American Journal of Community Psychology*, *62*, 135–149. doi:10.1002/ajcp.12268

Main, T. (1993). Hard lessons on homelessness: The education of David Dinkins. *The City Journal*, *3*(Summer), 30–39.

Malpezzi, S., & Green, R. K. (1996). What has happened to the bottom of the US housing market? *Urban Studies*, *33*(10), 1807–1820. doi:10.1080/0042098966385

Malpezzi, S., & Vandell, K. (2002). Does the low-income housing tax credit increase the supply of housing? *Journal of Housing Economics*, *11*, 360–380. doi:10.1016/S1051-1377(02)00123-7

Marr, C., Huang, C.-C., Murray, C., & Sherman, A. (2016). *Strengthening the EITC for childless workers would promote work and reduce poverty.* Retrieved from Center on Budget and Policy Priorities website: https://www.cbpp.org/sites/default/files/atoms/files/4-11-16tax.pdf

Martin, J. A., Hamilton, B. E., Osterman, M. J. K., Driscoll, A. K., Drake, P., & Division of Vital Statistics (2018). Births: Final data for 2017. *National Vital Statistics Report*, *67*(8), 1–49.

Massey, D. S., & Denton, N. A. (1993). *American apartheid: Segregation and the making of the underclass.* Cambridge, MA: Harvard University Press.

Mathews, T. J., & Hamilton, B. E. (2002). Mean age of mother, 1970–2000. *National Vital Statistics Report, 51*(1), 1–13.

Matthew, D. B., Rodrigue, E., & Reeves, R. V. (2016). Time for justice: Tackling race inequalities in health and housing. Retrieved from Brookings website: https://www.brookings.edu/research/time-for-justice-tackling-race-inequalities-in-health-and-housing

Mauer, M., & Chesney-Lind, M. (2002). Introduction. In M. Mauer & M. Chesney-Lind (Eds.), *Invisible punishment: The collateral consequences of mass imprisonment* (pp. 1–12). New York, NY: New Press.

Mayberry, L. S. (2016). The hidden work of exiting homelessness: Challenges of housing service use and strategies of service recipients. *Journal of Community Psychology, 44*(3). doi:10.1002/jcop.21765

Maycock, P., & Bretherton, J. (2016). *Women's homelessness in Europe.* London, UK: Macmillan.

Mazzara, A., & Knudsen, B. (2019). *Where families with children use housing vouchers: A comparative look at the 50 largest metropolitan areas.* Retrieved from Center on Budget andPolicyPrioritieswebsite:https://www.cbpp.org/research/housing/where-families-with-children-use-housing-vouchers

McCauley, E., & Samples, L. (2017). Navigating the disability determination process from the perspective of incarcerated adults with serious mental illness. *Community Mental Health Journal, 53*(8), 905–915. doi:10.1007/s10597-017-0140-9

McChesney, K. Y. (1990). Family homelessness: A systematic problem. *Journal of Social Issues, 46*(4), 191–205. doi:10.1111/j.1540-4560.1990.tb01806.x

McClure, K. (2017). *Length of stay in assisted housing.* Retrieved from Policy Development & Research website: https://permanent.access.gpo.gov/gpo86808/LengthofStay.pdf

McFate, K., Lawson, R., & Wilson, W. J. (1995). *Poverty, inequality and the future of social policy: Western states in the new world order.* New York, NY: Russel Sage Foundation.

McGrath, L., & Pistrang, N. (2007). Policeman or friend? Dilemmas in working with homeless young people in the United Kingdom. *Journal of Social Issues, 63*(3), 589–606. doi:10.1111/j.1540-4560.2007.00525.x

McKay, C., Pollack, E., & Fitzpayne, A. (2018). *Modernizing unemployment insurance for the changing nature of work.* Retrieved from Aspen Institute website: https://assets.aspeninstitute.org/content/uploads/2018/01/Modernizing-Unemployment-Insurance_Report_Aspen-Future-of-Work.pdf

Mears, T. (2015). Could you survive in 150 square feet? The lowdown on tiny homes. *U.S. News.* Retrieved from https://loans.usnews.com/factors-to-consider-before-joining-the-tiny-house-movement

Meehl, P. E. (1954). *Clinical versus statistical prediction: A theoretical analysis and review of the literature.* Minneapolis, MN: University of Minnesota Press.

Mervosh, S. (2018). Minneapolis, tackling housing crisis and inequity, votes to end single-family zoning. *New York Times.* Retrieved from https://www.nytimes.com/2018/12/13/us/minneapolis-single-family-zoning.html

Metraux, S., Byrne, T., & Culhane, D. P. (2010). Institutional discharges and subsequent shelter use among unaccompanied adults in new York City. *Journal of Community Psychology, 38*(1), 28–38. doi:10.1002/jcop.20349

Metraux, S., & Culhane, D. P. (2004). Homelessness shelter use and reincarceration following prison release. *Criminology & Public Policy*, *3*(2), 139–160.

Metraux, S., & Culhane, D. P. (2006). Recent incarceration history among a sheltered homeless population. *Crime & Delinquency*, *52*(3), 504–517. doi:10.1177/0011128705283565

Metraux, S., Hunt, D., & Yetvin, W. (forthcoming). Criminal Justice Reentry and Homelessness.

Metro Housing Boston. (2017). *RAFT in review: Annual overview and analysis of Metro housing/Boston's FY17 Residential Assistance for Families in Transition program*. Retrieved from https://www.mahomeless.org/images/raft_report_12-17.pdf

Montgomery, A. E., Fargo, J. D., Kane, V., & Culhane, D. P. (2014). Development and validation of an instrument to assess imminent risk of homelessness among veterans. *Public Health Reports*, *129*, 428–436. doi:10.1177/003335491412900506

Morris, P. A., Hill, H. D., Gennetian, L. A., Rodrigues, C., & Wolf, S. (2015). *Income volatility in U.S. households with children: Another growing disparity between the rich and the poor?* (IRP Discussion Paper No. 1429–15). Retrieved from University of Wisconsin Madison, Institute for Research on Poverty website: https://www.irp.wisc.edu/resource/income-volatility-in-u-s-households-with-children-another-growing-disparity-between-the-rich-and-the-poor

Morrow, G. D. (2013). *The homeowner revolution: Democracy, land use and the Los Angeles slow-growth movement, 1965–1992* (Doctoral dissertation). UCLA. Retrieved from https://escholarship.org/uc/item/6k64g20f

Morton, M. H., Dworsky, A., Matjasko, J. L., Curry, S. R., Schlueter, D., Chavez, R., & Farrell, A. F. (2018). Prevalence and correlates of youth homelessness in the United States. *Journal of Adolescent Health*, *62*, 14–21.

Morton, M. H., Dworsky, A., & Samuels, G. M. (2017). *Missed opportunities: Youth homelessness in America. National estimates.* Retrieved from Voices of Youth Count website: https://voicesofyouthcount.org/wp-content/uploads/2017/11/VoYC-National-Estimates-Brief-Chapin-Hall-2017.pdf

Munthe-Kaas, H. M., Berg, R. C., & Blaasvaer, N. (2018). Effectiveness of interventions to reduce homelessness. *Campbell Systematic Reviews*, *14*. doi:https://doi.org/10.4073/csr.2018.3

Murray, M. P. (1999). Subsidized and unsubsidized housing stocks 1935 to 1987: Crowding out and cointegration. *Journal of Real Estate Finance and Economics*, *18*(1), 107–124. doi:10.1023/A:1007741630145

Mykyta, L., & Macartney, S. (2011). *The effects of recession on household composition: "Doubling up" and economic well-being* (SEHSD Working Paper Number 2011-4). Retrieved from https://www.census.gov/library/working-papers/2011/demo/SEHSD-WP2011-04.html

National Academies of Sciences Engineering and Medicine (2019). *A roadmap to reducing child poverty*. Washington, DC: The National Academies Press. http://nap.edu/25246

National Alliance to End Homelessness. (2015). The role of long-term, congregate transitional housing. Retrieved from https://endhomelessness.org/resource/the-role-of-long-term-congregate-transitional-housing

National Alliance to End Homelessness. (2016). *Rapid re-housing performance benchmarks and program standards*. Retrieved from https://endhomelessness.org/resource/rapid-re-housing-performance-benchmarks-and-program-standards

National Center for Homeless Education. (2017). The McKinney-Vento Definition of Homeless. Retrieved from https://nche.ed.gov/mckinney-vento-definition

National Head Start Association. (2016). National Head Start fact sheet. Retrieved from https://www.nhsa.org/facts

National Homeless Information Project. (2017). Homeless Data. Retrieved from http://www.nhipdata.org/homeless-data-1

National Housing Trust Fund. (2015). *About the National Housing Trust Fund.* Retrieved from https://nlihc.org/sites/default/files/01_NHTF_About_0615.pdf

National Low Income Housing Coalition. (2016). *The long wait for a home.* Retrieved from https://nlihc.org/sites/default/files/HousingSpotlight_6-1.pdf

Nelson, G., Caplan, R., MacLeod, T., Macnaughton, E., Cherner, R., Aubry, T., ... Goering, P. (2017). What happens after the demonstration phase? The sustainability of Canada's At Home/Chez Soi Housing First programs for homeless persons with mental illness. *American Journal of Community Psycholgy, 59*(1–2), 144–157. doi:10.1002/ajcp.12119

Nelson, K. P., Burns, M., Khadduri, J., & Vandenbroucke, D. A. (1998). *Affordable rental housing: When to build, when to preserve, when to subsidize?* Washington, DC: HUD Office of Policy Development and Research.

Nelson, K. P., Vandenbroucke, D. A., Lubell, J. M., Schroder, M. D., & Rieger, A. (2003). *Trends in worst case needs for housing, 1978–1999: A report to congress on worst case housing needs.* Retrieved from U.S. Department of Housing and Urban Development website: https://www.huduser.gov/portal//Publications/PDF/trends.pdf

New Calcutta; At least help the homeless off the street; (1988, December 25). Editorial. *The New York Times.*

New York City Commission on the Homeless (1992). *The way home: A new direction in social policy.* New York, NY: Self.

OECD. (2019). *Income distribution and poverty* [Table]. Retrieved from: https://stats.oecd.org/Index.aspx?DataSetCode=IDD

O'Flaherty, B. (1996). *Making room: The economics of homelessness.* Cambridge, MA: Harvard University Press.

O'Flaherty, B. (2004). Wrong person and wrong place: For homelessness, the conjunction is what matters. *Journal of Housing Economics, 13*, 1–15. doi:10.1016/j.jhe.2003.12.001

O'Flaherty, B. (2010). Homelessness as bad luck: Implications for research and policy. In I. G. Ellen & B. O'Flaherty (Eds.), *How to house the homeless* (pp. 143–182). New York, NY: Russel Sage Foundation.

O'Flaherty, B., Scuttel, R., & Tseng, Y.-P. (2018). Private information, exits from homelessness, and better ways to operate rehousing programs. *Journal of Housing Economics, 41*, 93–105. doi:10.1016/j.jhe.2018.05.006

O'Flaherty, B., & Wu, T. (2006). Fewer subsidized exits and a recession: How New York City's family homeless shelter population became immense. *Journal of Housing Economics, 15*(2), 99–125. doi:10.1016/j.jhe.2006.08.003

Okamoto, Y. (2007). A comparative study of homelessness in the United Kingdom and Japan. *Journal of Social Issues, 63*(3), 525–542. doi:10.1111/j.1540-4560.2007.00522.x

Oliveira, V., Prell, M., Tiehen, L., & Smallwood, D. (2018). *Design issues in USDA's supplemental nutrition assistance program: Looking ahead by looking back.* Retrieved from Economic Research Service website: https://www.ers.usda.gov/webdocs/publications/86924/err-243.pdf?v=0

Olivet, J., Dones, M., & Richard, M. K. (2018). The intersection of homelessness, racism, and mental illness. In M. Medlock, D. Shatsel, N. T. Trinh, & D. R. Williams (Eds.), *Racism and psychiatry* (pp. 55–69). Cham, Switzerland: Springer Nature.

Olmstead v. L.C., 98 U.S. 536 (U.S. 11th Cir. 1999).

Olsen, E. O. (2010). Fundamental housing policy reforms to end homelessness. In I. G. Ellen & B. O'Flaherty (Eds.), *How to house the homeless* (pp. 89–109). New York, NY: Russell Sage Foundation.

O'Regan, K. M., & Horn, K. M. (2013). What can we learn about the low-income housing tax credit program by looking at the tenants? *Housing Policy Debate, 23*(3), 597–613. doi:10.1080/10511482.2013.772909

OrgCode Consulting Inc., & Community Solutions. (2015). *Vulnerability Index - Service Prioritization Decision Assistance Tool (VI-SPDAT): Prescreen triage tool for single adults: American version 2.01.* Retrieved from http://pehgc.org/wp-content/uploads/2016/09/VI-SPDAT-v2.01-Single-US-Fillable.pdf

Osher, F., Steadman, H. J., & Barr, H. (2003). A best practice approach to community reentry from jails for inmates with co-occuring disorders: The APIC model. *Crime & Delinquency, 49*(1), 79–96. doi:10.1177/0011128702239237

Padgett, D. K., Henwood, B. F., & Tsemberis, S. J. (2016). *Ending homelessness, transforming systems, and changing lives.* New York, NY: Oxford University Press.

Pager, D. (2003). The mark of a criminal record. *American Journal of Sociology, 108*(5), 937–975. doi:10.1086/374403

Park, J. M., Metraux, S., & Culhane, D. P. (2004). Childhood out-of-home placement and dynamics of public shelter utilization among homeless adults. *Children and Youth Services Review, 27*, 533–546. doi:10.1016/j.childyouth.2004.10.001

Parrot, S., & Sherman, A. (2007). TANF's results are more mixed than is often understood. *Journal of Policy Analysis and Management, 26*(2), 374–381. doi:10.1002/pam.20254

Pearson, C. L., Locke, G., Montgomery, A. E., & Buron, L. (2007). *The applicability of Housing First models to homeless persons with serious mental illness.* Retrieved from U.S. Department of Housing and Urban Development website: https://www.huduser.gov/portal/publications/homeless/hsgfirst.html

Pergamit, M., Cunningham, M., & Hanson, D. (2017). The impact of Family Unification housing vouchers on child welfare outcomes. *American Journal of Community Psychology, 60*, 103–113. doi:10.1002/ajcp.12136

Pergamit, M., Cunningham, M., Hanson, D., & Stanczyk, A. (2019). *Does supportive housing keep families together?* Retrieved from Urban Institute website: https://www.urban.org/research/publication/does-supportive-housing-keep-families-together

Pettigrew, T. F. (2004). Justice deferred: A half century after *Brown v. Board of Education. American Psychologist, 59*, 521–529. doi:10.1037/0003-066X.59.6.521

Pettigrew, T. F., Jackson, J. S., Ben Brika, J., Lemaine, G., Meertens, R. W., Wagner, U., & Zick, A. (1998). Outgroup prejudice in Western Europe. In W. Stoebe & M. Hewstone (Eds.), *European review of social psychology* (Vol. 8, pp. 241–273). Chichester, UK: Wiley.

Pettigrew, T. F., & Meertens, R. W. (1995). Subtle and blatant prejudice in Western Europe. *European Journal of Social Psychology, 25*, 57–75. doi:10.1002/ejsp.2420250106

Pettit, B., & Sykes, B. (2017). *Incarceration* (State of the Union 2017). Retrieved from Stanford Center on Poverty and Inequality website: https://inequality.stanford.edu/sites/default/files/Pathways_SOTU_2017_incarceration.pdf

Phelan, J. C., & Link, B. G. (1999). Who are "the homeless"? Reconsidering the stability and composition of the homeless population. *American Journal of Public Health, 89*(9), 1334–1338. doi:10.2105/AJPH.89.9.1334

Philippot, P., Lecocq, C., Sempoux, F., Nachtergael, H., & Galand, B. (2007). Psychological research on homelessness in Western Europe: A review from 1970 to 2001. *Journal of Social Issues, 63*(3), 483–503. doi:10.1111/j.1540-4560.2007.00520.x

Piketty, T. (2014). *The economics of inequality.* Cambridge, MA: The Belknap Press of Harvard University Press.

Pleace, N. (2016). Exclusion by definition: The under-representation of women in European homelessness statistics. In P. Maycock & J. Bretherton (Eds.), *Women's homelessness in Europe* (pp. 105–126). London, UK: Macmillan Publishers Ltd.

Pleace, N. (2017). The action plan for preventing homelessness in Finland 2016–2019: The culmination of an integrated strategy to end homelessness? *European Journal of Homelessness, 11*(2), 95–115.

Pritchett, W. E. (2008). *Robert Clifton Weaver and the American city.* Chicago, IL/ London, UK: University of Chicago Press.

Quillian, L., Pager, D., Hexel, O., & Midtbøen, A. H. (2017). Meta-analysis of field experiments shows no change in racial discrimination in hiring over time. *Proceedings of the National Academy of Sciences of the United States of America, 114*(41), 10870–10875. doi:10.1073/pnas.1706255114

Raphael, S. (2010). Housing market regulation and homelessness. In I. Gould-Ellen & B. O'Flaherty (Eds.), *How to house the homeless* (pp. 110–135). New York, NY: Russel Sage Foundation.

Ribton-Turner, C. J. (1887). *A history of vagrants and vagrancy, and beggars and begging.* London, UK: Chapman and Hall.

Riccio, J., Deitch, V., & Verma, N. (2017). *Reducing work disincentives in the housing choice voucher program: Rent reform demonstration baseline report.* Retrieved from U.S. Department of Housing and Urban Development website: https://www. huduser.gov/portal/sites/default/files/pdf/Reducing-Work-Disincentives-Housing-Choice.pdf

Rice, D. (2018). *Congress should increase HUD funding in 2019 to prevent voucher cuts, help children escape poverty.* Retrieved from Center on Budget and Policy Priorities website: https://www.cbpp.org/sites/default/files/atoms/files/5-14-18housing.pdf

Ridgway, P., & Zipple, A. M. (1990). The paradigm shift in residential services: From linear continuum to supported housing approaches. *Psychosocial Rehabilitation, 13* (4), 11–31.

Rodriguez, J. M., & Eidelman, T. A. (2017). Homelessness interventions in Georgia: Rapid re-housing, transitional housing, and the likelihood of returning to shelter. *Housing Policy Debate, 27*(6), 825–842. doi:10.1080/10511482.2017.1313292

Roeper, T. (1989, March 23). Letter to the Editor. *The New York Times.*

Rog, D. J., & Gutman, M. (1997). The homeless families program: A summary of key findings. In S. L. Isaacs & J. R. Knickman (Eds.), *To improve health and health care* (pp. 209–231). San Francisco, CA: Jossey-Bass.

Rog, D. J., Henderson, K. A., Greer, A. L., Kulbicki, K. M., & Weinreb, L. (2017). *The growing challenge of family homelessness: Homeless assistance for families in Massachusetts: Trends in use FY2008–FY2016.* Retrieved from The Boston Foundation website: https://www.tbf.org/~/media/TBFOrg/Files/Reports/Homelessness%20Report_Feb2017R.pdf

Rog, D. J., Henderson, K. A., Wagner, C. A., & Greer, A. L. (2017, June). *High needs families: Fact sheets* (Unpublished paper). Rockville MD: Westat, December 2018.

Rog, D. J., Holupka, C. S., & McCombs-Thorton, K. L. (1995). Implementation of the homeless families program: 1. Service models and preliminary outcomes. *American Journal of Orhtopsychiatry*, 65(4), 502–513. doi:10.1037/h0085057

Rog, D. J., Marshall, T., Dougherty, R. H., George, P., Daniels, A. S., Ghose, S. S., & Delphin-Rittman, M. E. (2014). Permanent supportive housing: Assessing the evidence. *Psychiatric Services in Advance*, 65(3), 287–294. doi:10.1176/appi.ps.201300261

Rolston, H., Geyer, J., Locke, G., Metraux, S., & Treglia, D. (2013). *Evaluation of the Homebase Community Prevention Program: Final Report*. Retrieved from Abt Associates website: https://www.abtassociates.com/sites/default/files/migrated_files/cf819ade-6613-4664-9ac1-2344225c24d7.pdf

Roncarati, J. S., Baggett, T. P., O'Connell, J. J., Hwang, S. W., Cook, F. E., Krieger, N., & Sorensen, G. (2018). Mortality rates among unsheltered homeless adults in Boston, Massachusetts, 2000–2009. *JAMA Internal Medicine*, 178(9), 1242–1248. doi:10.1001/jamainternmed.2018.2924

Rosenheck, R., & Fontana, A. (1994). A model of homelessness among male veterans of the Vietnam War generation. *American Journal of Psychiatry*, 151(3), 421–427. doi:10.1176/ajp.151.3.421

Rosenheck, R., Kasprow, W. J., Frisman, L., & Liu-Mares, W. (2003). Cost-effectiveness of supported housing for homeless persons with mental illness. *Archives of General Psychiatry*, 60, 940–951. doi:10.1001/archpsyc.60.9.940

Rosenthal, S. S. (2014). Are private markets and filtering a viable source of low-income housing? Estimates from a "repeat income" model. *American Economic Review*, 104(2), 687–706. doi:10.1257/aer.104.2.687

Rossi, P. H. (1989). *Down and out in America: The origins of homelessness*. Chicago, IL: University of Chicago Press.

Rossi, P. H., Wright, J. D., Fisher, G. A., & Willis, G. (1987). The urban homeless: Estimating composition and size. *Science*, 235(4794), 1336–1341. doi:10.1126/science.2950592

Rothstein, R. (2017). *The color of law: A forgotten history of how our government segregated America*. New York, NY: Liveright Publishing Corporation.

Rubinstein, G., & Mukamal, D. (2002). Welfare and housing: Denial of benefits to drug offenders. In M. Mauer & M. Chesney-Lind (Eds.), *Invisible punishment: The collateral consequences of mass imprisonment* (pp. 37–49). New York, NY: New Press.

Saez, E., & Zucman, G. (2016). Wealth inequality in the United States since 1913: Evidence from capitalized income tax data. *The Quarterly Journal of Economics*, 131(2), 519–578. doi:10.1093/qje/qjw004

Samuels, J., Fowler, P. J., Ault-Brutus, A., Tang, D. I., & Marcal, K. (2015). Time-limited case management for homeless mothers with mental health problems: Effects on maternal mental health. *Journal of the Society for Social Work and Research*, 6(4), 515–539. doi:10.1086/684122

Sard, B., Cunningham, M., & Greenstein, R. (2018). *Helping young children move out of poverty by creating a new type of rental voucher*. Retrieved from Center on Budget & Policy Priorities website: https://www.cbpp.org/research/housing/helping-young-children-move-out-of-poverty-by-creating-a-new-type-of-rental-voucher

Sawhill, I. V., & Karpilow, Q. (2014). *Raising the minimum wage and redesigning the EITC*. Retrieved from Brookings website: https://www.brookings.edu/wp-content/uploads/2016/06/30-Raising-Minimum-Wage-Redesigning-EITC-sawhill.pdf

Schaak, G., Sloane, L., Arienti, F., & Zovistoski, A. (2017). *Priced out: The housing crisis for people with disabilities*. Retrieved from Technical Assistance Collaborative Inc. website: http://www.tacinc.org/media/59493/priced-out-in-2016.pdf

Schott, L., & Hill, M. (2015). *State general assistance programs are weakening despite increased need.* Retrieved from Center on Budget and Policy Priorities website: https://www.cbpp.org/research/family-income-support/state-general-assistance-programs-are-weakening-despite-increased

Schuetz, J., Meltzer, R., & Been, V. (2011). Silver bullet or trojan horse? The effects of inclusionary zoning on local housing markets in the United States. *Urban Studies, 48*(2), 297–329. doi:10.1177/0042098009360683

Schuetz, J. (2018). *Under US housing policies, homeowners mostly win, while renters mostly lose.* Retrieved from Brookings website: https://www.brookings.edu/research/under-us-housing-policies-homeowners-mostly-win-while-renters-mostly-lose/?utm_campaign=Metropolitan%20Policy%20Program&utm_source=hs_email&utm_medium=email&utm_content=64585736

Scull, A. (1981). Deinstitutionalization and the rights of the deviant. *The Journal of Social Issues, 37*(3), 6–20. doi:10.1111/j.1540-4560.1981.tb00825.x

Seron, C., Frankel, M., van Ryzin, G., & Kovath, J. (2001). The impact of legal counsel on outcomes for poor tenants in New York City's housing court: Results of a randomized experiment. *Law and Society Review, 35*(2), 419–434. doi:10.2307/3185408

Shaefer, H. L., & Edin, K. (2013). Rising extreme poverty in the United States and the response of federal means-tested transfer programs. *Social Service Review, 87*(2), 250–268. doi:10.1086/671012

Shapiro, T. M. (2017). *Toxic inequality: How America's wealth gap destroys mobility, deepens the racial divide, and threatens our future.* New York, NY: Basic Books.

Sheward, R., Bovell-Ammon, A., Ahmad, N., Preer, G., Ettinger de Cuba, S., & Sandel, M. (2019). Promoting caregiver and child health through housing stability screening in clinical settings. *Zero to Three, 39*(4), 52–59.

Shinn, M. (1997). Family homelessness: State or trait? *American Journal of Community Psychology, 25*(6), 755–769. doi:10.1023/A:1022209028188

Shinn, M. (2010). Foreword. In S. Tsemberis (Ed.), *Housing first: The Pathways model to end homelessness for people with mental illness and addiction* (pp. xiii–xiv). Center City, MN: Hazelden.

Shinn, M. (2011). Is violence at the root of homelessness for women? *Sex Roles, 64*, 585–588. doi:10.1007/s11199-010-9898-8

Shinn, M., Brown, S., & Gubits, D. (2017). Can housing and service interventions reduce family seperations for families who experience homelessness? *American Journal of Community Psychology, 60*(1–2), 79–90. doi:10.1002/ajcp

Shinn, M., Brown, S. R., Spellman, B. E., Wood, M., Gubits, D., & Khadduri, J. (2017). Mismatch between homeless families and the homeless service system. *Cityscape, 12*(3), 293–307.

Shinn, M., Gibbons-Benton, J., & Brown, S. R. (2015). Poverty, homelessness and family break-up. *Child Welfare, 94*(1), 105–122.

Shinn, M., Gottlieb, J., Wett, J. L., Bahl, A., Cohen, A., & Ellis, D. B. (2007). Predictors of homelessness among older adults in New York City: Disability, economic, human and social capital and stressful events. *Journal of Health Psychology, 12*(5), 696–708. doi:10.1177/1359105307080581

Shinn, M., Greer, A. L., Bainbridge, J., Kwon, J., & Zuiderveen, S. (2013). Efficient targeting of homelessness prevention services for families. *American Journal of Public Health, 103*(S2), S324–S330. doi:10.2105/ajph.2013. 301468

Shinn, M., Gubits, D., & Dunton, L. (2018). *Behavioral health improvements over time among adults in families experiencing homelessness.* (OPRE Report No. 2018–61).

Retrieved from Administration for Children & Families website: https://www.acf.hhs. gov/sites/default/files/opre/opre_behavioral_health_brief_09_06_2018_508.pdf

Shinn, M., Knickman, J. R., & Weitzman, B. C. (1991). Social relationships and vulnerability to becoming homeless among poor families. *American Psychologist, 46*(11), 1180–1187. doi:10.1037/0003-066X.46.11.1180

Shinn, M., Samuels, J., Fischer, S. N., Thompkins, A., & Fowler, P. J. (2015). Longitudinal impact of a family critical time intervention on children in high-risk families experiencing homelessness: A randomized trial. *American Journal of Community Psychology, 56*(3–4), 205–216. doi:10.1007/s10464-015-9742-y

Shinn, M., Schteingart, J. S., Williams, N. C., Carlin-Mathis, J., Bialo-Karagas, N., Becker-Klein, R., & Weitzman, B. C. (2008). Long-term associations of homelessness with children's well-being. *American Behavioral Scientist, 51*, 789–810. doi:10.1177/0002764207311988

Shinn, M., Weitzman, B., Stojanovic, D., Knickman, J., Jimenez, L., Duchon, L., … Krantz, D. (1998). Predictors of homelessness among families in New York City: From shelter request to housing stability. *American Journal of Public Health, 88*(11), 1651–1657. doi:10.2105/AJPH.88.11.1651

Shlay, A. B., & Rossi, P. H. (1992). Social science research and contemporary studies of homelessness. *Annual Review of Sociology, 18*, 129–160. doi:10.1146/annurev. so.18.080192.001021

Shlay, A. B., Weinraub, M., & Harmon, M. (2010). Child care subsidies post TANF: Child care subsidy use by African American, White and Hispanic TANF-leavers. *Children and Youth Services Review, 32*, 1711–1718. doi:10.1016/j.childyouth. 2010.07.014

Silverbush, M., Albanese, T., McEvilley, M., Kuhn, J., & Southcott, L. (2015). *Supportive Services for Veteran Families (SSVF) FY 2015 annual report*. Retrieved from U.S. Department of Veterans Affairs website: https://www.va.gov/HOMELESS/ssvf/ docs/SSVF_Annual_Report_for_FY_2015.pdf

Smeeding, T. M. (2005). Public policy, economic inequality, and poverty: The United States in comparative perspective. *Social Science Quarterly, 86*(Supplement), 955–983. doi:10.1111/j.0038-4941.2005.00331.x

Smith, N., Flores, Z. D., Lin, J., & Markovic, J. (2005). *Understanding family homelessness in New York City: An in-depth study of families' experiences before and after shelter*. New York, NY: Vera Institute of Justice.

Smith, T. W., Davern, M., Freese, J., & Hout, M. (2017). *General social surveys, 1972–2016: Cumulative codebook* (National Data Program for the Social Sciences Series, no. 24). Retrieved from https://library.uvm.edu/sites/default/files/gss/ 2016_GSS_Codebook.pdf

Snyder, R. L. (2019). *No visible bruises: What we don't know about domestic violence can kill us*. New York, NY: Bloomsbury Publishing.

Social Security Administration. (2006). *Trends in the Social Security and Supplemental Security Income Disability programs* (No. 13-11831). Retrieved from https://www. ssa.gov/policy/docs/chartbooks/disability_trends/trends.pdf

Social Security Administration. (2015). Social security: What prisoners need to know. Retrieved from https://www.ssa.gov/pubs/EN-05-10133.pdf

Social Security Administration. (2018a). *2018 Red Book: A summary guide to employment supports for persons with disabilities under the Social Security Disability Insurance*

(SSDI) and Supplemental Security Income (SSI) programs. Retrieved from https://www.ssa.gov/redbook/documents/TheRedBook2018.pdf.

Social Security Administration. (2018b). *Fast facts and figures about social security, 2018. Research, statistics, and policy analysis.* Retrieved from https://www.ssa.gov/policy/docs/chartbooks/fast_facts/2018/fast_facts18.html#page24

Solari, C. D., & Khadduri, J. (2017). Family options study: How homeless families use Housing Choice Vouchers. *Cityscape: A Journal of Policy Development and Research, 19*(3), 387–412.

Solari, C. D., Shivji, A., de Sousa, T., Watt, R., & Silverbush, M. (2017). *The 2016 Annual Homeless Assessment Report (AHAR) to Congress part 2: Estimates of homelessness in the United States.* Retrieved from U.S. Department of Housing and Urban Development website: https://www.hudexchange.info/resources/documents/2016-AHAR-Part-2.pdf

Solenberger, A. W. (1911). *One thousand homeless men.* New York, NY: Russell Sage.

Somers, J. M., Moniruzzaman, A., Patterson, M., Currie, L., Rezansoff, S. N., Palepu, A., & Fryer, K. (2017). A randomized trial examining Housing First in congregate and scattered site formats. *PLoS One, 12*(1), 1–14. doi:10.1371/journal.pone.0168745

Souza, M. T., Collinson, R. A., Martin, M., Steffen, B. L., Vandenbroucke, D. A., & Yao, Y.-G. D. (2011). *Supplemental findings of the* Worst Case Housing Needs 2009: Report to Congress. Retrieved from U.S. Department of Housing and Urban Development website: https://www.huduser.gov/portal/Publications/pdf/WorstCaseDisabilities03_2011.pdf

Spellman, B., Henry, M., Finkel, M., Matthews, N., & McCall, T. (2014). *Brief #3. Rapid Re-Housing for Homeless Families Demonstration program: Subsequent returns to shelter for all families served.* Retrieved from Office of Policy Development and Research website: https://www.huduser.gov/portal/sites/default/files/pdf/RRHD-Brief-3.pdf

Spellman, B., Khadduri, J., Sokol, B., & Leopold, J. (2010). Costs associated with first-time homelessness for families and individuals. Retrieved from SSRN website: http://dx.doi.org/10.2139/ssrn.1581492

Stegman, M. A., Davis, W. R., & Quercia, R. (2004). The earned income tax credit as an instrument of housing policy. *Housing Policy Debate, 15*(2), 203–260. doi:10.1080/10511482.2004.9521500

Stergiopoulos, V., Hwang, S. W., Gozdzik, A., Nisenbaum, R., Latimer, E., Rabouin, D., ... Goering, P. (2015). Effect of scattered-site housing using rent supplements and intensive case management on housing stability among homeless adults with mental illness: A randomized trial. *Journal of the American Medical Association, 9*(313), 905–915. doi:10.1001/jama.2015.1163

Stojanovic, D., Weitzman, B. C., Shinn, M., Labay, L., & Williams, N. P. (1999). Tracing the path out of homelessness: The housing patterns of families after exiting shelter. *Journal of Commuity Psychology, 27*(2), 199–208. doi:10.1002/(SICI)1520-6629(199903)27:2<199::AID-JCOP7>3.0.CO;2-G

Stone, C. (2018). *A guide to statistics on historical trends in income inequality.* Retrieved from Center on Budget and Policy Priorities website: https://www.cbpp.org/research/poverty-and-inequality/a-guide-to-statistics-on-historical-trends-in-income-inequality

Sullivan, B. J., & Burke, J. (2013). Single-room occupancy housing in New York City: The origins and dimensions of a crisis. *CUNY Law Review, 17*(113), 113–143.

Susin, S. (2002). Rent vouchers and the price of low-income housing. *Journal of Public Economics, 83*(1), 109–152. doi:10.1016/S0047-2727(01)00081-0

Susser, E., & Roche, B. (1996). Coercion and leverage in clinical outreach. In D. L. Dennis & J. Monahan (Eds.), *Coercion and aggressive community treatment: A new frontier in mental health law* (pp. 73–84). New York, NY: Plenum Press.

Susser, E., Valencia, E., Conover, S., Felix, A., Tsai, W.-Y., & Wyatt, R. J. (1997). Preventing recurrent homelessness among mentally ill men: A "critical time" intervention after discharge from a shelter. *American Journal of Public Health, 87*(2), 256–262. doi:10.2105/AJPH.87.2.256

Tanzman, B. (1993). An overview of surveys of mental health consumers' preferences for housing and support services. *Hospital and Community Psychiatry, 44*(5), 450–455. doi:10.1176/ps.44.5.450

Taylor, J., Gibson, B., & Hurd, K. (2015). Parental preschool choices and challenges when young children and their families experience homelessness. *Child and Youth Services Review, 56*, 68–75. doi:10.1016/j.childyouth.2015.06.010

The City of New York Independent Budget Office. (2014). *Estimate of the cost of legal counsel in housing court and potential homeless shelter savings due to averted evictions.* Retrieved from http://www.ibo.nyc.ny.us/iboreports/2014housingco urtletter.pdf

The White House. (2016). *Fact sheet: Improving economic security by strengthening and modernizing the unemployment insurance syste*m [Press release]. Retrieved from https://obamawhitehouse.archives.gov/the-press-office/2016/01/16/fact-sheet-improving-economic-security-strengthening-and-modernizing

Tomita, A., & Herman, D. B. (2012). The impact of Critical Time Intervention in reducing psychiatric rehospitalization after hospital discharge. *Psychiatric Services, 63*(9), 935–937. doi:10.1176/appi.ps.201100468

Tonry, M. (1997). Ethnicity, crime and immigration. In M. Tonry (Ed.), *Crime and justice, a review of research, Vol. 21: Ethnicity, crime and immigration: Comparative and cross-national perspectives* (pp. 1–29). Chicago, IL: University of Chicago Press.

Toohey, S. M., Shinn, M., & Weitzman, B. C. (2004). Social networks and homelessness among women heads of household. *American Journal of Community Psychology, 33*(1–2), 7–20. doi:10.1023/B:AJCP.0000014315.82860.d2

Toro, P. A., Dworsky, A., & Fowler, P. (2007). *Homeless youth in the United States: Recent research findings and intervention approaches.* Retrieved from U.S. Department of Housing and Urban Development website: https://www.huduser.gov/portal/publications/homeless/p6.html

Toro, P. A., Tompsett, C. J., Lombardo, S., Philippot, P., Nachtergael, H., Galand, B., … Harvey, K. (2007). Homelessness in Europe and the United States: A comparison of prevalence and public opinion. *Journal of Social Issues, 63*(3), 505–524. doi:10.1111/j.1540-4560.2007.00521.x

Toros, H., Flaming, D., & Burns, P. (2019). *Early intervention to prevent persistent homelessness: Predictive models for identifying unemployed workers and young adults who become persistently homeless.* Retrieved from Economic Roundtable website: https://economicrt.org/publication/early-intervention-to-prevent-persistent-homelessness

Tsemberis, S. (1999). From streets to homes: An innovative approach to supported housing for homeless adults with psychiatric disabilities. *Journal of Community Psychology, 27*(2), 225–241. doi:10.1002/(SICI)1520-6629(199903)27:2<225::AID-JCOP9>3.0.CO;2-Y

Tsemberis, S. (2010). *Housing First: The Pathways model to end homelessnes for people with mental illness and addiction.* Center City, MN: Hazelden.

Tsemberis, S. (2013). Housing First: Implementation, dissemination, and program fidelity. *American Journal of Psychiatric Rehabilitation, 16*(4), 235–239. doi:10.1080/15487768.2013.847732

Tsemberis, S., & Eisenberg, R. F. (2000). Pathways to Housing: Supported housing for street-dwelling homeless individuals with psychiatric disabilities. *Psychiatric Services, 51*(4), 487–493. doi:10.1176/appi.ps.51.4.487

Tsemberis, S., Gulcur, L., & Nakae, M. (2004). Housing First, consumer choice, and harm reduction for homeless individuals with a dual diagnosis. *American Journal of Public Health, 94*(4), 651–656. doi:10.2105/AJPH.94.4.651

Tsemberis, S., Moran, L., Shinn, M., Asmussen, S. M., & Shern, D. (2003). Consumer preference programs for individuals who are homeless and have psychiatric disabilities: A drop-in center and a supported housing program. *American Journal of Community Psychology, 32*(3–4), 305–317. doi:10.1023/B:AJCP.0000004750.66957.bf

Turner, M. A., & Ross, S. L. (2003). *Discrimination in metropolitan housing markets: Phase 3.* Retrieved from U.S. Department of Housing and Urban Development website: https://www.huduser.gov/portal/Publications/pdf/hds_phase3_final.pdf

Turner, M. A., Santos, R., Levy, D. K., Wissoker, D., Aranda, C., & Pitingolo, R. (2013). *Housing discrimination against racial and ethnic minorities 2012.* Retrieved from U.S. Department of Housing & Urban Development website: https://www.huduser.gov/portal/Publications/pdf/HUD-514_HDS2012.pdf

U.S. Census Bureau. (2017). *Selected housing characteristics, 2013–2017 American Community Survey 5-year estimates.* Retrieved from: https://factfinder.census.gov/faces/tableservices/jsf/pages/productview.xhtml?pid=ACS_17_5YR_DP04&src=pt

U.S. Census Bureau. (2018). *Annual estimates of the resident population by single year of age and sex for the United States: April 1, 2010 to July 1, 2018* [data file and code book]. Retrieved from: https://www.census.gov/data/tables/time-series/demo/popest/2010s-national-detail.html

U.S. Census Bureau. (2019). *Poverty thresholds.* Retrieved June 12, 2019 https://www.census.gov/data/tables/time-series/demo/income-poverty/historical-poverty-thresholds.html

U.S. Conference of Mayors. (2006). *The United States Conference of Mayors' hunger and homelessness survey: A status report on hunger and homelessness in America's cities, a 23-city survey, December 2006.* Retrieved from https://www.usmayors.org/category/reports

U.S. Conference of Mayors. (2015). *The United States Conference of Mayors' hunger and homelessness survey: A status report on hunger and homelessness in America's cities a 22-city survey December 2015.* Retrieved from https://www.usmayors.org/category/reports

U.S. Department of Health and Human Services. (2014). *Results from the 2014 national survey on drug use and health: Detailed tables.* Washington, DC. Retrieved from Substance Abuse and Mental Health Services Administration website: https://www.samhsa.gov/data/sites/default/files/NSDUH-DetTabs2014/NSDUH-DetTabs2014.htm#tab6-93b.

U.S. Department of Health and Human Services (2016a). Runaway and Homeless Youth Act. *Federal Register, 81*(244), 93030–93064.

U.S. Department of Health and Human Services. (2016b). *Fiscal year 2017: Justification of estimates for appropriations committees.* Retrieved from https://www.acf.hhs.gov/sites/default/files/olab/final_cj_2017_print.pdf

U.S. Department of Health and Human Services. (2019). *U.S. federal poverty guidelines used to determine financial eligibility for certain federal programs.* Retrieved from http://columbiacollege-ca.libguides.com/apa/websites#government

U.S. Department of Housing and Urban Development. (1994). *Worst case needs for housing assistance in the United States in 1990 and 1991.* Retrieved from https://www.huduser.gov/portal//Publications/pdf/wc_90-91.pdf.

U.S. Department of Housing and Urban Development. (2007). *Affordable housing needs 2005: Report to Congress.* Retrieved from https://www.huduser.gov/Publications/pdf/AffHsgNeeds.pdf.

U.S. Department of Housing and Urban Development. (2013). *Guidance on housing individuals and families experiencing homelessness through the Public Housing and Housing Choice Voucher programs.* (Notice PIH 2013-15 (HA)). Retrieved from https://www.hud.gov/sites/documents/PIH2013-15.PDF

U.S. Department of Housing and Urban Development (2015a). Homeless Emergency Assistance and Rapid Transition to Housing: Defining "chronically homeless". *Federal Register, 20*(233), 75791–75806.

U.S. Department of Housing and Urban Development. (2015b). *Assessment tools for allocating homelessness assistance: State of the evidence.* Retrieved from https://www.huduser.gov/portal//publications/pdf/assessment_tools_Convening_Report2015.pdf

U.S. Department of Housing and Urban Development. (2016). *Homelessness Prevention and Rapid Re-housing Program (HPRP): Year 3 and final program summary.* Retrieved from https://www.hudexchange.info/resources/documents/HPRP-Year-3-Summary.pdf

U.S. Department of Housing and Urban Development. (2017). *Annual Report to Congress FY 2017.* Retrieved from https://www.hud.gov/sites/dfiles/FHEO/images/FHEO_Annual_Report_2017-508c.pdf

U.S. Department of Housing and Urban Development. (2018a). Code of Federal Regulations: Section §578.3 – Definitions. Washington, DC. Retrieved from https://www.gpo.gov/fdsys/pkg/CFR-2018-title24-vol3/xml/CFR-2018-title24-vol3-sec578-3.xml.

U.S. Department of Housing and Urban Development. (2018b). *Picture of subsidized households.* Retrieved from https://www.huduser.gov/portal/datasets/assthsg.html

U.S. Department of Housing and Urban Development. (n.d.). *Coordinated entry core elements.* Retrieved from https://www.hudexchange.info/resources/documents/Coordinated-Entry-Core-Elements.pdf

U.S. Department of Labor. (2019a). *Labor force statistics from the current population survey.* Retrieved from https://www.bls.gov/web/empsit/cpsee_e16.htm

U.S. Department of Labor. (2019b). *Unemployment rates, 1990–2019.* Retrieved from: https://data.bls.gov/pdq/SurveyOutputServlet

U.S. Department of Labor. (2019c). Usual weekly earnings of wage and salary workers: Fourth quarter 2018 [Press release]. Retrieved from http://www.publicnow.com/view/078E5D4BDAABE03A4BFE7DD1658F9C3AE39F0BCA

U.S. Department of Veterans Affairs. (2019). *Ending veteran homelessness: A community by community tally.* Retrieved from https://www.va.gov/homeless/endingvetshomelessness.asp

U.S. General Accounting Office. (2001). *Federal housing programs: What they cost and what they provide.* (GAO-01-901R). Retrieved from https://www.gao.gov/assets/100/90783.pdf.

U.S. Interagency Council on Homelessness (2010). *Opening doors: Federal strategic plan to prevent and end homelessness.* Washington, DC: United States Interagency Council on Homelessness.

U.S. Interagency Council on Homelessness. (2016). *Housing First checklist: Assessing projects and systems for a housing first orientation.* Retrieved from https://www.usich.gov/resources/uploads/asset_library/Housing_First_Checklist_FINAL.pdf

U.S. Interagency Council on Homelessness. (2017a). *Criteria benchmarks for achieving the goal of ending veteran homelessness.* Retrieved from https://www.usich.gov/resources/uploads/asset_library/Vet_Criteria_Benchmarks_V3_February2017.pdf

U.S. Interagency Council on Homelessness. (2017b). *Ten strategies to end veteran homelessness.* Retrieved from https://www.usich.gov/resources/uploads/asset_library/Ten-Strategies-to-End-Veteran-Homelessness-v3.pdf

U.S. Interagency Council on Homelessness. (2018a, August 2). Ending veteran homelessless: A community by community tally. Retrieved from https://www.va.gov/homeless/endingvetshomelessness.asp

U.S. Interagency Council on Homelessness. (2018b). *Home, together: The federal strategic plan to prevent and end homelessness.* Retrieved from https://www.usich.gov/resources/uploads/asset_library/Home-Together-Federal-Strategic-Plan-to-Prevent-and-End-Homelessness.pdf

U.S. Office of Management and Budget. (2019). Table 1.1—Summary of receipts, outlays, and surpluses or deficits: 1789–2024.

United Nations. (1948). *Universal Declaration of Human Rights.* Retrieved from United Nations: http://www.un.org/en/universal-declaration-human-rights

VA National Center on Homelessness Among Veterans. (2016). *Annual report fiscal year 2015: Universal screening for homelessness and risk in the Veterans Health Administration.* Retrieved from https://content.govdelivery.com/attachments/USVHACENTER/2018/05/19/file_attachments/1009944/AnnualReport_FY15_EXTERNAL_2.17.2016.pdf

van Huizen, T., & Plantenga, J. (2015). *Universal child care and children's outcomes: A meta-analysis of evidence from natural experiments* (Discussion Paper Series 15–13), Retrieved from Utrecht University website: file:///Users/shinnm/Downloads/vanHuizen_Plantenga_TKI_15_13.2pdf.pdf

Vespa, J. (2017). *The changing economics and demographics of young adulthood: 1975–2016.* Retrieved from U.S. Census Bureau website: https://www.census.gov/content/dam/Census/library/publications/2017/demo/p20-579.pdf

Villarreal, J. (2019). Innovative solutions to support non-traditional ownership of manufactured housing communities. *Perspective.* Retrieved from Fannie Mae website: http://www.fanniemae.com/portal/research-insights/perspectives/manufactured-housing-solutions-villareal-070219.html

Waldfogel, J. (2001). International policies toward parental leave and child care. *The Future of Children, 11*(1), 98–111. doi:10.2307/1602812

Wallace, R., Struening, E., & Susser, E. (Eds.) (1993). *Homelessness and psychopathology.* New York, NY: Springer.

Walmsley, R. (2018). *World prison population list.* Retrieved from World Prison Brief website: http://www.prisonstudies.org/sites/default/files/resources/downloads/wppl_12.pdf

Walton, D., Dastrup, S., & Khadduri, J. (2018). *Employment of families experiencing homelessness* (OPRE Report No. 2018–56). Retrieved from Office of Planning, Research & Evaluation website: https://www.acf.hhs.gov/sites/default/files/opre/opre_employment_brief_06_15_2018_508.pdf

Walton, D., Dunton, L., & Groves, L. (2017). *Child and partner transitions among families experiencing homelessness.* Washington, DC: Administration for Children and Families. Retrieved from https://www.acf.hhs.gov/opre/resource/child-partner-transitions-among-families-experiencing-homelessness

Walton, D., Wood, M., & Dunton, L. (2018). *Child separation among families experiencing homelessness.* (OPRE Report No. 2018-39). Washington, DC: OPRE & Abt Associates.

Wamsley, L. (2019). Oregon legislature votes to essentially ban single-family zoning. *National Public Radio.* Retrieved from https://www.npr.org/2019/07/01/737798440/oregon-legislature-votes-to-essentially-ban-single-family-zoning?utm_medium=RSS&utm_campaign=news&mc_cid=a92d4d741c&mc_eid=328b4ae809

Watson, N. E., Steffan, B. L., Martin, M., & Vandenbroucke, D. A. (2017). *Worst case housing needs: 2017 report to Congress.* Retrieved from: U.S. Department of Housing and Urban Development website: https://www.huduser.gov/portal/sites/default/files/pdf/Worst-Case-Housing-Needs.pdf

Weicher, J. C. (2012). *Housing policy at a crossroads: The why, how, and who of housing assistance programs* (978-0-8447-4258-8). Retrieved from American Enterprise Institute website: http://www.aei.org/publication/housing-policy-at-a-crossroads-the-why-who-and-how-of-assistance-programs

Weicher, J. C., Eggers, F. J., & Moumen, F. (2017). *The long-term dynamics of affordable rental housing.* Retrieved from Hudson Institute website: https://www.hudson.org/research/13339-the-long-term-dynamics-of-affordable-rental-housing

West, R., Dutta-Gupta, I., Grant, K., Boteach, M., McKenna, C., & Conti, J. (2016). *Strenthening unemployment protections in America: Modernizing unemployment insurance and establishing a Jobseeker's Allowance.* Retrieved from Center for American Progress website: https://cdn.americanprogress.org/wp-content/uploads/2016/05/31134245/UI_JSAreport.pdf

Wilson, W. J. (1996). *When work disappears: The world of the new urban poor.* New York, NY: Knopf.

Wong, Y.-L. I., Culhane, D. P., & Kuhn, R. (1997). Predictors of exit and reentry among family shelter users in New York City. *Social Service Review, 71*(3), 441–462. doi:10.1086/604265

Wood, D., Valdez, B., Hayashi, T., & Shen, A. (1990). Homeless and housed families in Los Angeles: A study comparing demographic, economic, and family function characteristics. *American Journal of Public Health, 80*(9), 1049–1052. doi:10.2105/AJPH.80.9.1049

Wood, M., Turnham, J., & Mills, G. (2008). Housing affordability and family well-being: Results from the housing voucher evaluation. *Housing Policy Debate, 19*(2), 367–412. doi:10.1080/10511482.2008.9521639

Wright, S., & Kamensky, J. (2019). *Greater Los Angeles homeless count shows 12% rise in homelessness.* Retrieved from https://www.lahsa.org/news?article=558-greater-los-angeles-homeless-count-shows-12-rise-in-homelessness&ref=hc

Y-Foundation (2017). *A home of your own: Housing First and ending homelessness in Finland.* Keuruu, Finland: Otava Book Printing Ltd.

Yoshikawa, H., Weiland, C., Brooks-Gunn, J., Burchinal, M., Espinosa, L., Gormley, W. T., ... Zaslow, M. (2013). *Investing in our future: The evidence base on preschool education.* Retrieved from Foundation for Child Development website: https://www.fcd-us.org/assets/2016/04/Evidence-Base-on-Preschool-Education-FINAL.pdf

Ziliak, J. P. (2016). *Modernizing SNAP benefits.* Retrieved from The Hamilton Project website: http://www.hamiltonproject.org/assets/files/ziliak_modernizing_snap_benefits.pdf

Zlotnick, C., Robertson, M. J., & Lahiff, M. (1999). Getting off the streets: Economic resources and residential exits from homelessness. *Journal of Community Psychology, 27*(2), 209–224. doi:10.1002/(SICI)1520-6629(199903)27:2<209::AID-JCOP8>3.0.CO;2-2

Index

In the Midst of Plenty: Homelessness and What to Do About It, First Edition.
Marybeth Shinn and Jill Khadduri.
© 2020 Marybeth Shinn and Jill Khadduri. Published 2020 by John Wiley & Sons Ltd.